THE BOOK OF SAMPLER QUILTS

THE BOOK OF

SAMPLER

QUILTS

DOROTHY FRAGER

CHILTON BOOK COMPANY   RADNOR, PENNSYLVANIA

Copyright © 1983 by Dorothy Frager
All Rights Reserved
Published in Radnor, Pennsylvania 19089, by Chilton Book Company

Designed by Jean Callan King/Visuality
Manufactured in the United States of America

Library of Congress Cataloging in Publication Data

Frager, Dorothy.
  The book of sampler quilts.

  Includes index.
    1. Quilting—Patterns.   2. Patchwork—Patterns.
I. Title.
TT835.F696 1983   746.9′7041   82-73540
ISBN 0-8019-7267-1
ISBN 0-8019-7268-X (pbk.)

  2 3 4 5 6 7 8 9 0   2 1 0 9 8 7 6 5 4 3

CONTENTS

Acknowledgments   ix

Chapter 1 Sampler Quilts: Fabrics, Patterns and Designs   1

What is a Quilt?   3

Using the Sampler Quilt as a Learning Tool   3

The No-Fail Color System   4

Quilt Size   5

Quilting Fabrics   7

Background Fabric   8

Border Bands   9

Outer Borders   12

Patternmaking   13

The Importance of Grain Line   17

Additional Supplies   18

Using This Book   19

Chapter 2 Patchwork   20

History   20

Basic Design Formula   21

Four-Patch Block Design   23

Nine-Patch Block Design   23

Patchwork Assembly Techniques   25

Hand Sewing vs. Machine Sewing   28

Four-Patch Designs   30

Dutchman's Puzzle   30

Clay's Choice   31

Nine-Patch Designs, Even Size   35

Monkey Wrench   35

Variable Star and Star-Within-a-Star   36

Nine-Patch Designs, Uneven Size   40

Duck and Ducklings   40

Stepping Stones   46

Time-Saving With Mixed Stripes   47

Country Roads   49
Water Wheel   52
Time-Saving with the Sawtooth Edge   53
Bear's Paw   57
Pine Tree   60
Three-Pieced Corners   65
Aunt Sukey's Choice   67
Weathervane   68
Working from the Center Out   73
Union Square   73
Autograph   79
Curved Seam Patchwork   81
Chinese Fan   85
Drunkard's Path   85
Mohawk Trail   86
Eight-Point Stars   87
Eight-Point   89
LeMoyne Star   92
Whirling Star   93
Dahlia   94
Log Cabin   95
Log Cabin String Quilt   98

Chapter 3 Pieced Applique   103

Fabrics for Applique   104
Templates and Fabric Marking   104
Working Order   104
Slashing and Mitering   106
Using Opaque Fabric   106
Basting the Appliques to the
Background   107
Hidden Slipstitch   107
Finishing the Applique   109
Wedge Designs   109
Friendship Ring   110
Small Fans   112
Victorian Fan   114
Parallelograms   117

Tumbling Blocks   117
The Six-Sided Hexagon   121
Grandmother's Flower Garden   121
Patchwork Background with Applique
on Top   124
Honey Bee   124
Patchwork Basket Plus Applique   128
Orange Basket   128

Chapter 4 Applique   131

Applique for the Sampler Quilt   132
Crossed Diagonal Designs   133
Crossed Tulip and Dutch Tulip   134
Turkey Tracks   137
Common Center Designs   140
Pineapples   140
Hearts All Round   142
The Reel Designs   144
Reel and Buds   144
Oak Leaf and Reel   146
Single Motifs   148
Butterfly   148
The Cat   150
Wreaths   157
Rose Wreath   157
Bridal Wreath   159
President's Wreath   162
Laurel Leaf Wreath   162
Upright Patterns   164
Jack and Jill   164
Triple Tulip   171
Pomegranates   175
Bird in the Bush   175
The Central Floral   178
Whig Rose   178
Effective Use of Diagonal Designs   181
The North Carolina Lily   182
Pictorial Applique Designs   185

Pascack Historical Society Quilt   *194*
The Putnam County Quilt   *198*
Faces and Fashion Quilt   *198*

Chapter 5 Quilting and Finishing   **200**

Assembling the Face, Batting and Backing   200
The Frame   202
The Stretcher Bars   205
Strapping the Quilt   207
Round and Oval Frames   209
How to Quilt   209
Starting and Ending the Stitches   211
Where to Quilt   213
Patchwork Quilting   213

Quilting Sawtooth Edge Patchwork   214
Pieced Applique Quilting   214
Applique Quilting   215
Border Band Quilting   220
The Outer Border Design   220
Finding Quilt Designs   220
Making Solid Templates for Quilting Designs   220
Stencil Templates   223
Binding the Finished Quilt   225

Source List   **242**

Index   **244**

ACKNOWLEDGMENTS

I am grateful for all the support given to me by my family. My husband, Victor, took most of the pictures of the black and white blocks and the color photos of the small quilts. My son, Colin, worked hand and glove with me in taking the ''in class'' pictures of the quilt finishing techniques. He wove his way professionally between the eighteen busy women who were hard at work at Pascack Valley High School, Hillsdale, New Jersey, putting their quilts into frames. He helped with the black and white photos and offered many sound judgments on the photo work in general. To Hal Linderman of Target Photo, many thanks again. This must be the fifth time I have said this but I am grateful for all the special attention given to the color photos of the large quilts.

To my jolly and stalwart quilt club companions who generously loaned their quilts made during club sessions, thank you all. I am pleased to have had such a terrific response to the sampler quilt course offered in the Pascack Valley area of New Jersey. After teaching for 14 years, I was so pleased to see students work so hard in the 10 weeks we were together and their hard work shows here in the text.

Special thanks to Kathryn Conover, Senior Editor, for her enthusiastic response to *The Sampler Quilt Book* and for all her help on editing this text. Between every author and her editor, there works a paragon of patience and skill, the typist. Thank you, Mary Lou Hemingway, for performing that task so well again.

Particular thanks to the talented Gladys Boalt, who designed and coordinated the Putnam County Quilt. In my opinion, it is the most beautiful and artistic quilt made to commemorate the 1976 Bicentennial. I am proud to present it in all its colorful glory as an ultimate model for quilters across the country.

THE BOOK OF SAMPLER QUILTS

1

SAMPLER QUILTS: FABRICS, PATTERNS AND DESIGNS

The contemporary sampler quilt is a well-designed quilt composed of a variety of patterns. Its colors and proportions unite a series of design vignettes into a harmonious object. The ever-popular sampler quilt is an excellent teaching tool: each block should be a progression of needlecraft skill. And the sampler provides an opportunity for the quilter to satisfy a desire for variety: here every block is a different but related design; each block offers an opportunity to experiment with shape, color, and texture, and to excel in workmanship.

This text is built on a sound educational process of developing quilting skills. Once these skills are mastered, they may be manipulated in any number of combinations. Each skill will draw upon another. A good teacher chooses the methods that will enable the artist to achieve her goals in the shortest possible time. I have been teaching, writing and lecturing on quilting and other needlearts for 14 years. Most of the work in this book is mine or my students—the best testament to a teacher's success.

The patterns included here were chosen for technical skill building, each skill strengthening the next. Upon completion of the work in this text, the novice will be a confident and competent needlecrafter, accomplished in all aspects of quilting. These skills will remain with you all your life and will improve the quality of your work in other needlearts.

Read all of Chapter 1 so that you will understand all the elements of quiltmaking. Read the introductory material presented with each chapter before moving on to the individual block techniques. Remember that this material is set up just the way the quilter will be making the quilt. First the face, then putting the three layers together, then the actual quilting and then the final binding suggestions. Study the color section and the black and white photographs of finished work before starting.

The most wonderful way to learn a needlecraft is by experimenting. Very often in other needlecrafts, the end product is rather small or hard to display (crewel, needlepoint) or trendy (dressmaking). The sampler quilt is not only a useful learning tool, but can become a family heirloom. There is always a bed to display it on or someone to be kept warm and cozy.

In my classes, I ask for a block a week. Others may set a goal of only a block a month. The fun of a project of this nature is the anticipation of moving on to the next technique and the feeling of accomplishment with each block worked.

In a sampler, the crafter has a unique opportunity to test her color sense. If an individual block turns out rather weak or excessively strong in its coloration, it still will find a place in the overall structure of the sampler quilt. The most important experience is the extension of oneself into an artistic object that has a true, no-fail system built into it. It grants the opportunity to work with color, design and texture in one item.

The patterns in this book are traditional, best-loved Americana designs. They have been chosen because they work well in a multi-unit quilt. They offer the optimal teaching tools for the techniques taught; plus each has been carefully considered for best use of color in a sampler quilt. Over the years, the repeated use of standard patterns in any needlecraft has been to satisfy a need of unity, symmetry and harmony.

Each pattern presented here will include a discussion on how best to use the pattern in both a sampler quilt and an overall single pattern quilt. Suggestions are given for patterns which are to be used without framing borders to give a kaleidoscope effect. So the reader gains immediate technical skill and the long range knowledge of how effectively to use each pattern.

What is a Quilt?

A quilt is a three layered blanket containing the elements of *color, design* and *texture*. The color and design portions are primarily in the eye-catching top layer of the quilt known as the *face*. This is placed over a filler used for warmth, known as the *batting*. The batting material is generally polyester but may be cotton or even wool. Batting is made in large sheets for quilting. The fibers are covered on both sides by a light glazing finish so the material is easily handled. It is purchased in approximate quilt sizes such as 108 × 96 inches, 86 × 96 inches or 45 × 60 inches. It may be cut to fit any size.

The under layer of the quilted blanket is called the *backing*. It can be one large piece or several strips of material sewn together to match the size of the face. When the face of the quilt is finished, it is placed over the batting and backing, and the three layers are basted together. It is the batting that sets the stage for the element of texture. To hold the three layers together permanently, they are stitched or quilted with a small needle called a *between*, strong thread called quilting thread and a small running stitch. It is the quality and the design of the stitching that creates the texture, thus exhancing the elements of color and design found in the face.

Using the Sampler Quilt as a Learning Tool

The text will carry the reader from conception to completion of a single quilt. All the patterns given are the same finished size, 16 × 16 inches. To a quilter, finished size means without seam allowance. The seam allowance in this craft is $\frac{1}{4}$ inch. *All pattern pieces given will not have the $\frac{1}{4}$ inch seam allowances added.* The 16-inch size block makes the sewing easy, even if the design has over 50 pieces, such as Stepping Stones (Fig. 2-26).

There are three major techniques in this craft. *Patchwork* is the art of sewing together small pieces of fabric one to another (Fig. 2-11). *Applique* is the art of applying small pieces of fabric in an overlaying fashion onto a solid background material (Chapter 4). *Mixed media or pieced applique* is the technique of piecing a portion of a design as in patchwork and then appliqueing it to the background (Chapter 3).

Each of the above techniques with variations will be discussed, beginning with the easy ones and progressing to the more difficult. No one quilt can be made with all the design blocks offered here. Either progress from the beginning to end of this text, making several quilts and using the blocks in the order they appear; or make a first quilt, using one block of each technique in the order that they appear in the text. This way growth will be constant.

For each technique, there is a general discussion, pointing up advantages and labor-saving tricks to increase speed and accuracy. Two or more examples of each technique are offered for experimentation. For each design block, you will find the following: photo of sample block, cutting instructions, general information on the design, ideas for using the block in a full quilt, step-by-step assembling instructions and suggestions on actual quilt stitching for best textured effects.

Each design block appears in the finished quilts in the color section. Many of the designs will appear in several quilts. This offers the opportunity to see and compare how the designs look in different color and fabric combinations, and with various quilting designs.

Actual pattern pieces are clearly labeled with arrow markings for straight of grain. Some of the patterns appear within or overlapping other pattern pieces.

It is important to note that care has been taken to prepare line drawings or photos showing the steps completing each block. Hold the work in your hands as it appears in the pictures unless it is obviously photographed from the reverse position.

In each line drawing, the background is indicated by the absence of color, prints and solids by the use of various shadings. This will help the crafter produce attractive, properly colored blocks. Taking the guess work out of the color and pattern area gives that added touch of confidence. Most of the design blocks are shown in the color photos and some of the blocks are shown in black and white photos of entire quilts. This will help show how these blocks look when made into full size quilts.

The No-Fail Color System

A sample in any needleart is generally worked in scraps. Years ago, due to the shortage of paper, the quilter would practice her technique in a block made of scraps. Thus she was left with a block assortment of unrelated colors and sizes. Our forebears, being parsimonious, would stitch all these blocks together to form a quilt top with a very hodgepodge look. It would keep someone warm on a cold night but it was far from a beautiful artifact.

The sampler quilt today has come a long way. It is usually color coordinated to be used in a particular room. To make a sampler quilt of heirloom quality begin with at least two important statement colors. Then add a background color that will define the two statement colors. This is why off-white muslin has played such a strong part in quilting. The calico prints and strong vibrant solid colors are warmed by the softness of the off-white. It is a good place for a beginner to start. Any artist needs a good color palette to work from or the work becomes sterile. For one of your statement colors, choose $\frac{1}{2}$ yard each of two or three very small calico type prints of the same color and intensity. This will give you an opportunity to experiment with different prints. If you run out of the above assortment and cannot replace with the exact same print, then choose another similar print with the same color intensity. It keeps the color the same but the variety of prints adds interest. If you are not up to an assortment of prints, then select $1\frac{1}{2}$ yards of one print. If you want a very modern look, you could choose to work in only solids or you may choose to put the two solids onto a pale small print background. (Study the color photos.)

The second color should complement the first in intensity, but it should be $1\frac{1}{2}$ yards of solid color broadcloth. If you really like this second color, add $\frac{1}{4}$ yard of the same color in a small print—either slightly warmer or cooler in intensity than the solid color. Be sure that this secondary color print works well with at least one of the original prints.

Place all your colors against a background of pale intensity—either off-white or a pastel is generally best. Purchase 2 yards for a small quilt (40 × 64 inches) and 3 yards (84 × 84 inches) for a larger quilt. The off-white muslin is the most consistently available fabric. The reverse combination may be choosen, darker background with light colors on top (see color photos).

You can begin to see what fun it is to have a nice palette of colors to work from. Part of the fun of choosing a design block is coloring it. A formula will be suggested with each design block offered but your response to the shapes and design in the block will allow for final color selection.

Do not select stripes and try to stay away from checks. The only checks that work for most of the patterns given here are "pin" checks about $\frac{1}{8}$ inch each. Small pin dots on strong color background add a nice variety.

The suggested yardages will be sufficient for at least 9 to 12 blocks. The bordering band yardage is not included. The bordering bands frame each of the blocks. This will be discussed and purchased later, or you may have enough left over from one of the colors already in use. As you work through the sampler blocks, you will begin to develop a personal style of coloring. Some crafters will develop a dramatic style with dark bordering bands. Others will be more comfortable working in paler tones and softer colors with bordering bands for definition.

Quilt Size

In determining the size of a quilt you might have in mind, first remember that the blocks are finished 16 × 16 inches. The band sizes can be anywhere from 2 to 4 inches but 4 inches is suggested. It then becomes easy to compute the width and length of the quilt (see Fig. 1-1). If you are going to make a baby quilt or wall hanging, then choose four patches. This would make a 44 × 44-inch square quilt, including the 4-inch bordering bands. Choose from the first set of techniques. A baby quilt can be made of one 16 × 16-inch square by placing it on the diamond and filling in the corners with background colors to make a 22-inch square. Then add several more bands of graduated widths—2, 3 and 4 inches, to make a 40 × 40-inch finished quilt (Fig. 1-2).

For a twin size quilt, it is suggested you make two blocks across and four blocks down, using 4-inch bordering bands plus a 5-inch outer border. The finished size would be 54 × 84 inches (Fig. 1-6).

A smaller or childs' quilt could be two blocks wide and three blocks down, using 4-inch bands. It would finish 44 × 64 inches. Moving up to double bed size, use three

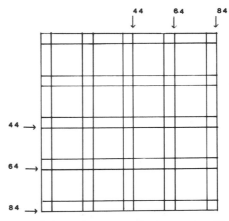

Fig. 1-1 *Chart of various quilt sizes, using 16" × 16" blocks and 4" border bands.*

5

Fig. 1-2 *A small quilt or wall hanging, using one block set on the diamond with filled in corners and various size outer borders.*

blocks across and three blocks down which would be 64 × 64 inches. Now three blocks across and four down would be a finished quilt of 64 × 84 inches. All this is based on using 4-inch bands between blocks. Add a 5-inch border all the way around and it would accommodate a double or queen size bed, 74 × 94 inches.

Additional wide outer borders are very attractive and help to frame the quilt. They also enlarge the quilt. It is not a good idea for these quilts to reach to the floor but rather to the dust ruffle or side board of the bed.

Follow the text to make the number of blocks you will need, trying a new technique for each block. If you start at the

beginning of the text and only need nine blocks for a quilt, select the first nine patchwork blocks, or the first five patchwork blocks and the first four applique blocks. Some experienced students may have already mastered the easier skills; if so pick up where you find a new challenge. If you are a skilled patchworker and wish to advance to the art of applique, be sure to read the patchwork section for time-saving tricks and then move forward to applique. For someone with no skills, begin at the beginning and select one block from each technique. Quilting is a little like vegetable soup. The more variety you put into the pot, the better the end product.

After enough blocks have been made

to complete a selected size quilt, refer to Figs. 1-3 to 1-5 for the yardage requirements for bordering bands.

Quilting Fabrics

Calicoes are first and foremost everyones favorite quilting fabric. They are small close pattern prints generally of a floral nature. The smaller the prints and the more cheerful the colors, the more popular they are. Calicoes most often have a colored background. It is this colored background that identifies them as a particular color. The print generally helps to intensify the background color by being a complement in the color spectrum to the background color. Most calicoes are cotton, some are blends of cotton and polyester. Quilters generally like to obtain all cotton for two reasons: they are softer and easier to sew by hand and they are more traditional in appearance and touch. The cotton and polyester blend calicoes are sometimes a little stiffer and are very good to use for machine sewing of patchwork. As a general rule they are harder to quilt through. Occasionally, they come from the manufacturer quite soft and are delightful to work with. Sometimes the prints are so perfect that the difficulties they present have to be overlooked in favor of the total look the quilter wants to achieve. The question most asked is can the cotton and cotton and polyester combinations be combined in one quilt face? The answer is yes; there is very little difference in the overall look if the weights of the fabrics are the same. Don't pass up a fabric blend if it is the right print or color to make your quilt sparkle. Fabrics should be of dress and shirt weights; do not use traditional skirt or pants weights in quilts.

Broadcloth is an even-weave solid color fabric. The quilter is looking for lightweight solid colors similar to those used in dresses and shirts. It is in the broadcloth range that cotton and polyester combinations are found most abundantly. There is a wide variety of grades in this lightweight fabric because it is an all-purpose fabric for home sewing. It too is available in all cotton or cotton and polyester blends. The retail fabric shop has more call for the fabric blend for general purpose clothing where wash and wear is important. For quilting purposes, select a broadcloth that has a higher percentage of cotton than polyester. All bolts are marked with fabric content and manufacturers minimum shrinkage. Ask for colorfastness guarantee at the point of purchase. It is a good practice to wash and press all fabric before using. The dark color broadcloths have a tendency to run and need two or three baths to get rid of the excess dye. Sometimes colors can be set by using a small amount of salt in a rinse: let the fabric dry and check with another rinse to make sure the dye is still not bleeding.

It is in the broadcloth family of fabrics that the color range is the greatest—from jewel tones to creamy pastels. Shops stock basic colors but will also carry seasonal colors. In the fall it would be easy to get rust and purple while in the spring hot pink and lime green would be easy to find. The variety of tones available in the solid color broadcloth act as a compliment to the prints, as good compliments to each other and as tinted background colors.

Muslin is an even-weave fabric of off-white color, traditionally made with a high thread count but with slight irregularities in the yarn. This gives the cloth a home-spun look. It comes in varying weights from lightweight to bed sheeting. It is the former that the quilter is interested in. Although it is traditionally a cotton fabric, it is now available in cotton and polyester blends. It has a lovely soft feel and is very desir-able in traditional quilting. It most often serves as a background for the calicoes and solids. Its soft coloring allows the prints and bright shades to rise up from the back-ground and have sharp definition. If you want a stark white, then muslins' off-white effect is not the answer—choose a white broadcloth.

Batiste and lawns are lightweight, even-weave cotton and cotton and polyester blends used for lightweight summer cloth-ing. Both should be very soft and silky to the touch and come in prints and solids. These fabrics are harder to work with be-cause they are soft and lack body but they do make marvelous baby quilts and quilts for old or confined people.

Ginghams are yarn-dyed woven checks of varying sizes. For the quilter, the small-est size called "pin" checks are used. Any size check larger must be carefully con-sidered. For applique, the patterns are cut on the bias to eliminate the linear look of the checks. The checks form diagonal lines or appear as little diamonds rather than squares.

Lightweight wool is used generally as a background for applique. Wool quilts in patchwork were a thrifty way for New Englanders and Pennsylvania Dutch quil-ters to use up their scraps. Wool is not a common medium but certainly has been used; designs are always simple.

Silk and silk-like blends of fabrics can be used for a very dressy look and are often combined with intricate embroidery stitchery. Silky fabrics require great care in handling and are hard to work with. The lighter the better, they are beautiful to quilt. They are most reminiscent of Victorian decor. Silk is not for the novice.

BACKGROUND FABRIC

In almost all blocks, patchwork or appli-que, there is a portion of the design that serves as a quiet area. It is from this quiet area that the rest of the design moves for-ward so the eye can easily discern the pat-tern. In a standard quilt one pattern is re-peated many times. The background is extremely important as it can "make or break" the look of a quilt. If the back-ground is too strong in color, it can over-power the rest of the design. The central design must have enough quiet space around it so as not to overpower the overall quilt design and cause confusion.

Many people do not know where the background is when looking at a line draw-ing of a quilt design. In this text the back-ground is identified in three ways. You will see it in the photos that accompany the text. In all line drawings, an absence of color represents the background. In the cutting instructions, the number of back-ground pieces are separately indicated. Some novices at this craft try to use the background fabric in the design portion it-self. This causes the appearance of holes in the design. A typical example of this is the Variable Star pattern (Fig. 2-17). If any portion of that star—particularly the cen-ter—is made of the background fabric, it looks as if the star has a hole in it, giving it an unfinished look. The viewer would not be satisfied. The eye would be searching out the symmetry trying to be expressed.

I explained this once to a mother and daughter who came to a class of mine many years ago. They both decided to work with the same colors. I explained that the star was to be wine colored and the background a white with a wine colored floral print. I envisioned how grand these large wine colored stars were going to look. I had done my job in explaining that the print was to be used only for the background and was busy patting myself on the back—until both quilt faces came back to class eight weeks later. The background print had been used in the middle of the star and the stars were put together without framing borders. The star was no longer the central design and what looked like a series of intersecting borders had appeared. The mother and daughter were delighted and excited but they were the only ones who knew where the stars were. I learned a valuable lesson: to demand to see the work in progress. One way to avoid this problem is to draw the selected design block in the proposed colors onto graph paper. If you don't have the time to make a full graph, make at least half. First make a line drawing then color it in with colors as close as possible. Any big stationery store or art supply store carries colored pencils in a myriad of colors. This will help you to visualize your quilt design. It will make the design clearly recognizable against its background. If you want to use a dark background, you will find out if it overpowers the colors for the design.

In this text the quilter gets to see a variety of backgrounds in the color photographs. Notice the gold color Album Quilt with the applique designs. There is a great deal of yellow background space around each applique. If the appliques were crowded against the cherry red bordering bands the quilt would lose a great deal of its picture quality.

BORDER BANDS

In a sampler quilt, the use of bands running both horizontally and vertically helps to frame the individual blocks, making each a composition unto itself. All the patterns given here show a consistent amount of background so the design in the block will have more definition. The patterns have all been planned for a 16 × 16-inch finished block size. Quilters speak of patterns or portions of patterns by their finished size. *That does not include the seam allowance of $\frac{1}{4}$ inch.* This offers an opportunity for the novice to get started without much difficulty. The smaller the pieces, the more dexterity is required. The bands suggested are 4 inches wide but they can vary from 2 to 4 inches. (Study color photos for reference.)

Buy the suggested yardage for the blocks and work each technique as it comes along. After six blocks are finished, you will get a feel for the blocks that are dark or light. A natural color sense will come through. At this point, border material can be chosen. Remember the bands act as frames for your blocks. The blocks must sit close together so the bands generally are strong colors to help delineate the work.

Many quilts are designed with bands that are interspersed with small squares in each corner. The student's first reaction is that this is more difficult to make than solid bands. There are several reasons for the contrast corner. The chief reason is that the yardage requirement is less, followed by the fact that this style of band is easier to make than solid-color bands and, last but not least, the addition of the patch in the corner adds variety to the bands. This little patch sets up a diagonal eye movement in the quilt, detracting from that horizontal/vertical look.

After at least six blocks are finished, take the blocks into the room it is planned for and place it on the bed, couch or floor.

When looking at the quilt, it may be apparent that:

There is an overwhelming amount of one color which must be balanced with another color.

There is a need for the addition of another color.

There is a need to strengthen a particular color family because it will be used in a room where that color dominates.

The bands should coordinate with a dust ruffle or some other decoration.

The overall colors used may be very dark (such as a dark background) and a light color band may be needed.

The color selected for the corner is an accent color. It will be some color that adds a little spark to the quilt in general. It may be leftover from the accent colors used on the main body of the quilt. This type of band is a very old technique. From one yard of 45-inch fabric, 20 strips can be cut (Fig. 1-3a). The strips are cut $16\frac{1}{2} \times 4\frac{1}{2}$ inches on the raw edge with a marked sew-

ing line of 16 × 4 inches. The corners are cut $4\frac{1}{2} \times 4\frac{1}{2}$ inches and marked 4 × 4 inches for the sewing line. Make solid cardboard template patterns.

For each completed block, attach a small square to the end of one long band (Fig. 1-3b). Stitch a 16 × 4-inch band to the left side of a finished and pressed block (Fig. 1-3c). Stitch the small square and long band combination to the top (Fig. 1-3d). The block is now banded on the top on the left. As each block is finished this way, it is enlarged from 16 × 16 inches to 20 × 20 inches, including the bands. The blocks with these bands can then be treated as one completed block. Spread them out on the work surface in an arrangement that

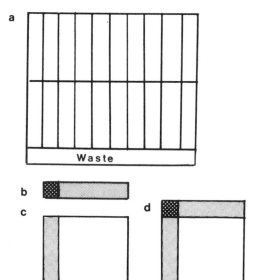

Fig. 1-3 (a) Cutting chart for bands that will be 16" × 4" when finished, 1 yard makes 20 bands. (b,c,d) Attaching a top and left band to each block.

pleases you and stitch together to form one large face. The missing right hand and bottom bands can be added by piecing it to those blocks selected for the right hand side or bottom: or one long, l-shaped band can be striped together and then stitched to the side and bottom. In this way the quilter is assured that the bands would fit accurately and easily into the quilt.

Years ago when a hand quilter adopted this method, each block was not considered complete until the bands were added. Today, I find that even if the blocks are all beautifully handmade, the bands are usually put on by machine and the banded blocks then assembled into a whole by machine.

If solid color bands are used, then yardage must be purchased the length of the quilt. With fabric being 45 inches wide, this means a great deal of waste. The lengthwise bands must all be cut first since they require so much continuous fabric. Then the crosswise pieces are cut and set aside. Keep in mind that first a plan on graph paper should be made. It will act as a road map and will help to estimate the amount needed for the bands. A standard size bed is 75 inches long and extra long is 80 inches. It would require a minimum purchase of $2\frac{1}{4}$ yards (81 inches) to 3 yards (108) inches for solid color bands.

Press all fabric before cutting and marking. It is best to mark all the sewing lines. Seam allowances still remain $\frac{1}{4}$ inch on all bands. Cut; do not tear. Tearing fabric cuts down on accuracy. People who suggest tearing and mumble something about grain line have been told some false stories. The only time tearing of fabric is accepted is for the rag bag. Be professional and accurate and use a sharp scissors. Long vertical bands are cut to go between the long strips of blocks and at the outer right and left hand of the quilt. Cut two more long horizontal bands to go across the top and the bottom. Set the long bands aside. Either roll them up or place over a hanger and allow them to fall free. Try not to fold or you will have to press before using. Next, cut the appropriate number of short horizontal bands.

Stitch the short horizontal bands between the blocks, starting below the first block and ending above the last. Do not put a short band at the top or bottom. Continue to assemble in rows (Fig. 1-4). When the long strips of assorted blocks are assembled, press the seam allowances to the dark side and press on the right too. Next add the vertical bands between the strips; press again both seam allowance and right side. Now you are ready to add outer right

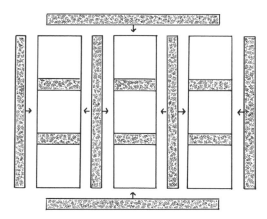

Fig. 1-4 *For solid color border bands, first place the short horizontal bands between the blocks, then the long vertical bands, then long horizontal top and bottom bands.*

and left hand vertical bands and finally the long horizontal bands, top and bottom. (Study color section, Album Quilt.)

OUTER BORDERS

Study the color section for reference. Additional outer borders can be added to enlarge the quilt and also to act as a frame for the entire work. This is an optional feature. Add it to the main body of the quilt after the blocks and bands are put together. It is an integrated part of the face. There are two ways to approach the addition of an outer border to a sampler quilt. Generally all the assorted block patterns will fit on the top of the bed so the outer border may be a large solid or print band. This would fall down the side of the bed to meet the dust ruffle. This is then embellished with beautiful quilt stitchery. The outer border may be a series of assorted colored bands, most often using the fabrics that appear in the quilt. These bands may be the same size or may vary in width. The narrowest width band will be closest to the assorted blocks. These bands will be quilted with running border-type quilting patterns such as those in Fig. 5-23. The most intricate quilting should be in the solid color bands since the bands made of busy prints will show only a textured look. Keep adding bands to the perimeter of the quilt until the desired look is achieved.

Yardage for the additional outer borders is very easy to figure. Take the longest measurement—that would be the head to foot—and purchase a length of fabric to equal this plus another $\frac{3}{4}$ yard. Fold that lengthwise in half, then in half again lengthwise. Cut into four equal panels; since most fabrics for quilting come 44 to 45 inches wide, the panels will be approximately 11 inches each. That will generally cover the mattress and come to the dust ruffle. If you need less, make a lengthwise fold every 9 inches and this will yield five lengths. This lengthwise folding is a very old trick that quilters have used for years to add the colored border.

If applying this optional border, stitch a band to the top and one to the bottom. Add the two side lengths, stitching from top to bottom (Fig. 1-5).

These borders can be assorted strips of graduated sizes. You could first stitch on a 1½-inch wide outer border, then a 3-inch band, then a 5-inch, as shown in Fig. 1-6. All kinds of combinations are possible.

Fig. 1-5 *Border bands with contrasting corners.*

A few tips: plan for a contrasting color above the dust ruffle. Do not make the outer band of the quilt the same color as the dust ruffle, since it will not show up very well. Small assorted patchwork bands could also be added for variety.

Patternmaking

Keep in mind that the accuracy developed in good patternmaking is the first step to quality workmanship in this craft. Attention to detail at this point will show up dramatically in the end product. Do not try to skimp on time at this point. I learned to respect the art of the original pattern from my grandfather who made metal templates for my grandmother. His patience, time and accuracy were always rewarded.

Patterns are provided for all the traditional blocks offered. They are all graded to the 16-inch block. To grade a pattern means to create a particular composition of shapes to fit a particular size block. All the blocks offered here are the same size so they can go into one quilt—uniformity of block size is one of the unifying features of a many patterned quilt.

It is important that a good quilter know how to grade patterns. All it requires is a large piece of paper, a ruler and a sharp pencil. Most quilters work on $\frac{1}{4}$-inch graph paper which can be purchased in large sheets (16 × 20 inches) at art supply stores or large stationery stores. To grade or resize a pattern, first draw the outline of the block. Most often in patchwork, the patterns are divided into four or nine portions, then further subdivided into squares, triangles, parallelograms or other shapes. In applique the pieces are applied to the background. To get the right proportions, divide the block up with very light lines—in quarters or lightly mark two crossed diagonal lines to help with placement of the designs. Then draw the design lightly in pencil or cut from colored paper the shapes needed. With this method, you get a feeling for the proportions of design. Place the colored shapes on the ground. Pencil in lightly. If a piece is too small or too large, recut and retrace on the background, adjusting the pattern to please your eye.

The pattern grading has been done for you in this text. Each 16-inch block has its accompanying pattern pieces. The number of pieces to be cut will be given under the cutting directions. This will necessitate making template patterns from the text.

Window-Frame Templates

The best kind of template for a beginner is the picture-frame or window-frame type (Fig. 1-7b). Retrace separately each one of the pattern pieces given onto graph paper, leaving about one inch around the outside of each shape. If tracing paper with a $\frac{1}{4}$-inch grid can be used, so much the better. Trace these pieces exactly, checking your tracing against the page. Add a $\frac{1}{4}$-inch seam allowance all the way around each piece. If you use graph paper, then the $\frac{1}{4}$-inch grid on the paper gives you an immediate seam allowance in many instances. Glue this to a firm piece of cardboard, such as bristol board (art supply store) or heavy oak tag and allow to dry flat. Cut the template out on the two lines given so the pattern resembles a picture frame. The outside line is the cutting line and the inside line is the sewing line. This

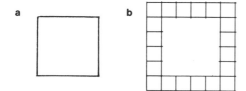

Fig. 1-7 *Templates: (a) exact pattern to be drawn; (b) window-frame template, showing inside cut out so that sewing line may be marked correctly. The outside of the template will mark the cutting line.*

then gives very accurate markings. Label each pattern piece with the name of the pattern and the grain line direction and indicate how many pieces to cut (for example, four solid and eight print). Place the template on the fabric and draw *both* cutting and sewing lines. This is the ideal way for beginners to work. All my classes begin with this method. First, draw or grade a pattern on paper and then make window-frame templates (Fig. 1-8).

Sometimes large window-frame templates are very hard to hold down onto the fabric to mark. First use a good strong ruler, the best you have. If you can procure a steel ruler with a cork nonskid back, at least 12 inches long, you will be treating yourself to a precious lifelong tool. Place the template down and the ruler over the top to hold the edge secure. The pressure from your hand will hold the ruler down over an extended distance that your hand cannot reach.

Fig. 1-6 *Note three different colored outer borders. These can be any size in any combination of widths. This quilt has just been basted; it is being prepared to go into the quilt frame. Twin bed size quilt made by Sue Sinton.*

Double Solid Templates

As an alternate to the window-frame method, try a double solid template. First make a solid template the exact size of the pattern piece with no seam allowance. Cut this out. Redraw this outline on another piece of bristol board, add the seam allowance and then cut out this second one as a solid template (Fig. 1-9). Place the larger one on the fabric and draw on the cutting line. It will be easy to hold down with your fingertips. Take it off and place the smaller sewing line template $\frac{1}{4}$ inch within the larger outline. Use this method for large pieces in a pattern that normally would use the window-frame templates. The window-frame template works very well for small pieces, but the large pieces work best with a double solid template. Finding the method that works most accurately is what is important.

Single Templates

This is an advanced technique. Each pattern piece is traced onto graph or plain paper, then glued onto bristol board or oak tag and no additional seam allowance is added. The piece is cut from the cardboard as a solid shape. Each piece is marked with the name of the pattern, the grain line direction and number of pieces to be cut. This is placed on the fabric and the outline is carefully penciled around the template (Fig. 1-9a). The $\frac{1}{4}$-inch seam allowance is then estimated by eye. Without the experience of the first method, the window-frame template, it is very difficult to adjust to cutting the $\frac{1}{4}$-inch seam allowance by eye. All home sewers who are used to the $\frac{5}{8}$-inch seam allowance must mentally erase that from their minds.

15

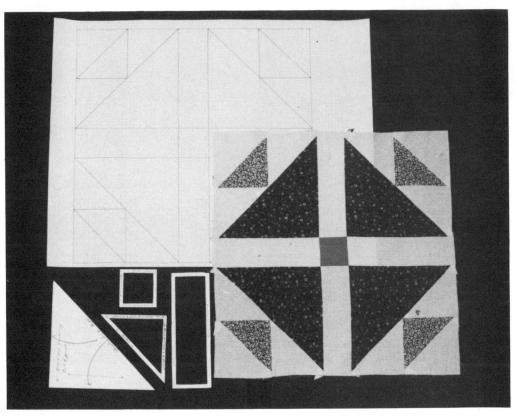

Fig. 1-8 *The elements of pattern making: graph of full block; sample block assembled; three window-frame templates; one solid template.*

To test your patterns for accuracy, cut out one block and assemble it. Check the paper patterns against the stitched work. Marking and cutting should be done in short sessions when concentration is at its highest level. Be sure you have a sharp scissors before attempting the cutting. Hardware stores generally sharpen scissors. Use a 5 to 7-inch dressmaking scissors. Never anything bigger. Never use a pinking shears.

Fabric Marking

After the pieces have been made into patterns, the *patchwork* patterns are placed on the *wrong* side of the fabric. They are marked with a medium to dark pencil on light colored material or with white or light colored dressmarkers (usually purchased anywhere fabric is sold) on very dark colored fabric. These markers look like regular pencils but have light colored lead. The

16

reason the markings are drawn on the wrong side of the fabric is because you will be sewing on the wrong side. For *applique*, draw the patterns on the face or *right* side of the fabric because the seam allowances are turned to the wrong side and then applied to the background. There is no mystery to this process—only common sense.

Use a contrasting but sharp pencil. As soon as the point starts to wear down, sharpen it again. Do not use a ball-point pen for two reasons: the color will not wash out and the color comes off on your hands when you work. Never use a felt-tip marker; they will bleed through after washing and the points are too broad for stitching. There is a washable felt-tip marker being sold but this grand invention has the same drawbacks as the regular felt-tip marker. The broad point creates a very broad line; very dissatisfying to a fine quilter.

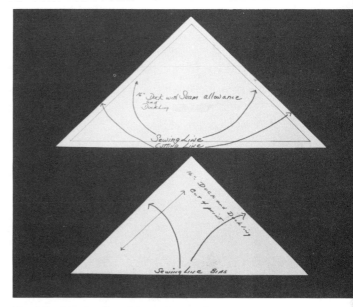

Fig. 1-9 *The double solid template: at bottom, the solid exact size template to mark sewing line; at top, same template with ¼-inch seam allowance added to mark cutting line.*

The Importance of Grain Line

The word grain in woven fabric refers to the lengthwise and crosswise threads in fabric. The lengthwise grain runs parallel to the selvage. It is called the straight of the grain. The crosswise grain runs from selvage to selvage.

The bias grain is found when the fabric is folded so that crosswise threads run parallel to the lengthwise threads or selvage (Fig. 1-10). This can be called the diagonal grain. It is easy to test for the bias on a piece of evenly cut fabric. Fold back one corner to form a diagonal fold line, making sure the crosswise and lengthwise sides are the same length, say 8 inches.

The diagonal fold is the true bias of the fabric (Fig. 1-10).

When cutting assorted pieces for patchwork, they should generally be placed on the straight of the grain. The reason for this is when they are stitched back together they will fall naturally in line with each other and not buckle. Some confusion may arise when marking a triangle! Remember that, for our purposes, a triangle is a square cut in half on the diagonal. Two sides will be of equal size and they are to be placed on the lengthwise and crosswise grain. The longest side or the diagonal side of the triangle will be placed on the bias grain. When putting two triangles together, both the bias

17

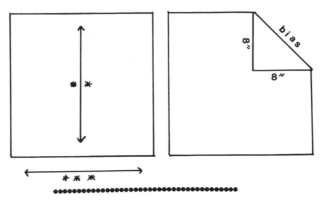

Fig. 1-10 *Grain lines: at left, ** shows lengthwise grain and *** crosswise grain; at right, bias grain is formed when fabric is folded so that crosswise threads run parallel to lengthwise threads.*

sides are sewn together. In this way when the seam is opened, the lengthwise and crosswise threads remain straight.

In the text and drawings, pattern pieces that meet this simple standard will have no grain markings. The pieces that need special grain line instruction will be marked with an arrow. Bias edges will be indicated on patterns with a line of dots.

Applique work presents less of a problem. The background material that forms the block should be cut on the straight of the grain. The applique pieces will be sewn to this background in a variety of methods. If the grain line gives a special advantage, it will be mentioned in the discussion of the design block.

Additional Supplies

Needles

Did you know needles have names and sizes too? The needle most commonly associated with quilting is called a *between*

needle. The packages are marked betweens or "quilting needles". They are short, medium thick needles with a rather large eye. This is used for hand stitching patchwork and for stitching the three layers of the quilt together, forming the textural surface. Many people like this needle so much they use it for applique too. Another popular needle for applique is called a *sharp*, a slender needle with a larger eye.

The size of a needle is indicated by numbers. The shorter the needle, the higher its number. A #9 between is a favorite of a good quilter and it is shorter than a #6. The shorter needle will force the quilter to make smaller stitches. It is important for a needleworker, especially a beginner, to do all quilting with the same size needle because it will promote even stitches. Small even stitches are important in making a strong product that will have a long life. The use of one size and type needle will help the needle artist to build dexterity in her hands.

Thread

The use of a thread called *quilting thread* is very popular. It is a rather stiff thread that is heavier and stronger than dressmaker thread but not as heavy and course as *buttonhole twist*. The spool should be marked *quilting thread* and it comes in white, off-white and many colors. It is used primarily for two techniques: to stitch patchwork together and in the actual quilt stitching. It is in the latter that long lengths of thread are used to make many small stitches in and out of the three layers of material. A thread of lesser quality would break under this kind of wear. For the applique techniques, generally dressmaker thread is used and in colors to match the fabric being applied.

To stitch patchwork on the machine, use dressmakers thread.

Pins

This craft uses a lot of pins and it behooves the quilter to have the best dressmaker or silk pins with the sharpest point she can afford. The pins with the plastic or glass heads are nice if they are not too long. Do not use very long pins that are used for knits or very short pins used for sequin crafting.

Scissors

A 7-inch dressmaker scissors is ideal for cutting most of the materials used in quilting. An additional small thread scissors, 2 to 3 inches long, is nice to have when hand sewing and quilting. Many people hang it from a ribbon around their necks so it will not get lost.

Thimble

If you have been taught to work with a thimble or if you find you need additional protection on the pushing finger, select a thimble at any sewing store. The metal ones are best. Some come with the crown open so air will circulate more freely around the covered area. There are also leather thimbles but you have to shop around for them. They are in short supply. Quilt or needle-arts shops generally have them.

Using This Book

Read through all the material presented—the general information and all the exact details. Try to visualize what is being taught. As you move along, stop and review what you have read.

Carefully cut out the appropriate pieces, lay them on your work surface, and check grain lines. As you progress, there will be new techniques to master. If they aren't clear to you at first reading, take the actual work in your hands. The directions will be easier to follow.

Along the way, there are many choices to be made between the old, tried and true methods, which are certainly still valid, and the modern techniques used by quilters today.

PATCHWORK

History

As a design form, patchwork is a unique American folk art. The strong graphic qualities of the designs are tempered with the picturesque names given to the patterns. Patchwork is created by sewing together small pieces of fabric to form a large block. This block is most often square but need not be. Design blocks are repeated a number of times to create a complete face or outer top portion of a quilt.

All the charm and inventiveness characteristic of American folk art is captured in patchwork. Understanding its origins will help to bridge the gap between yesterday and today. In America, cotton was not a money crop until Eli Whitney invented the cotton gin. The type of cotton that could be grown abundantly in the southern states had a large seed, like an apple seed. In 1793 Eli Whitney was credited with inventing the gin. But it was later, as the gin became more effective, that cotton became a large scale agricultural crop. By the early 1800s, America was producing vast quantities of raw and finished cotton cloth. And as America expanded westward at an unprecedented rate, this land of opportunity was attracting all kinds of people. While it was first and foremost an agricultural society, the need for goods and services followed on the heels of the farmers. After the first priorities of food and shelter came the need to clothe people. While wool and linen cloth had been made at home for years, there was a growing demand for factory-made cotton goods. The lines of transportation were slow and uncertain. Cotton goods as well as homespun fabric became very precious. First clothing was made. Then the remainder of the fabric was used to make three-layered quilted blankets. The smallest scraps were stitched together to create decorative tops for the bed quilts. The large scrap yardages were stitched together to create the backings or undersides and the upper and bottom layers were filled with loose cotton fiber. To prevent the cotton from slipping and sliding, running stitches were sewn in straight lines and novel designs to pocket the batting into small areas. This process of applying the stitchery for holding the batting evenly throughout the two layers is most accurately called *quilting*.

Another factor that contributed to the rising popularity of quilt making was the dreariness of life in the home. Whether it was a snug log cabin, a prairie mud hut or a simple clapboard farmhouse, the work was hard and drab. During the 1800s women owned very little. Everything belonged to the men and generally passed to the son or sons who were to take care of their mothers. The men owned the land, house, farm and it's trappings, the silver clocks, the kitchen utensils and any furnishings. Women had only their dowry gifts. To brighten the scene and add a touch of their own personalities, they took to needlearts. While the interiors of the houses were plain, the outdoor landscape was rich and spectacular, affording constant joy. That joy was repeated in the needlearts they produced. In studying needlearts I am constantly amazed at the endless depictions of floral forms and wildlife. It is easy to see the source of their inspiration.

When the colonial woman wanted to reproduce what she saw, she moved to her bag of scraps. It is here we feel the richness of the American creative spirit. It is here, with scraps of squares, rectangles, diamonds and hexagons, that the reflections of everyday life are most strongly felt. This unique inventiveness created hundreds of patterns with names that shine out with vivid images: Rocky Road to Kansas, Drunkard's Path, Bear's Paw, Stepping Stones, Union Square, Mohawk Trails, Pine Tree, Country Roads, Honey Bee, Turkey Tracks, Open Reel or the Log Cabin. Each pattern is simply an assortment of shapes. It is the proportion of these shapes, the selection of the colors and the quality of the stitchery that makes each of these designs special to creator and viewer. Patterns were traded, copied and sometimes borrowed without consent. The making of samples in scrap fabric was a common way to record designs since paper was equally as scarce as fabric.

Basic Design Formula

Patchwork is the art of geometrical form. A patchwork quilt is composed of a series of repeated blocks of the same design. The various shapes of small pieces of fabric are generally stitched into easy-to-handle design blocks. When enough of these blocks are accumulated, they are sewn together to form the top layer of the quilt. This is a single large sheet when finished.

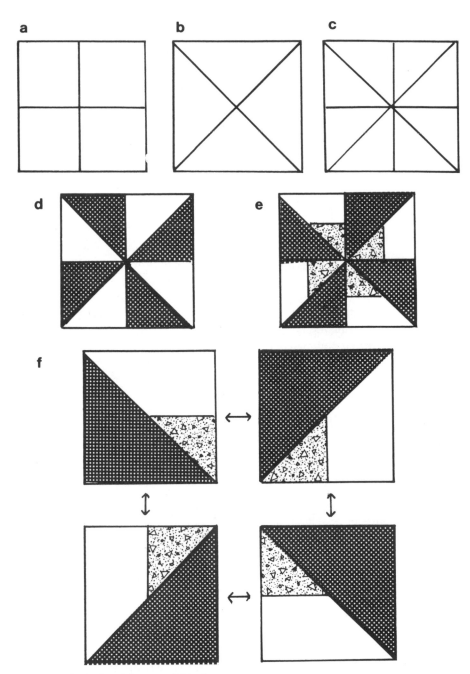

Fig. 2-1 *Designing a four-patch block: (Pinwheel) (a,b,c) divide in equal portions; (d,e) add color to some of the pieces and the design moves forward; (f) unite three small pieces to form one patch and four patches to form one block.*

There is a basic formula for designing and making a block. The greater the understanding of the design technique, the less complicated the process becomes.

FOUR-PATCH BLOCK DESIGN

The first breakdown of a patchwork block is to divide it in half both horizontally and vertically, or perhaps twice on the diagonal (Fig. 2-1a-c). If shading is added, a windmill effect appears, the dark color moving forward to our eye (Fig. 2-1d). If the light portion of each eighth is further divided and shaded to a medium color, a pinwheel effect is created (Fig. 2-1e). If four equal portions are put together, each portion would be called a *patch* (Fig. 2-1f). Each patch would have three *pieces* and ultimately each block would have twelve pieces. A piece is one individual element of a patch. So our progression of assembly goes from individual *pieces* to *patches* to the completed *block*. When enough blocks are joined together, the face is completed. The four-patch offers a limited design form.

NINE-PATCH BLOCK DESIGN

If the block is broken into nine individual patches, the range of design becomes much greater (Fig. 2-2a). By manipulating the size, shape, color and placement of pieces within each patch, a wide variety of patterns are created. If four of the outer corners are cut on the diagonal, half of which are shaded the same as the center patch, a pattern named Shoo Fly is created (Fig. 2-2b). If each of the remaining solid patches are divided into rectangles, and the four resulting rectangles nearest the center are shaded, a pattern called Monkey Wrench appears in Fig. 2-2c and Fig. 2-14.

If only four of the patches in a block are divided twice on the diagonal, a confusing figure appears (Fig. 2-2d). When the same color is added to thirteen of the pieces, a star emerges (Fig. 2-2e and 2-17). Change the proportion of the nine patches contained in one block to make them uneven in size. First, a cross with four empty corners appears (Fig. 2-2f). These can then be divided again on the diamond, creating a block called Garden of Eden (Fig. 2-2g). This is very geometric. Look at Duck and Ducklings further on in the text (Fig. 2-22). Here is a more picturesque breakdown of an uneven nine-patch. Then look at Stepping Stones (Fig. 2-26), a varied but balanced breakdown of a nine-patch. Four of the corner patches are mini nine patches and four others form arrow-like shapes— all adding up to a very interesting uneven nine-patch design. We can go on dividing blocks into all sorts of breakdowns but the most popular is still the nine-patch, even or uneven.

The basic block can be any size from 6 to 26 inches, depending on what kind of work the quilter is looking for.

The patchwork designs shown here were carefully selected with a sampler quilt in mind. Most have a design composition that rises from the background. The second criteria for choosing a block was its merits of technical skill. To teach new skills without repetition, techniques have been arranged from simple to more complex, from straight line patchwork to curved seam patchwork. There are ten techniques and twenty-five design blocks to be tried. The most varied and popular are the nine-patch designs. From each category try one at least. Hopefully you will be so intrigued you will try them all. If you want only a

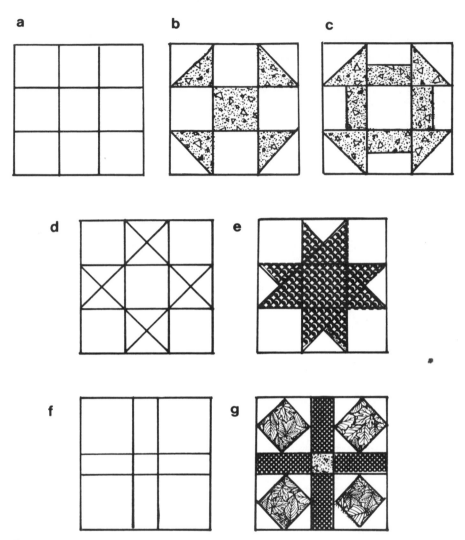

Fig. 2-2 *Designing a nine-patch: (a) even nine-patch (b) Shoo Fly (c) Monkey Wrench (d) An even nine-patch with four squares divided twice on the diagonal (e) Thirteen pieces of (d) shaded to form a star (f) Uneven nine-patch (g) Garden of Eden.*

few pieces of patchwork for your first quilt, select one nine-patch, one sawtooth, one curved seam, one star and a log cabin.

Years ago patterns were conceived and carried out based on the basic patch concept of the design. Each patch was first broken down into squares and further down into triangles and so on. When some of these pieces were put together, small triangles were put back to back to form parallelograms such as the four large windmill-looking pieces in the center of Clay's Choice (Fig 2-11). I have altered the patterns so that each patch contains one parallelogram flanked by two small triangles (Fig. 2-3). The one parallelogram piece is cut instead of two triangles, thus eliminating one seam (Fig. 2-3b).

It makes the work go faster, more efficiently and is ultimately more attractive. Instead of cutting nine little squares for the corners of Stepping Stones (Fig. 2-26), cut five squares and two rectangles. The effect

of a nine-patch is maintained but the work is shortened by deleting two separate squares and two short seams. This type of efficiency may not seem necessary in a sampler when dealing with only one block of each design; but if the block were to be repeated many times, the time saved in cutting and seaming would be considerable. Learning these techniques will only help to step up work here and in other areas of the quilt craft. Each generation of crafters builds on, and often improves upon, past techniques.

Patchwork Assembly Techniques

The first step is selection of a design block. The art of patternmaking has been outlined earlier. Working patterns will be made to accommodate each of the pattern pieces given. Remember to add $\frac{1}{4}$-inch seam allowance around each of the pattern pieces or the finished block will not measure 16 × 16 inches. When working on patchwork all patterns are placed, marked and cut on the *wrong* side of the fabric because all sewing is worked on the *wrong* side. After cutting, the pieces should be placed right side up on the work surface so you will get an idea how the pieces correspond to the finished block. Patches are formed first. Work the simplest seams first, pinning pieces right side to right side. Disregard raw cut edge and concentrate only on the marked sewing lines from this point on. Place the first pin in the right corner of the marked seam line, checking to see that the pins come out in the exact same matching corner. Place a pin in the left hand corner and repeat checking on the back (Fig. 2-

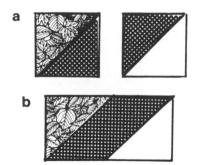

Fig. 2-3 *To upgrade patterns that would create a finished look of a parallelogram with four pieces of patchwork (a), combine and cut one parallelogram and two triangles (b) reducing work to three pieces to cut and sew. (See Clay's Choice, Fig. 2-11.)*

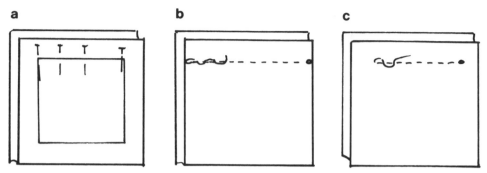

Fig. 2-4 *(a) Pinning seam lines together; (b) stitch from raw edge to raw edge; (c) stitch on the marked seam line only.*

4a). Continue pinning the two marked seam lines together. There are two ways to sew:

1. *From raw edge to raw edge:* This is most common for straight-line patchwork. Start with a knot at the raw edge; stitch on the line with small stitches, using a between needle and a short (10 to 15 inches) length of thread. When stitching, keep checking to make sure you are precisely on *both* marked seam lines. If the needle goes off one of the lines, unthread the needle and, with wrong end of needle, pull out stitches, rethread and stitch again in the right place. When you reach the opposite side, stitch past marked corner almost to raw edge and make two back stitches over the last stitch. Then make one or two return stitches in the existing stitches or in the seam allowance. This is called reweaving the thread. All needlearts are finished by reweaving of thread (Fig. 2-4b).

2. *Stitching on the seam line only:* This is popular where intricate piecing is required. It is used when small pieces are put together. It offers freedom in seam pressing. Start with a knot but begin stitching where the first pin intersects both marked corners. Continue along seamline, stopping where the other corner intersects. Back stitch and reweave (Fig. 2-4c). All stitching in this technique will be on marked line only.

The Raised Seam

This is a technique used by accomplished patchworkers to allow freedom in pressing seams when uniting four individual seams of differing colors. Look at the outer corners of Aunt Sukey's Choice (Fig. 2-45). Here a background square has been joined to a print square to form a rectangle; a solid color square has been joined to a background to form a rectangle. Each of the background seam allowances have been pressed to the dark side. When uniting the two rectangles to form a checkerboard square, each seam must still be pressed to the dark. To accomplish this the seams are not sewn down but are raised between the

26

thumb and the index finger. The needle is passed under the seam and is free to continue on to finish the rest of the seam. The two short seams on either side of the long seam are now free to be pressed down in either direction (Fig. 2-5). This technique is only a hand technique. The advanced version of this seam is the three-piece corner (Fig. 2-44).

While individual patterns will dictate what is best for each block design, the raised seam technique must become a part of your basic knowledge. While working a block in hand, it will become apparent when it is needed.

Sew all simple seams by uniting the combined pieces into patches. Press seams to the dark and press fabric on right side as well. Clip any points that may show around the edges. The best to work is to organize like an assembly line. Work the first patch, checking the patterns and sewing to make sure you cut, marked and stitched correctly. Then proceed in an orderly fashion.

In making a four-patch block, it's easy to see that top and bottom right patches would be combined; then top and bottom left patches. Both pieces are pressed and finally the center seam sewn. With a nine-patch block, combine three right-hand patches, then three left-hand patches and finally three middle patches. You now have three separate strips. Sew the long vertical seams, matching the corners of the center square first and then the edges of the blocks.

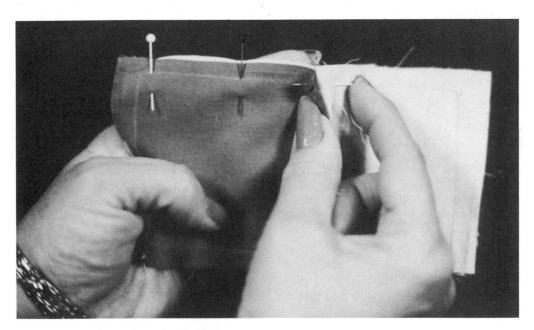

Fig. 2-5 *Raised seam allows freedom to press seams in either direction.*

A trick that many quilters use to make sure of the accuracy of the work is to pin from the center out; first pin down one side, turn the work over and pin down the other side. Stitch from the center out (Fig. 2-6). This means you can work with shorter threads for each seam and the stress in the middle is reinforced from each side. If the seam is bulky at the center patch, use the raised seam technique.

Hand Sewing vs. Machine Sewing

A great deal of the patchwork done today is stitched on the machine because the seams do not show and the seams are often straight. The machine work is generally limited to blocks with few pieces and straight lines. Advanced patchwork requires hand sewing techniques that have a great degree of dexterity which the machine does not have. There is no reason why some parts of a block cannot be done on the machine and some parts by hand, thus combining the best of two worlds. Listed below are the advantages and disadvantages of the two techniques. Combine them to make them work for you.

Hand Sewing

Hand sewing offers great accuracy because as you stitch you can check both sides.

If a mistake is made, it is easy to take out hand stitching.

Fewer pins are needed when hand sewing since fingers are constantly adjusting seams.

The raised seam (Fig. 2-5), not available to the machine stitcher, is an absolute necessity in certain work such as Grandmother's Flower Garden and Tumbling Blocks.

Hand sewing is delightfully quiet and pieces can be put into a pocket or handbag to be stitched at any time or any place. Many crafters like to do this in the evening in their easy chairs.

When using a between needle and quilting thread, the product is very strong and the needle is easy to thread.

Hand sewing is more traditional and of greater heirloom quality. Any hand crafted article is intrinsically more valuable.

Machine Sewing

Machine sewing is relatively quick if you use a lot of pins placed in line with the marked seam line rather than at right angles. Make sure the pins' points face the machine and the heads are to the face of the sewer. Withdraw the pins one

Fig. 2-6 *When uniting long seams of patchwork, stitch from the center out.*

at a time as the machine comes to them. This pinning technique will help assure the even feeding of the fabric on the machine.

The use of assembly line techniques of feeding one piece of patchwork in after another helps speed up the process on straight line patchwork.

To accomplish good work on the machine, use a small hole throat plate and small straight-stitch presser foot; not the wide open hole throat plate used in zigzagging (Fig. 2-7). The needle should be a #11 but a #14 may also work.

It is very easy to stretch the bias edge of the goods. Make sure the thread tension and pressure on the foot are just right. Sample a few pieces by measuring the bias edge before and after stitching.

While the machine has the advantage of speed, the disadvantage is that the seamstress cannot see the reverse side. To protect seams on the wrong side

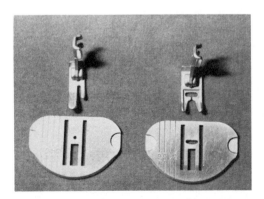

Fig. 2-7 *For machine patchwork sewing, use dressmaker foot and throat plate shown at left. The other set is used for zigzag.*

from turning when passing under the foot, pin all seams in place.

The work on the machine will be stronger because 10 to 12 stitches to the inch can be made with regular dressmaker thread.

Seams take time to undo because a small seam ripper or a very pointed scissors must cut every third stitch at right angles. Pull out the back thread and pull apart the two pieces. Do not rip apart.

On long seams, accuracy can be increased if the seam starts in the center of the block and goes to the raw edge and then work is turned and sewn to the opposite edge (Fig. 2-6).

When starting and stopping at the raw edge, begin and end a few threads from the edge. The overcast stitch and knot don't have to be used with the machine. When starting and ending the stitching on the marked seam line, start just inside the marked seam line below the corner. Backstitch one stitch to the corner, push the machine switch to forward and proceed to the other end of the marked seam line and at the end backstitch one or two stitches.

Trim all threads when the work is finished. There is a tendency in machine work to have a lot of threads.

Pressing

The importance of pressing seams for patchwork cannot be overstated. Each piece will fit better to the next piece if both pieces have been pressed. The rule of thumb is to press as much as possible. After pressing the wrong side, turn and press the right side too. Be careful not to stretch bias seams or edges. Press both seams to the darker, more opaque fabric. There are two reasons for this. First, when batting and backing are placed behind the face of the quilt, the seams sometimes show through light-colored fabric. Second, quilt stitching is placed just at the edge of the folded seam allowance. The quilter will stitch through only three layers of material. If a seam should open and separate in time, the seam has two seam allowances laying in one direction. This will not allow the batting to pop out through the open hole.

Four-Patch Designs

DUTCHMAN'S PUZZLE

Dutchman's Puzzle is a whimsical Pennsylvania Dutch design based on a four-patch combination (Fig. 2-8). The basic block is divided into four equal parts. Then each

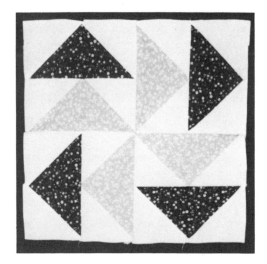

Fig. 2-8 *Dutchman's Puzzle, a four-patch block.*

square is divided in half again, forming two rectangles. Each rectangle is further divided into triangles. These triangles, offset by a pale background, are called *geese* or *birds*. The triangle shape being pictured as a bird in this and many different patterns links us to our forefathers. Flying birds are always a joy to see; there are no patterns, such as boll weevil or mosquito patch that refer to unpleasant elements.

This is a simple pattern that can use scraps or can be made to look very modern with stark solid colors or can be specially coordinated with a common background in a sampler quilt. In a full quilt, the blocks are set up one after the other, further heightening the circular motif of the bird-like triangles in each block.

Materials and Cutting
PATTERN A: Cut 8, 4 prints and 4 contrast prints (as shown), or 4 prints and 4 solids or 8 assorted prints
PATTERN B: Cut 16 solid color background

Note: Be careful to follow the grain line indicated when cutting.

Assembly
Stitch from raw edge to raw edge throughout the block.

1. Stitch a B piece to the right sides of each A piece (Fig. 2-9a). Open and press to the dark side.

2. Stitch the remainder of the B's to the left side of the eight pieces just made (Fig. 2-9b). Open and press to the dark.

3. Stitch two contrasting rectangles together so the points of the triangles face the same way (Fig. 2-9d). Press seams to the dark.

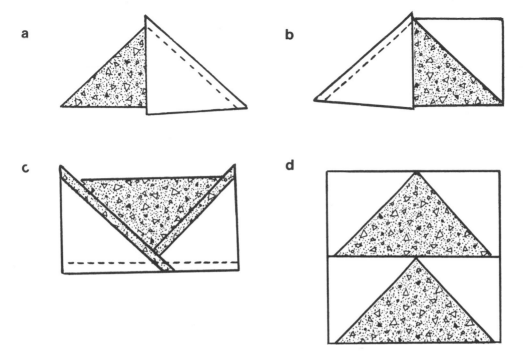

Fig. 2-9 *Dutchman's Puzzle assembly.*

4. Repeat step 3 until there are four individual patches. Using Fig. 2-8 as a guide, assemble blocks. The birds will appear to be flying out of the block. Press all seams to the dark.

Quilting Suggestions
The quilting should be simple. Follow the outline of each of the individual triangles if the minimum quilting is desired. If more quilting is desired, add a little pattern in each background triangle.

CLAY'S CHOICE

This was named for the famous statesman and orator Henry Clay (1777–1852). There are many patterns named to honor and commemorate famous people such as Dolly Madison's Star or Mr. Lincoln's Platform. In days gone by, Clay's Choice was made by dividing the original block into sixteen small squares, requiring cutting of many small squares and triangles to make a very time-consuming piece of work.

Studying this pattern, it is clearly a four-patch, or one block divided into four repeating parts (see Fig. 2-11 and 2-12c for one patch). To call this pattern authentic, you must pay special attention to the coloring. The parallelogram that forms the center pinwheel-like design is always a solid color with a small print toward the inside and on the outer corners; all the rest is

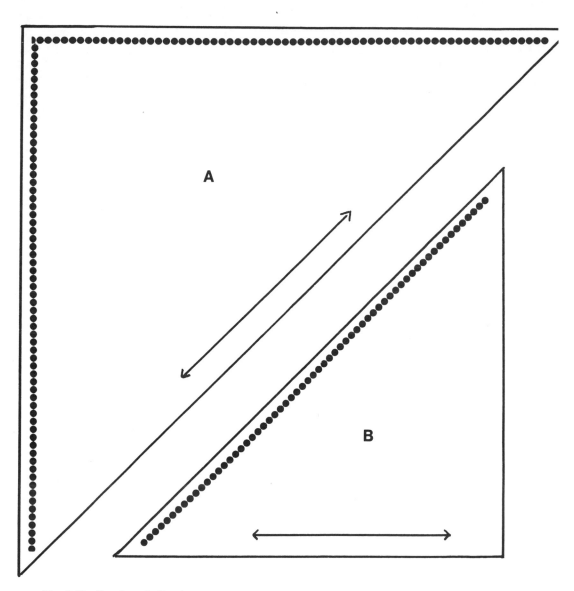

Fig. 2-10 *Dutchman's Puzzle pattern.*

background color, generally in off-white. If you are not concerned with authenticity, then color this as you like, using two prints or two solids with the background.

This pattern is generally put into a large quilt with bordering bands running between the blocks. The bands are generally the color of the parallelogram, with a corner patch of the print used in the block.

Materials and Cutting

PATTERN A: Cut 4 background and 4 small print

PATTERN B: Cut 4 very strong solid colors

PATTERN C: Cut 4 background and 4 print (same as A)

Notice the grain line on the parallelogram piece (Fig. 2-13). The short ends should be cut on the straight of the grain. It does not matter if pinwheel appears to be moving to the right or to the left.

Assembly

Place the assorted pieces on the work surface in front of you and check the directions of the parallelogram, using Fig. 2-11 for reference.

1. Seam a background A and a print A to either side of the long sides of B, stitch from raw edge to raw edge and press seams to dark side. Repeat to complete the remaining three rectangles (Fig. 2-12a).

a

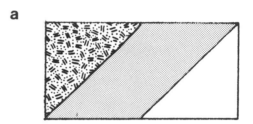

b

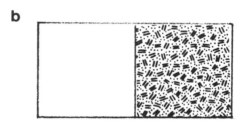

c

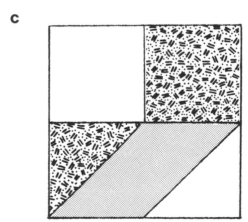

Fig. 2-11 *Clay's Choice, a four-patch block.*

Fig. 2-12 *Clay's Choice assembly.*

Fig. 2-13 *Clay's Choice pattern. Note grain line on B. Long sides will be cut on bias grain.*

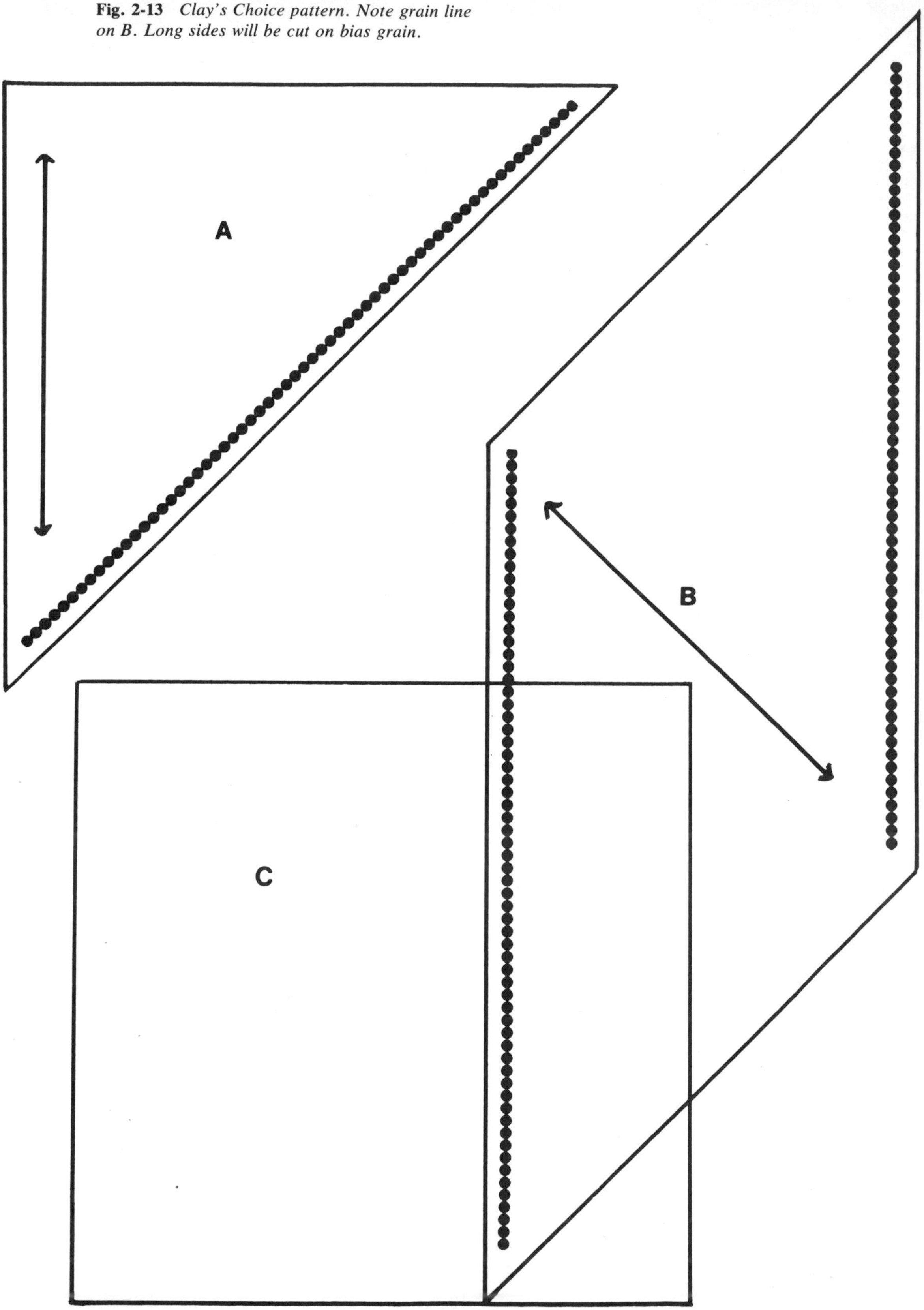

2. Stitch a print C to a background C. Stitch from raw edge to raw edge and press to the dark side. Repeat to complete the remaining three rectangles (Fig. 2-12b).

3. Stitch the A/B rectangle to the double C rectangle. Stitch from raw edge to raw edge and press to the dark side. Repeat to complete remaining three patches (Fig. 2-12c).

4. Place the patches right side up on the work surface. Make sure that the points of the parallelograms meet at the center. Stitch the two right patches, then the two left patches and finally the entire center seam.

Quilting Suggestions

Each parallelogram should be accented with rows of quilt stitching $\frac{1}{4}$ inch from the sewing line. To make it more distinctive, use two additional lines of stitching $\frac{1}{4}$ inch apart. The background can be treated as one unit with one line of stitching $\frac{1}{4}$ inch from the sewing line. Each of the print areas will be treated as above. A novel pattern of stitching such as a small leaf, can be placed in the background.

Nine-Patch Designs, Even Size

MONKEY WRENCH

Monkey Wrench is a simple division of a block into nine equal parts or patches (Fig. 2-14). Its symmetry keeps the eye moving around in a circle within this geometric configuration. Four of the equally divided patches are divided on the diagonal, forming triangles, and four are divided in half, forming rectangles. Sometimes the nine

Fig. 2-14 *Monkey Wrench, even nine-patch.*

original patches are made unequal, leaving the center larger and the eight perimeter patches a little smaller. Sometimes a smaller nine-patch is added to the center, enhancing the entire pattern. For simplicity, the novice should try this pattern. It makes a clean looking block with a broad expanse of background showing through. This 16-inch block is about as big as the pattern should be made and should only be repeated in an all over quilt that will be planned for a king size bed. However, it can be graded down to fit the proportion of any bed, even a crib. It is often seen as a scrap quilt and works very well if each geometric figure is a different color against a common ground, not necessarily a light color. This block as shown is planned for one color plus a background; bands can be used to border each patch to add a third color. If the pattern is made 10 inches or smaller, it could be placed alternating with a blank square. This shows a great deal of the background and is a good place to show off some imaginative quiltings. Another suggestion for using this as an overall pattern would be to make a bordering band the same color as the background color with a corner the same fabric as the Wrench, thus showing only a Wrench and small square on a common background.

Materials and Cutting
PATTERN A: Cut 4 background and 4 print
PATTERN B: Cut 4 background and 4 print
PATTERN C: Cut 1 background

Assembly
Stitch from raw edge to raw edge throughout.

1. Stitch a printed A to a background A. Press to the dark (Fig. 2-15a).

2. Stitch a printed B to background B. Press to the dark (Fig. 2-15b).

3. To make the left and right outer strips stitch two squares made in step 1 on either side of one square made in step 2. Arrange the colored points of the triangles so that they face the inside of the block and touch the colored

rectangles. Press to the dark; repeat for the other side (Fig. 2-15c).

4. To form the center strip, place the remaining two pieced squares on either side of piece C, with print side each touching the C patch. Press seams to the dark (Fig. 2-15d).

5. Place the center strip between the end strips, using Fig. 2-14 as a guide. Press to the dark.

Quilting Suggestions
Outline each of the print pieces $\frac{1}{4}$ inch from the sewing line and outline each of the background pieces. The large middle may be left unquilted but it is an excellent place to exhibit some interesting quilting. Three or four concentric squares or two upright diamonds would look neat. If this is made in soft colors or for a child, then use the open background for a floral type quilting.

VARIABLE STAR AND STAR-WITHIN-A-STAR

This legendary American star is a basic square divided into nine even squares or patches. Note the simplicity of the line

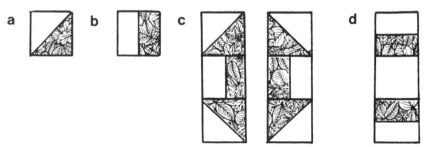

Fig. 2-15 *Monkey Wrench assembly.*

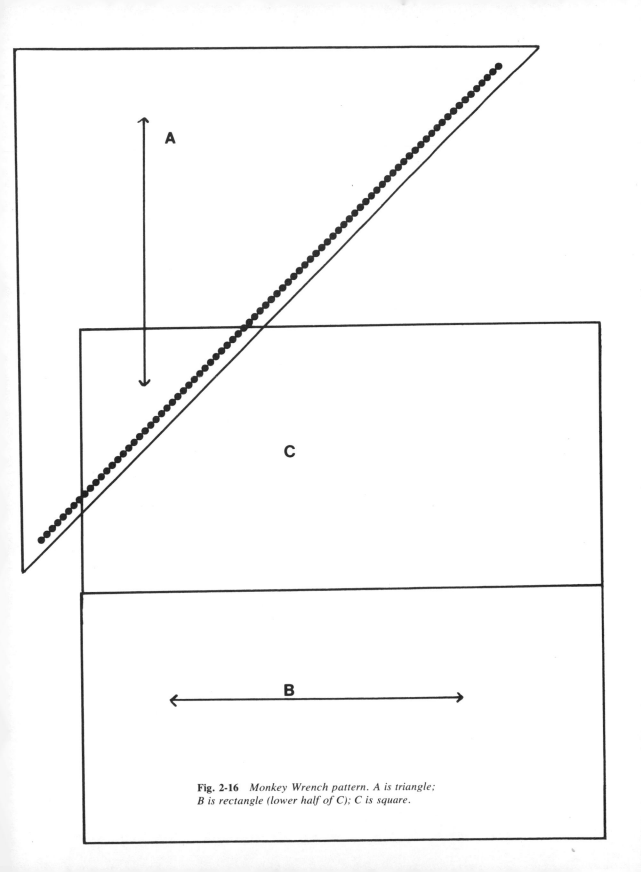

Fig. 2-16 Monkey Wrench pattern. A is triangle; B is rectangle (lower half of C); C is square.

Fig. 2-17 *Variable Star, even nine-patch.*

Fig. 2-18 *Star-Within-a-Star, even nine-patch.*

drawing (Fig. 2-20a) with four of the squares divided twice on the diagonal. It is in the arrangement of the colors within the star that makes the star interesting. It is important to identify the background of the star and never use any of the background color in your star, or it will look like it has a hole in it. It is a very powerful design when made in a strong color and used as an all-over design. It does need to be separated in some manner either by intersecting bands (2 to 3 inches wide) if block is 14 to 16 inches or by a blank block if graded to a 12-inch or smaller size. Even when working with a smaller star, the block looks good with the bands if they are scaled down (1 to $1\frac{1}{2}$ inches wide).

Another interesting version of Variable Star in an overall quilt design is to place it on "the diamond". This means instead of using the block as a square, it is turned on the bed for a diamond shape.

Fig. 2-19 *Variable Star can be made with two prints for its design but do not use the background fabric in the star. Made by Barbara Hennig.*

38

Use the bands to separate the stars. The drop or sides will have a sawtooth edge of stars. Fill this in with solid colored fabric, matching the background of the stars and filling in with a handsome quilt design.

Another stunning variation of this star is to divide the center patch into a star just like the main star. This is called a Star-Within-a-Star (Fig. 2-18). It is important here to watch colorations. The mini star should be a definite contrasting color from the main star. This way it looks like the mini star is emerging from the middle of the large star. The value of working with small pieces of patchwork should not be lost on poor coloration. It is not advisable to take on the Star-Within-a-Star as a novice since small pieces are hard to work with.

As proficiency develops then attempt the mini-star; the mini-star would replace pattern A and, after sewing, will be the same size as A.

The large star goes together very accurately on the machine making a very strong face. It can be beautifully worked in pastels for baby quilts. If you really get into working small pieces of patchwork, the mini-star can be repeated many times for a baby quilt, alternating with a blank block. You can begin to see how this pattern got the name Variable Star.

Materials and Cutting

PATTERN A: Cut 4 background and 1 print
    (which matches or contrasts with B)
PATTERN B: Cut 12 print and 4 background

For the Star-Within-a-Star use AA and BB to form mini-star in place of center A. Stitch from raw edge to raw edge.

Assembly

1. Stitch one print B to a second print B, along the bias cut edge. Press open seam; repeat three more times (Fig. 2-20b, left).

2. Stitch one print B to one background B, along the bias cut edge. Press seam to the dark; repeat three more times (Fig. 2-20b, right).

3. Unite a triangle from step 1 with a triangle of step 2, matching center seams. Stitch along the long bias edge and press to the dark. Press right side. Repeat to complete the three additional bi-colored patches (Fig. 2-20c).

4. Using Fig. 2-20d as a guide, place the 9 patch on the work surface, right side up, forming three vertical strips. Stitch one A background to one bi-colored patch completed in step 3; attach another A background below it. Repeat for the opposite side, keeping background fabric at outer edges. To form the center strip, sew one bi-colored unit to the print B (or mini-star if used) and add the remaining bi-colored patch, keeping the background toward the outside edge. Press seams to the dark and press the right side.

5. Unite the three strips with two vertical seams. Press long seams to the dark and press the right side.

Quilting Suggestions

This geometric design could hold softly curved lines of quilting, almost making a floral effect. Geometric quilt lines and perhaps the addition of diamond patterns in the center of the large patch would also work. If the mini-star is added, then quilt the outline of the mini-star. A trick quilters

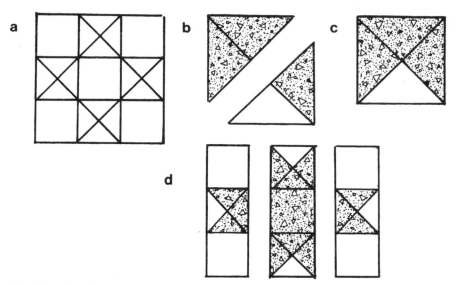

Fig. 2-20 *Variable Star assembly.*

use to give more definition to the mini-star is to baste a small square of batting, the size of the star patch, to the wrong side of the mini-star. When placed over the regular batting, this part will stand out more clearly, having a double layer. This trick can be used almost anywhere for more definition of a small area.

Nine-Patch Designs, Uneven Size

DUCK AND DUCKLINGS

The name of this block should draw on your imagination. The early settlers of this country had a great desire to record part of their life style in their craft articles. One common pleasure, then and now, is our love of birds. Many times triangles represent bird forms. In this case we are dou-

bly blessed with four ducks and four ducklings represented by the large and small colored triangles. This is still a nine-patch design but is greatly altered. The outer four corner patches are enlarged and the inner four patches are narrowed down to what looks like long strips, further reducing the remaining center patch.

Due to the pictorial nature of the block, it is best separated by bands if repeated in a single quilt. By placing it one after the other without bands, it would lose some of the impact of the design. The Duck and Ducklings can be the same color, two different solid colors, two different but compatible prints or a reverse print combination; but do not use assorted scraps. This pattern can be graded down somewhat but below 10 inches the pieces get very small. The center piece is occasionally referred to as the Rising Sun or the Moon as in the

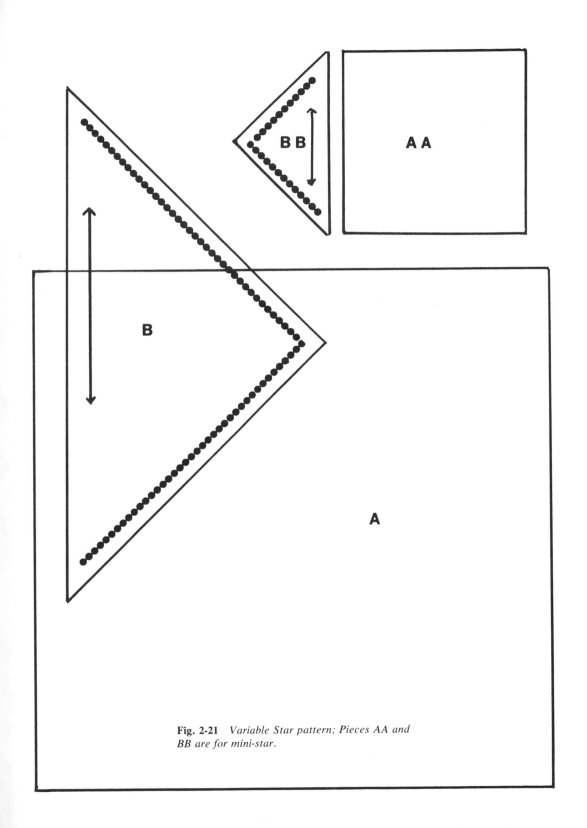

Fig. 2-21 *Variable Star pattern; Pieces AA and BB are for mini-star.*

Fig. 2-22 *Duck and Ducklings, uneven nine-patch. Made by Joan Shaw.*

early morning or evening when we sometimes see flocks of birds. For this reason, the center square is often colored sun or moon colors.

Materials and Cutting

PATTERN A: Cut 4 prints
PATTERN B: Cut 4 prints (same as A or complimentary) and 12 background
PATTERN C: Cut 4 background
PATTERN D: Cut 1 solid color

Assembly

Up to now the work has been concentrated on simple combinations of pieces within a patch and ultimately an entire block. Here, while the actual sewing is not hard, the success of the four corner patches will depend on an orderly method of work. The outer corner of each patch holds the figure of the duckling. It is important that when the entire duckling corner (the duck-

ling and three adjoining triangles) is finished, it will be equal to the large duck.

1. Stitch two B background pieces to either nonbias side of print B to form a strip. Stitch from raw edge to raw edge and press to the dark (Fig. 2-23a).

2. Add the remaining background B to the print B, uniting the bias edges. Stitch from raw edge to raw edge. Press to the dark and press the front of the entire piece (Fig. 2-23b).

3. Place the long bias edge of portion completed in step 2 against the long bias cut edge of A. Stitch raw edge to raw edge. Press to the dark (Fig. 2-23c). Repeat these three steps to complete the other three corner patches.

4. Stitch the narrow ends of two C's to either side of D (Fig. 2-23d). Do not stitch to the raw edge but merely on marked sewing line. Note that by keeping these corner seams open on the center piece D, they become easy to press to the dark side with the point of a warm iron.

5. Referring to Fig. 2-22, stitch the long edge of a corner patch finished in step 3 to either side of C. On the outer edge stitch to the raw edge; on the inner portion (the part where the duck will form the center of the design), stop stitching at the marked sewing line (Fig. 2-23e). Press to the dark and repeat for the other side.

6. Stitch the two outer strips to the newly made center strip, step 4. Stitch all the way to raw edges on the outer portion but, at the center where stitches are to cross the D piece seams, pass needle through seam allowance leaving seams free. Press seam to the dark side. (Refer to Fig. 2-5.) Accuracy in marking

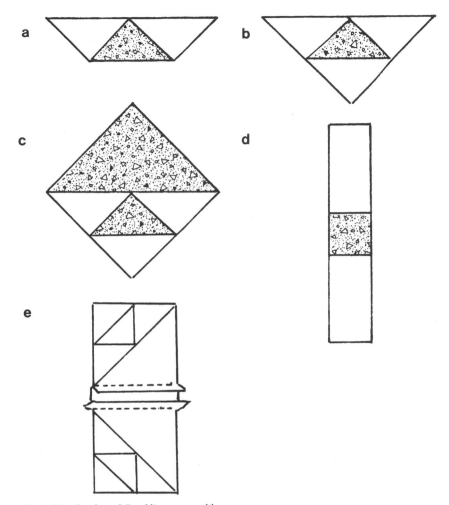

Fig. 2-23 *Duck and Ducklings assembly.*

and stitching on the sewing line to produce a neat block is very important in this block. If the work is not finished with the background closing each outer seam allowance, then rip out and check accuracy in patternmaking and/or marking.

Quilting Suggestions

Accent the bird forms and the center square by quilting $\frac{1}{4}$ inch from the seam line. That would be sufficient to hold the patch together but it would be more interesting to quilt in each of the background pieces as well.

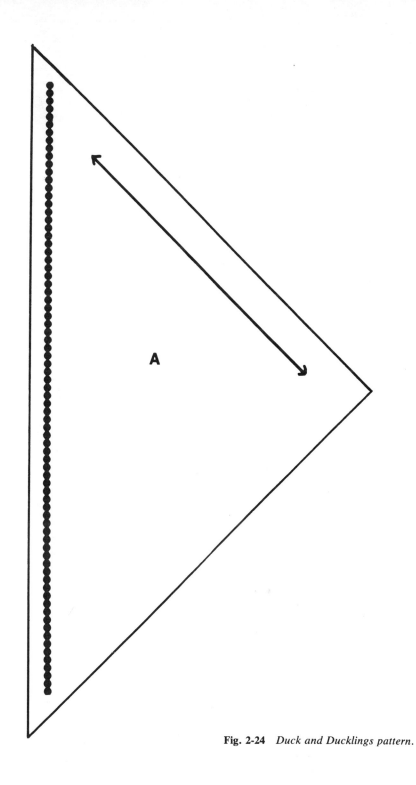

Fig. 2-24 *Duck and Ducklings pattern.*

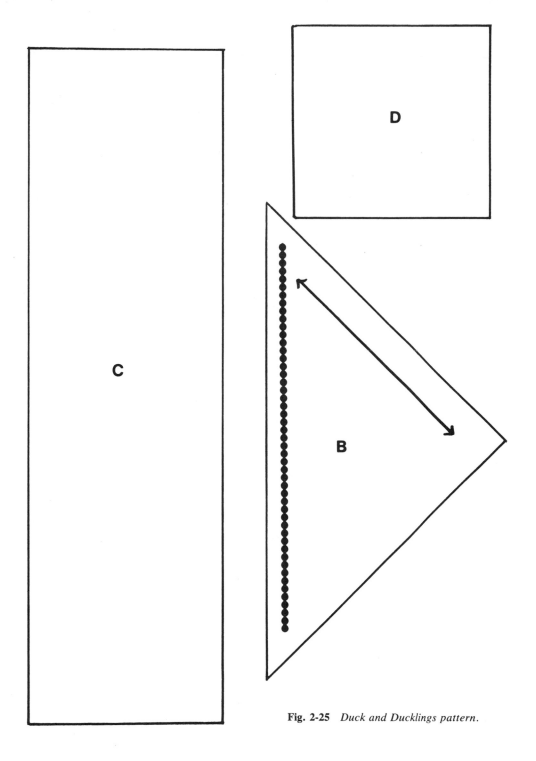

Fig. 2-25 *Duck and Ducklings pattern.*

Fig. 2-26 *Stepping Stones, uneven nine-patch.*

STEPPING STONES

Stepping Stones is an uneven nine-patch (Fig. 2-26). Its center section is one-fifth slimmer than the corner patches. Although it has many pieces, they go together very easily. In grading the pattern for this text, I eliminated eight seams and eight extra pieces to cut in the outer corner patches by using a rectangle in place of two small squares. Doing patchwork is a lot like a good detective story. You have to put all the pieces together to make them come out with the proper solutions.

This type of block design is placed one after the other in a large quilt so that a diagonal effect is achieved with the small diagonal lines of squares and a vertical-horizontal effect is presented with the chevrons and the center square.

This is also very effective as a two-color quilt playing light against dark with solid fabrics. This creates a strong silhouette pattern.

Materials and Cutting
PATTERN A: Cut 12 strong solid colors and 8 background
PATTERN B: Cut 8 background
PATTERN C: Cut 1 print, strong color
PATTERN D: Cut 8 prints (same as C)
PATTERN E: Cut 16 background

Assembly
There are two designs held in eight patches. Prepare the four outer corner patches. The entire piece of work should be stitched on the seam lines but not through to the raw edges.

1. Stitch a solid color A to background B. Repeat this again (Fig. 2-27a).

2. Stitch two background A's to either side of one solid color A and press (Fig. 2-27b).

3. Assemble for the diagonal effect, press (Fig. 2-27c). Repeat for other three corners.

4. Stitch two background E's to either end of one D. Repeat for the other half of patch. Press to the dark side.

5. Stitch the chevron centers together and press center seam open (Fig. 2-27d). Repeat steps 4 and 5 to complete the other three chevron-like patches.

6. Following Fig. 2-26, place all nine patches together on the work surface to be sure of placement. Stitch the two narrow ends of the chevron pieces (steps 4 and 5) to either side of the remaining C piece. Stitch two each of the checkered corner squares (step 3) to the wide side

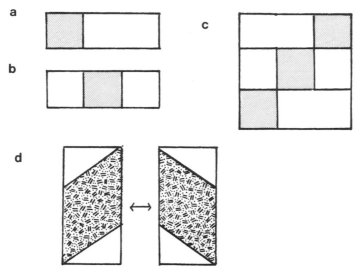

Fig. 2-27 *Stepping Stones assembly.*

of the remaining chevrons. The point of each chevron should face the center.

7. After the three strips are sewn together, assemble into one complete block.

Quilting Suggestions

Stitch $\frac{1}{4}$ inch off the seam line of all the important portions: the center square, the chevrons (treat as one design portion) and each of the small blocks leading up to the center. Treat the remaining space of the background as one and quilt within its perimeter.

Time-Saving with Mixed Stripes

Actual stripe fabric is generally avoided in most quilting techniques because it is difficult to cut accurate repeats. The viewer's eye picks up any mistakes very quickly.

There are patterns where stripe-like effects are created in certain areas of a design block. To speed up the process of making these stripe-like effects, specific widths of fabric are sewn together at one time on the machine. A template is placed against the wrong side and the square or specific shape is cut out all at once (Fig. 2-30e). The time saved in cutting small pieces would be increased considerably. This would be feasible when repeating a design block many times in a quilt that called for a stripe-like effect within one of its patches. It is the sewing machine that will relieve the tiresome task of matching small individually cut stripes.

There are two considerations when planning to utilize this time-saving method. First and foremost is the grain line. In utilizing this idea for a pattern like Country Roads, the grain is most important because when the outer four patches are completed

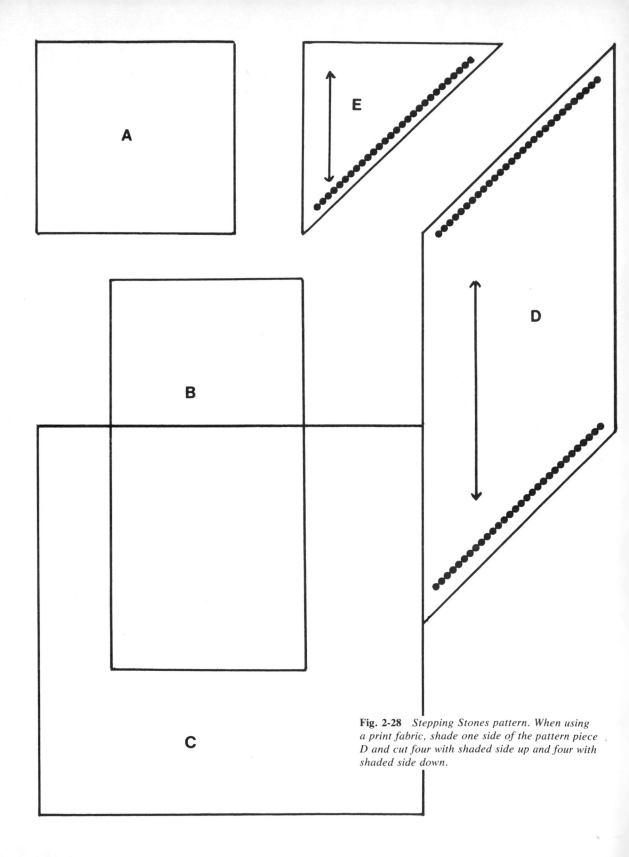

Fig. 2-28 *Stepping Stones pattern. When using a print fabric, shade one side of the pattern piece D and cut four with shaded side up and four with shaded side down.*

they will be in the straight of the grain. A careful look at this block will show that the center and four middle patches are assembled as the Variable Star given earlier. In order that the corner stripes remain on the straight of the grain, they must be cut on the bias. When seamed together on the bias, the stripes must be sewn together in the right color order too (Fig. 2-30e).

If a totally hand-sewn patch is desired, then the stripes for the corner patches are cut out and sewn individually. The pieces that form the stripes, pattern pieces C and D, are both cut with their longest edges on the bias.

In the pattern Water Wheel, stripes are cut on the straight of the grain because trying to cut and sew them all on the bias would be a difficult task. They will create a strong piece of work on the straight of grain. The four triangular background pieces will have the longest sides placed on the straight of the grain; the two short sides will be bias cut.

The second most important factor is cutting the stripes accurately and stitching on the sewing line only. The quickest way to do this is to cut a length of cardboard the size of the width required without seam allowance. Draw the width on the wrong side of the fabric and cut it estimating the seam allowance. When cutting any bias material, always have it pressed carefully before cutting so as not to stretch it. Stitch only on the sewing line. Press to the dark, but also examine and press the face.

COUNTRY ROADS

This is a strong geometric pattern to be worked in bright colors. It is used one after

Fig. 2-29 *Country Roads.*

the other in an all-over quilt. The outer dark tone will unite as the blocks come together. It is sometimes called Deer in the Woods. It is most important to get a good contrast in the colors. Note the similarity of the line drawing to that of Variable Star.

Materials and Cutting
PATTERN A: Cut 1 solid color
PATTERN B: Cut 4 solid colors, 8 medium light print, 4 dark print

For hand stitching:
PATTERN C: 4 medium light print, 4 dark print
PATTERN D: 4 solid colors, 4 background

If using time-saving method for C and D, cut four bias strips, each $1\frac{14}{16}$ inches wide without seam allowance. See step 5 below.

Assembly

1. Stitch the bias edge of one B solid color to one B medium print. Press to the dark and repeat three more times. Press seams to the dark (Fig. 2-30a).

2. Stitch on the bias one B medium print to one B dark print, repeat three more times. Press to the dark (Fig. 2-30b).

3. Stitch on the long bias one triangle from step 1 to one triangle from step 2. Repeat three more times (Fig. 2-30c). Press and set aside.

4. *For hand stitching only:* Stitch one medium print C to one solid color D. Repeat three more times. Stitch one dark print C to one background D. Repeat three more times. Stitch on the long bias edge of the two bicolored triangles, uniting the medium print C to

the dark print C. Press all seams to the dark. Repeat three more times.

5. *For machine work and time-saving methods:* Cut bias strips $1\frac{14}{16}$ inches wide at the marked seam allowance or $2\frac{6}{16}$ inches wide at the raw cut edge. Cut one solid color, one medium print, one dark print and one background color approximately 32 inches long for four squares. Sew strips together and use pattern piece A to cut a single square patch (Fig. 2-30e). Repeat for other three square patches. If many patches were needed for a full quilt, then the bias strips could be cut longer.

6. Place all the patches on the work surface, using (Fig. 2-29) as a guide. Make three patch strips, uniting two diagonal strip patches from step 4 or 5 on either side of a four-piece bias patch

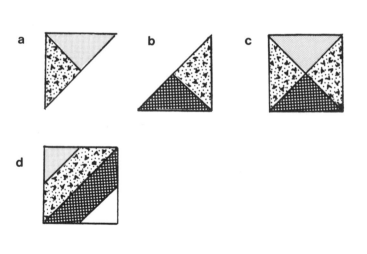
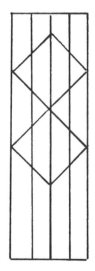

Fig. 2-30 *Country Roads assembly.*

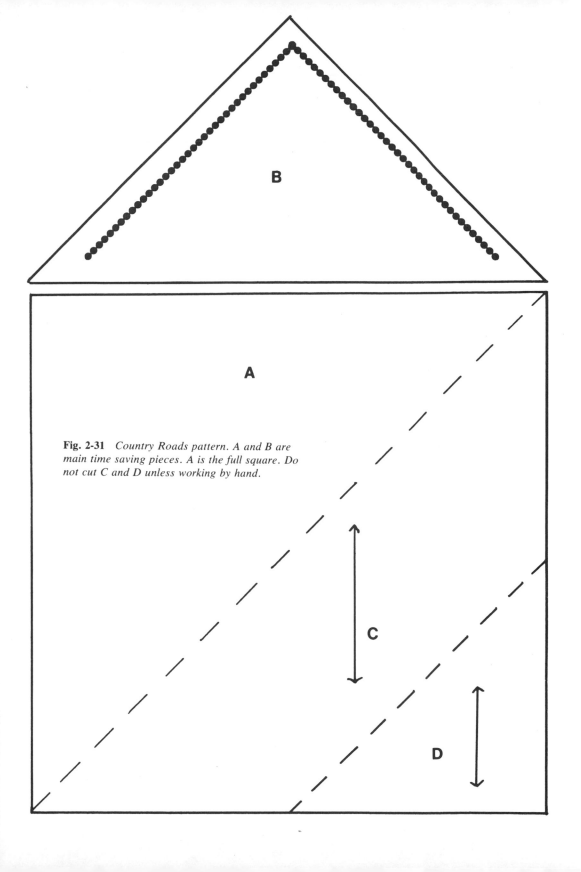

Fig. 2-31 *Country Roads pattern. A and B are main time saving pieces. A is the full square. Do not cut C and D unless working by hand.*

from step 3. Repeat for the opposite side, always keeping the dark print B to the inside of the block. Stitch the remaining two patches made in step 3 to either side of the solid color A. Keep the solid side of the two patches against the A above and below. Unite the three strips into one complete block, matching corner seams.

Quilting Suggestions

Outline the solid color center $\frac{1}{4}$ inch from the seam allowance and add some decorative stitches in this area. Outline both prints and the background $\frac{1}{4}$ inch off all the seam lines. If this was in a full quilt, the dark print would make a much larger area for quilting than in one single block.

This is not a beginner's block. This is a medium to difficult piece to assemble. The advantage here is that the quilt assembly line techniques are offered to complete a varied piece block in a short time. The coloring is interesting to study but the sewing is actually quite easy.

WATER WHEEL

This old pattern, while quite traditional, can be worked into a truly brilliant contemporary edition. The colors for a traditional design should have the strongest color on the longest stripe and colors should slowly diminish in intensity toward the shortest stripe. This gives movement to the three part wheel of stripes. For a modern look, use solid colors of the same intensity. It will look like a fire cracker exploding. It could be made with multi-stripes as a scrap quilt. This may fill the need to get rid of a lot of scraps but it will not give a feeling of movement to the pattern. Water Wheels' strong pattern and colors are well liked by the young set and the male population.

The strips can be cut on the straight of the grain. In a pattern like this, the stitching in the seams will hold the seams firm. Be careful not to stretch the diagonal cut across the stripes. The block may be enlarged and more stripes may be added. The block will have a stronger construction when finished especially when using this block in a full quilt. In a full quilt, this block will be set together one after the other with no bands. It is best to assemble these into a four-patch block first, as shown here.

The time-saving method of making stripes is to cut the stripes from the assorted fabrics first. Assemble into the stripe order needed; in this case, dark, medium and light shading. Press seams to the dark or all in one direction. For the block as shown, the stripes will be 1 by 34 inches long for each patch. It is best to cut a strip of cardboard this desired width and one the desired width plus the seam allowance (in this case $1\frac{1}{2}$ inches wide). This makes quick work of marking and cutting stripes. To speed your work, stitch these by machine until they form the width needed; in this case, $3\frac{1}{2}$ inches wide, including the outside seam allowances of the first and last stripe. Use pattern A to place over stripes on the wrong side, positioning it so it remains within the seam allowance. Mark the top and bottom sewing lines, add the seam allowance on top and bottom and cut out. A major portion of the work is done (Fig. 2-33a). You will quickly have 16 three-stripe pieces. There will be a waste of some portion of the stripes. This can be kept and

Fig. 2-32 *Water Wheel.*

used for a smaller project such as a pot-holder or pillow top.

Materials and Cutting

PATTERN A: Cut 16 multi-stripe pieces (as described above)

PATTERN B: Cut 16 background

Stitch from raw edge to raw edge.

Assembly

1. Stitch one background B to the shortest stripe of the piece A (Fig. 2-33b). This will make a triangle. Repeat for the other fifteen pieces; press to the dark.

2. Stitch two of these triangles together, using Fig. 2-33c as a guide. This will form half of the patch; seam will be on the diagonal. Repeat to complete seven more triangles; press to the dark.

3. Unite the diagonal seams to complete four patches (Fig. 2-32). Press seam open.

4. Using Fig. 2-32 as a guide, assemble the four patches into a 16-inch block. Press seams open or to the dark if possible.

Time Saving with the Sawtooth Edge

The element of design for a sawtooth edge is a square cut in half on the diagonal. Half of the square, or one triangle, is dark and the other light. When arranged in rows, these look like the teeth of a saw (Fig. 2-35a). If an authentic quilt is desired, then these triangles must have equal amounts of light and dark colors and must be stitched together on the bias edge. The machine can cut this tedious work in half. We know that triangles that will be half of a square have the bias cut edge on longest side. This allows for the outer corners, both the dark and the light, to remain on the straight of the grain. Cut bias strips of dark and light fabric the width from the bias seam to the corner point and add seam allowance to either side. As an example, a 2-inch square divided on the diagonal, measures $1\frac{7}{16}$ inches from center bias line to unjoined corner. Add the $\frac{1}{4}$-inch seam allowances to that and we get a full 2 inches (Fig. 2-35b). For safety, cut strips $2\frac{1}{4}$ inches wide on the bias from the light and dark fabric and stitch them together like stripes with $\frac{1}{4}$-inch seams (Fig. 2-36). The full 2-inch square pattern, with seam allowance, can be placed for marking on the diamond over one seam which unites a light and dark stripe. This is marked indicating both cutting line and sewing line. After cutting the diamond shape out, turn it so it appears as a square. The grain line will remain straight, with a bias seam uniting the two triangles of light and

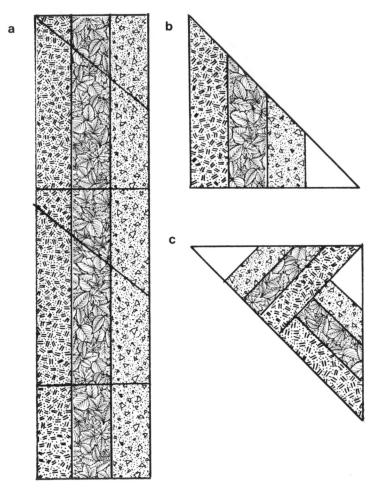

Fig. 2-33 *Water Wheel assembly, using pre-stitched multistriped units.*

dark. Use only two strips if you have only a few sawtooth squares to cut; however if the pattern calls for many sawtooth squares to be assembled, then cut and sew together many bias strips. The use of multi-stripes affords an opportunity to place one dia-mond pattern next to the other with waste only at the edges. Use 10 to 12 stitches to the inch on the machine and keep the ten-sion light when sewing any bias. The stitches will not open at the point ends if handled carefully. Strips need not be exactly even

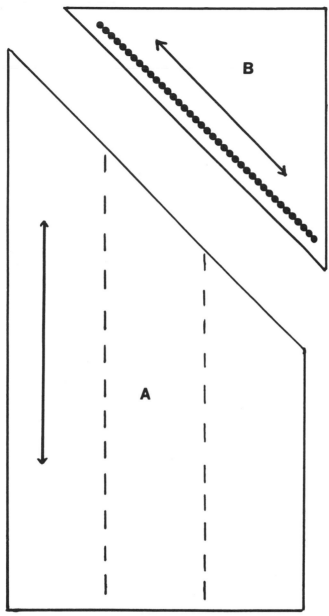

Fig. 2-34 *Water Wheel pattern.*

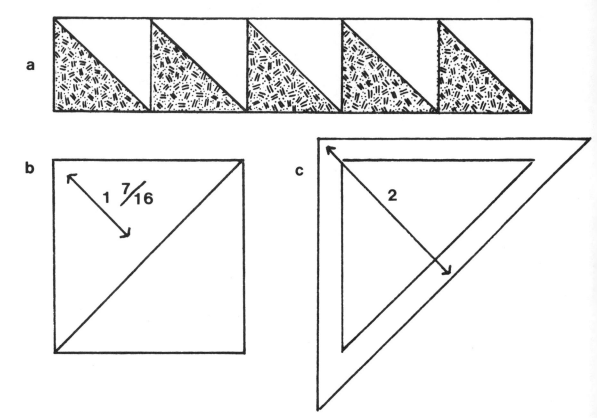

Fig. 2-35 *(a) Sawtooth edge row; (b) 2" square divided on the diagonal half equalling $1\frac{7}{16}$ (c) the same square with $\frac{1}{4}$-inch seam allowance added equalling 2".*

at the top and bottom. This method will cut your work time in half.

Now these strips are treated as dark and light diagonally split squares not as a lot of little triangles. Stitch them together in rows, pinning together the correct number and then working one after the other through the machine. The Pine Tree quilt in Fig. 2-37 was made that way. It used 36 diagonally split squares plus 6 individual

dark triangles on the ends for each block. The quilt has 9 blocks so 324 diagonally split squares were needed and 54 small dark triangles fill in on the edges. Each 20 × 20-inch block took nine experienced quilters about four to five hours or about 40 hours for a center top 60 inches square. It would have taken another 20 hours to assemble the little diagonal squares by hand and it would have meant cutting 324 dark trian-

Fig. 2-36 *Timesaving method for sawtooth edge. Cut bias lengths of fabric in both light and dark colors and stitch together, alternating the colors. Place a square window frame template on the diamond so the long end of the diamond is over the seam. Trace the inside sewing line and the outside cutting line. Trace as many as you need before cutting.*

gles and 324 light triangles. With the additional dark corners added, the top measures approximately 80 inches square.

BEAR'S PAW

Bear's Paw is a silhouette pattern of dark outlines against a light background (Fig. 2-

38). This is the traditional coloring. When this coloring is reversed, using a light color silhouette and a dark background, it is called Duck's Foot in the Mud. It is easy to see the block is an uneven nine-patch design. By making the corner patches and the center in one color, the paw print silhouette is obvious. There are many other quilt patterns with animal identification names like Goose Tracks, Snails Trail and even Spider Web.

Materials and Cutting

PATTERN A or B: If hand piecing, cut 12 dark A and 12 dark B. If using the time-saving method, cut 12 combined color pieces using B

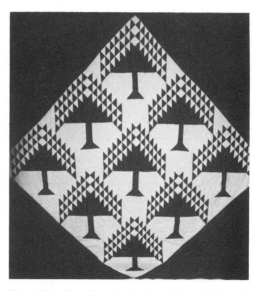

Fig. 2-37 *Pine Tree Quilt. Nine 20″ × 20″ blocks are used in the center. The trees stand upright because they are placed on the diamond. There are two horses quilted under each tree and snowflakes quilted into the four dark green corners. Designed by Dorothy Frager.*

Fig. 2-38 *Bear's Paw, uneven nine-patch, featuring a sawtooth edge. Made by Joan Shaw.*

PATTERN B: Cut 4 background
PATTERN C: Cut 4 same dark color as in A
PATTERN D: Cut 4 background
PATTERN E: Cut 4 same dark color as in A

Assembly

Stitch from raw edge to raw edge except when working on the E piece (steps 6 and 7).

1. If hand stitching, sew the bias edge of the background A to the bias edge of the dark A until all twelve squares are equal to pattern piece B. Press to the dark.

Alternate: For the time-saving method (Fig. 2-35, 2-36), select two bias strips (one background and one a dark color). Cut one strip 2½ × 58 inches, or four short strips each 2½ × 20 inches. This includes the ¼-inch seam allowance. Stitch the strips together on the bias

edges, alternating colors. Press to the dark side and press the right side too. Cut 12 squares, using pattern B (as suggested in Fig. 2-36).

2. Stitch together two of the finished squares from step 1 (Fig. 2-39a). Repeat three more times, press and set aside.

3. Stitch two of the finished squares from step 1 and one background B (Fig. 2-39b). Repeat three more rows; press to the dark.

4. Using Fig. 2-39c as a guide, stitch the two squares from step 2 along one side of the large dark C and add the three squares from step 3 along the adjoining side. Repeat until all four corners (or paws) are completed; press to the dark side.

5. Using Fig. 2-39d as a guide, stitch a patch from step 4 to one of the long sides of piece D. Stitch a second patch from step 4 to the other side of D. Keep the points of the paw patches pointing out of the block. Repeat for the opposite side and press to the dark.

6. Stitch the short end of one of the remaining D's to the single E. Stitch only on the seam line, not from raw edge to raw edge as you did in steps 1 to 5. This will give you flexibility in turning all seams at the middle of this block to the dark side. Add the remaining D to the opposite side of E, press to the dark (Fig. 2-39e).

7. Using Fig. 2-38 as a guide, assemble the two outer portions made in step 5 to either side of the narrow strip made in step 6. When stitching, begin at the raw edges and stitch past the first patch (or paw) to the point of joining the

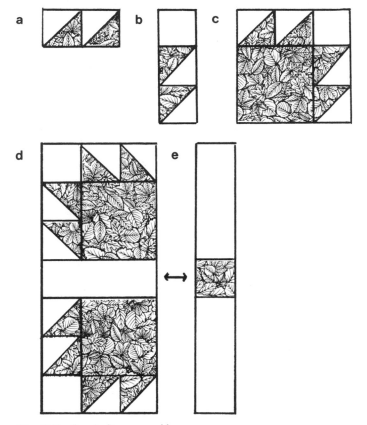

Fig. 2-39 *Bear's Paw assembly.*

E portions to the short end of D, sew only on the seam line. This will mean you will lift the seam allowances up pass the needle through at the bottom of the seam allowance and stitch only on the marked sewing line. This will allow freedom to turn the seam for piece E to the dark side.

The Bear's Paw is generally used as a single pattern in a full quilt. It is made with bordering bands running between the blocks of the same color or a shade closely matched to that used in the paws. The bands set off the blocks.

Quilting Suggestions

For simple quilting, outline each of the D pieces and each of the separate background pieces of triangles and squares $\frac{1}{4}$ inch in from the seam line. Outline the entire paw print as one piece $\frac{1}{4}$ inch off the seam line and another $\frac{1}{2}$ inch further in-

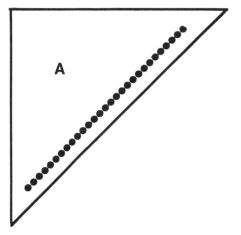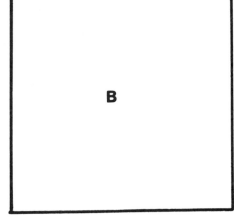

Fig. 2-40 *Bear's Paw pattern.*

ward; or another geometric design can be added within the paw print and perhaps echoed in a smaller version in the center square E. The bordering bands should have a small 2¼ inch running diamond design, or any other design that you feel flows.

This is an easy block to sew together, especially when using the methods suggested earlier. The method of leaving the seam allowance free at the center makes the block look very handsome as no dark seam allowances will show under the light color of the background. The coloring is simple and is the same throughout the quilt. This is a very good solid color quilt. The number of pieces allows us to do a lot of simple outline quilting. This is a favorite pattern of men and boys. As soon as they understand what the pattern depicts, they gravitate to it.

PINE TREE

This Pine Tree block chosen for a sampler quilt is worked on the diagonal. It is easy to make and will work very well being placed in a bottom outer corner of the sampler quilt. In the space allowed in a sampler quilt, 16 × 16 inches, it is better for the design to have a massive tree rather than a sapling. It will give the quilter a good test of her abilities to work out all the suggestions given earlier for time-saving techniques with the sawtooth. The Pine Tree is made mostly by forming rows of sawtooth-edge squares. Here it is imperative that the quilter make good use of her time.

The word Pine Tree immediately brings to mind the color green. It is not necessarily so in American quilting. I have seen stunning blue Pine Tree quilts and even

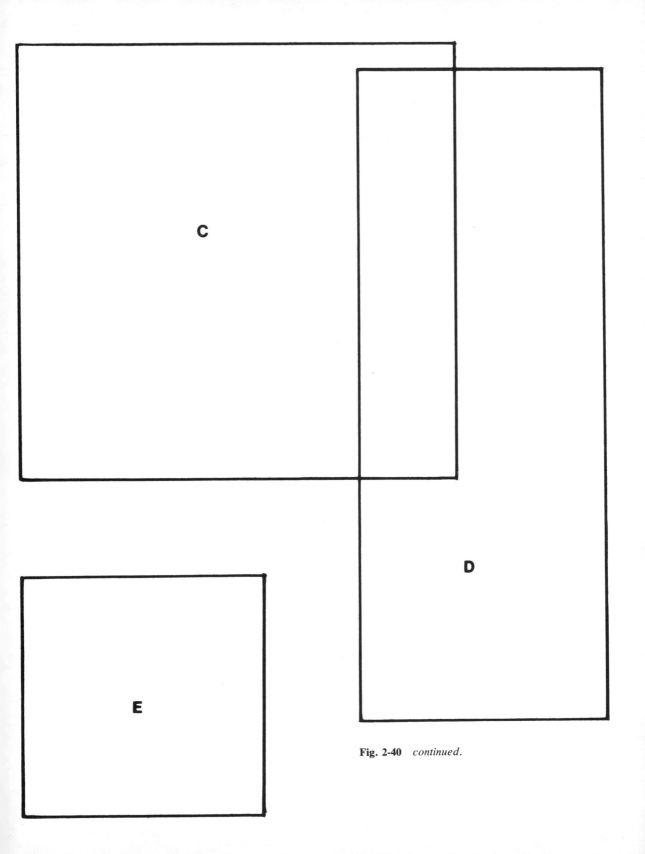

C

D

E

Fig. 2-40 *continued*.

Fig. 2-41 *Pine Tree with multi-sawtooth design.*

red ones. It would be possible to work out a light and dark combination of the same color against a light background. The traditional way is to use a dark tone with a light background. Sometimes this is called the Tree of Life.

It is traditional to place the Pine Tree on the diagonal in an overall quilt design but it can be placed upright. Pine Tree blocks may be placed one after another in the diamond form as shown in the almost finished quilt photo (Fig. 2-37). There nine Pine Tree blocks form the large center diamond, measuring 60 × 60 inches. The outer corners were added in the dark color to form the balance of the quilt, measuring approximately 80 × 80 inches. Horses are quilted under the trees and four large snowflakes finish off the outer corners. This top was placed over a backing of a holly floral print. Sometimes to enlarge quilts, a blank or empty block is alternated with the design block. This block is then enhanced with quilt stitchery. For a baby quilt or wall hanging, one 16 × 16 inch Pine Tree block may be placed on the diamond in an upright position with four 16 × 11½ × 11½ inch triangles surrounding it to form the square (Fig. 1-2) center. Then a 3-inch outer border of the dark color can be added to frame the entire piece. This would equal a piece 25 × 25 inches to make the piece into a large wall hanging or a small quilt.

Additional outer borders may be added, each one increasing in width. This adds a dramatic frame to the single design. Four compatible designs such as found in the four-piece wall hanging called Garden's Delight (see color section) can be used on the diamond, too, as the single pine tree. With additional borders, it makes a medium size quilt.

This gives the crafter an idea how this or any group of designs can be worked into larger quilt designs. When a quilt has a very large design in the center, with added borders, it is called a medallion design quilt.

Materials and Cutting

PATTERN A or B: If hand piecing, cut 30 dark A and 24 background A. If using the time-saving method as suggested earlier (Fig. 2-36), then cut 24 squares of the combined colors using pattern B and 6 dark color using pattern A

PATTERN B: Cut 3 background

PATTERN C: Cut 2 background

PATTERN D: To make pattern, on a separate piece of pattern board, draw a 10-inch square. Divide that in half on the diagonal, add seam allowance and cut one of dark color and one of the background.

PATTERN E: One tree trunk to be appliqued

62

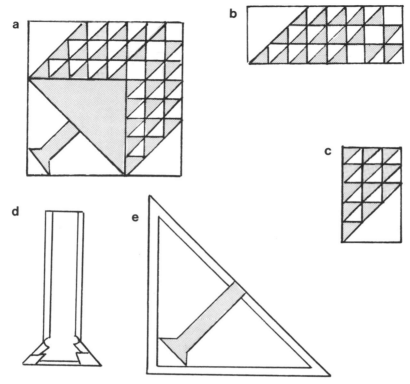

Fig. 2-42 *Pine Tree assembly.*

Assembly

Throughout this block, stitch from raw edge to raw edge, except for the tree trunk.

1. If hand stitching, sew the bias edge of background A to the bias edge of a dark color A until 24 squares are completed.

Alternate: If the time-saving technique is used, stitch together six alternating dark and background bias strips 2½ × 20 inches (Fig. 2-36). Use pattern B to cut 24 squares.

2. Using Fig. 2-42b as a guide, assemble three rows, using a total of fifteen combined color squares, three dark A's, three background B's and one background C. Assemble in rows, then sew the rows together and finish by adding the single C. This piece will finish 16 × 6 inches, not counting seam allowance. Press to the dark as each row is assembled.

3. Using Fig. 2-42c as a guide, stitch together 9 combined color squares from step 1, three dark A's and the remaining C piece. Combine into rows and finish

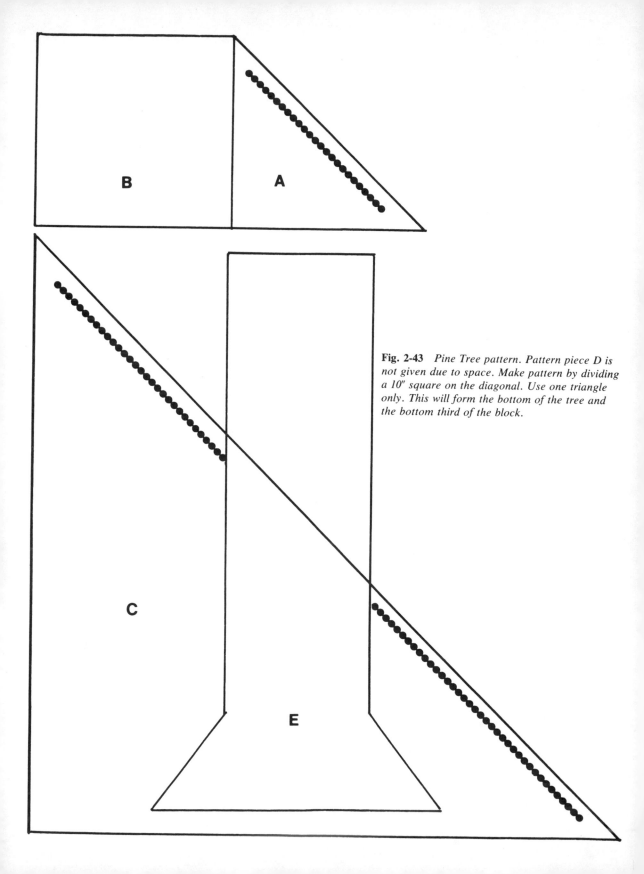

Fig. 2-43 *Pine Tree pattern. Pattern piece D is not given due to space. Make pattern by dividing a 10″ square on the diagonal. Use one triangle only. This will form the bottom of the tree and the bottom third of the block.*

by adding the C. The finished size will be 10 × 6 inches. Press to the dark as each row is assembled.

4. Turn the seam allowance to the wrong side of E, clipping in the corners to form bottom of tree trunk. Baste seam allowance to wrong side on all but top of trunk. Center and baste the trunk to the background D (Fig. 2-42d and e). Make sure the top of tree trunk seam allowance is not turned but is flush with the raw edge of the background seam allowance. Applique with *small* slipstitches (see applique) or small overcast stitches, using the same color thread as the applique or trunk.

5. Attach the background D with the trunk appliqued to the dark color D. Stitch across center, catching upper seam allowance of the trunk in seam. Press to the dark.

6. Stitch the portion made in step 3 (Fig. 2-42c) to the side of portion made in step 5, (Fig. 2-42a, lower portion). Press to the dark.

7. Stitch the remaining portion made in step 2 (Fig. 2-42b) above the portion assembled in step 6 and press (Fig. 2-42a and 2-41).

Quilting Suggestions

For simple quilting, stitch ¼ inch off the seam allowances of each background triangle. Outline quilt each C and D piece and around the trunk.

Three-Pieced Corners

This is one of the most important techniques in advanced patchwork art. Remember that up to this point, the work has concentrated mainly on squares, triangles made from diagonally divided squares and some parallelograms which were graded as single pattern pieces. There are, however, areas in the pattern making of a block where two pieces can be combined to form one solid pattern piece such as a triangle. This cuts down on both the cutting and sewing work. It also gives a more intricate look to the work. The intrinsic value is increased because this sewing technique requires a high level of dexterity and absolute accuracy in cutting, marking and stitching on the marked sewing line. Having made all or many of the blocks before this, the abilities needed for this technique can now be developed.

The point of the three-pieced corner is flanked by two bias edges of equal length. The longer edge is on the straight of the grain (Fig. 2-44a). Where a corner square, triangle or any other shape is to be joined, stitch only on the seam line that is to receive the point of the triangle. Stop stitching where the line stops. Backstitch to secure end of the sewn line (Fig. 2-44b). Open work in hand. Do not press seam.

Keep the wrong side of the work facing you. That would mean the seam that was just made in Fig. 2-44b. Keep the triangle behind, right sides together. The trick in putting in these corners accurately is to pin one bias cut edge to the right hand side of the work first. Place the first pin in the right hand side of the triangle where the bias and straight of the grain come together marked with *. Add additional pins to secure the two marked lines. Place all pins at right angles to the marked seam lines. The end of the line of the triangle marked ** will be placed exactly at point of the vertical seam made in Fig. 2-44b.

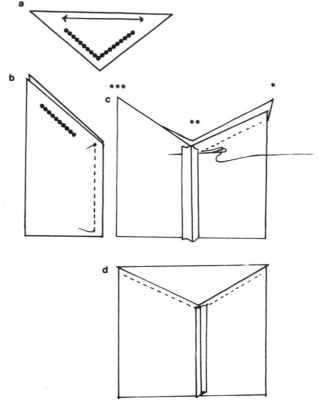

Fig. 2-44 *Three-pieced corner inset technique.*
Hold work as shown in picture with first seam
facing you.

Starting with a knot, stitch from the raw edge side of the line (*) to the pin on the left. Slip the needle through and under the seam allowance that is facing you (Fig. 2-44c). Do not sew seam allowance down. Without breaking the thread, withdraw the pins just stitched over. Freeing the seam, let it fall to the right. Lift the remaining bias cut edge of the triangle and line it up with the remaining seam allowances mark-

ing facing you. Place the first pin at the right hand side of seam where the needle has just come through marked **. Place the second pin at the other end of the seam line, marked ***. Add additional pins where necessary. With the needle, proceed down the rest of the seam line, overcast at end (Fig. 2-44d). When you are secure and comfortable in this technique and you don't feel like you're all thumbs, then place an extra backstitch before and after passing the thread under the seam allowance. The vertical seam in Fig. 2-44d can be pressed open or to the side and the seam allowance of the triangle can be pressed forward or back against itself, depending on where the dark side is.

This technique also can be used to place a square into a corner, see Eight-Point Star. This is an important technique to master since many patterns use this technique. It is the difference between the amateur and the artist.

AUNT SUKEY'S CHOICE

No one seems to have recorded exactly who Aunt Sukey was but everyone agrees she picked a winner (Fig. 2-45). This well-liked block is often chosen when an interesting geometric quilt is desired. It is interesting to cut and stitch as there are three

Fig. 2-45 *Aunt Sukey's Choice, with three-piece corner on the inside.*

separate patches to comprise the even nine-patch block. The center is a solid and the corner patches are four small squares set in a checkerboard pattern.

It is the four center blocks that combine the chevron pattern with the three-piece corner. The grain line comes into focus here if a good sturdy block is to be made. The long sides of the parallelogram are to be cut on the bias and the solid color triangle set toward the middle will match its bias edges with those of the parallelogram.

Materials and Cutting

PATTERN A: Cut 8 background, 4 prints, 4 solid

PATTERN B: Cut 8 parallelograms. After cutting out the cardboard pattern, shade one side lightly with pencil. In order that print material forms this chevron effect, four pieces are to be cut with *unshaded* patterns facing upward and four are to be placed on the fabric *shaded* side up. All this is worked on the wrong side of fabric. This is a trick to know in dealing with some pattern shapes. If this was to be cut from solid colors it would not be necessary to have a shaded side to the cardboard pattern. Then the crafter would turn half of the pieces to the wrong side to form the chevron.

PATTERN C: Cut 4 solid

PATTERN D: Cut 8 background

PATTERN E: Cut 1 print

Choose a very small opaque print and a contrast color solid; both in contrast to background.

Assembly

1. Stitch this patch only on the seam line, except around the perimeter. Stitch one A print to one A background and then one A solid to another A background. Stitch together the two rectangles formed above, keeping the solid ground pieces diagonally opposite each other. Slip the needle under the center seam to allow flexibility in pressing (Fig. 2-5). Repeat to complete the three other patches (Fig. 2-46a).

2. To create the set of chevron patches, place two B parallelograms together with print side touching. Stitch one of the short ends only on the marked seam line; do not press (Fig. 2-46b). Open the parallelogram; it will form a V shape (Fig. 2–46c). Stitch one solid color C into the V shape formed by the two B's. Use the three piece corner technique described earlier (Fig. 2-44 b,c and d). Press the center seams of the two B's open and the seam of C over the print toward the outside (Fig. 2-46d). To complete the patch, stitch the bias edge of a background D to the remaining bias edge of one B. Stitch from raw edge to raw edge and press open to the dark (Fig. 2-46e). Stitch on the remaining D, stitching from raw edge to raw edge. Press seam open (Fig. 2-46e) and repeat for the three remaining patches.

3. Using Fig. 2-45 as a guide, assemble the nine patches on the work surface in front of you. Place two of the checkerboard patches finished in step 1 (Fig. 2-46a) on either side of the chevron patch finished in step 2. Keep the points of the chevrons pointing out of the block. At the outer sides of the block stitch to the raw edge but on the inside edge where it will attach to the center, stop stitching at the end of the sewing line. This gives flexibility in pressing seams. Repeat for the opposite side of the block. Stitch the solid color portion of the two remaining patches finished in step 2 to either side of the single E. Stitch the three strips together matching corners carefully (Fig. 2-46f).

When using Aunt Sukey's Choice in a full quilt, place blocks one after the other. If blank blocks are placed between, the pattern becomes too big and open looking. The block forms a large diamond in the center and when it is added to an adjacent block the solid corners come up as large squares; very suitable for an interesting quilting design.

Quilting Suggestions

Place a fancy quilt stitching design in the center patch if it is not going to get lost in the print. If it will not show up well, use two concentric diamonds echoing the outlines of the main diamond shape. Quilt $\frac{1}{4}$ inch from the seam line on the solid color triangles flanking the center. Treat the outer diamond shape of the print as one, outlining both inside and outside lines of its shape, $\frac{1}{4}$ inch off the seam line. Outline the background, treating it as a single shape.

WEATHERVANE

Weathervane is a beautiful old design (Fig. 2-48). It's easy to make and uses strong colors. It has both a horizontal/vertical effect and a diagonal effect. It is most often

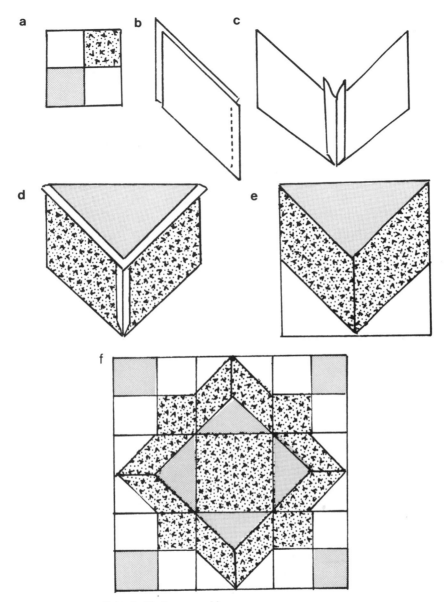

Fig. 2-46 *Aunt Sukey's Choice assembly.*

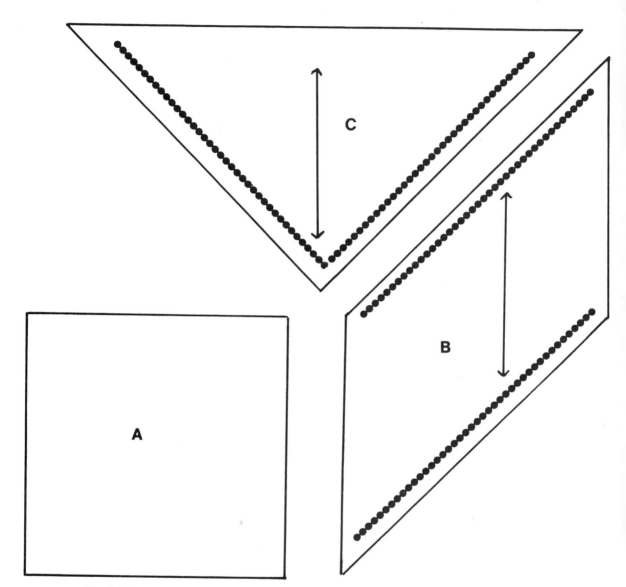

Fig. 2-47 *Aunt Sukey's Choice pattern.*

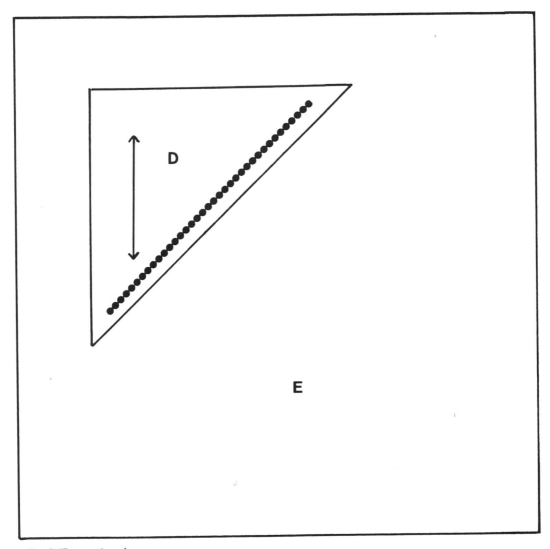

Fig. 2-47 *continued.*

used in a full quilt one block right after the other. The light color background enhances the strength of the pattern colors. Originally this was made with nine even-sized patches but it has been regraded here for eight triangles along the perimeter, us-ing the three-piece corner technique (Fig. 2-44). This reduces the number of small pieces needed to be cut and stitched. It also makes a more attractive way to attach one block to the next in a full quilt, rather than having a lot of little triangles to seam

Fig. 2-48 *Weathervane with three-piece corner on the outside of the block.*

together. Having more intricately sewn pieces increases the value of the finished product.

Materials and Cutting

PATTERN A: Cut 4 prints and 4 background
PATTERN B. Cut 8 prints (same as A)
PATTERN C: Cut 4 solid to complement print
PATTERN D: Cut 1 print (same as A and B)
PATTERN E: Cut 8 background

Stitch only on the seam line except at perimeter edges; stitch to raw edge there.

Assembly

1. Stitch 1 print B to 1 print A (Fig. 2-49a) and 1 print B to 1 background A (Fig. 2-49b). Seam this combination together to form three-quarters of the corner. Repeat for other three corner patches (Fig. 2-49C).

2. Start to form lengthwise strips at left side. Add partially finished corner to large piece C (Fig. 2-49d). Repeat to form righthand strip.

3. Form center strip by stitching two solid C's to print D (Fig. 2-49e).

4. Stitch the three newly formed strips together noting the outer edges will have a notched-out look.

5. Carefully fit in the remaining eight E background pieces, using three-piece corner method. The piece must lay flat and it must finish 16 × 16 inches sewing line to line, or $16\frac{1}{2}$ × $16\frac{1}{2}$ inches raw edge to raw edge. Refer to Fig. 2-44 in general discussion. There are eight points to the outer edge. The pattern pieces must be accurately drawn on the fabric and sewing lines must be checked back and front.

This is a broad strong pattern and would look best in 14 to 16-inch finished size. If the pattern were regraded smaller than this, it would lose its effectiveness. It would have a very modern look if you use two strong solid colors of equal color value.

Quilting Suggestions

Because the pieces are rather large and very geometric, it is best to accent this in the quilting. The printed portions can be outlined $\frac{1}{4}$ inch toward the inside, and the same for the background. The large solid pieces could be enhanced with three concentric outlines—the first $\frac{1}{4}$ inch from the sewing line, then two smaller lines $\frac{1}{2}$ inch from the original, following the contours of the pattern.

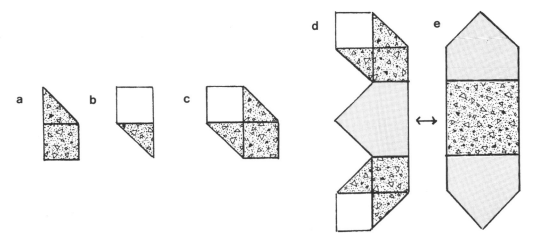

Fig. 2-49 *Weathervane assembly.*

Working from the Center Out

Until now patchwork has been broken down in the drafting stage into four, nine or more patches (such as Pine Tree). Just as the block was broken down into patches, it was reconstructed from pattern to fabric, to patches then into related strips and then into the block itself.

Throughout this text block patterns have been updated and pieces combined to make less work in cutting and sewing. Sometimes in graphing a design for a block, especially the complicated blocks, it is obvious that pieces of the basic pattern can be combined. It means less cutting and less stitching. But more importantly, it means a better looking and stronger block in the end because it reduces the number of small seams. The design block will keep its American pedigree look but will be easier to make. This means a change in the order of work. In this section, the patterns which

have been selected will be worked from the center out. First look at the basic graph to see how the pattern pieces were designed to achieve the final block design.

UNION SQUARE

A glance at this finished block reveals that it has four repeated corners (Fig. 2-51). Indeed, for many years it was conceived as a four-patch repeat design. If worked as a four-patch, it would have many seams in the center. Regraded to achieve the same authentic look, the center is a square, surrounded by four small and four larger triangles. It becomes apparent at once that it would be better to work from the center out. So the order for assembling this block changes from our previous methods (Fig. 2-52).

The name of this block evokes two most dearly held visions in the heart of every American; *Union*, the uniting of the

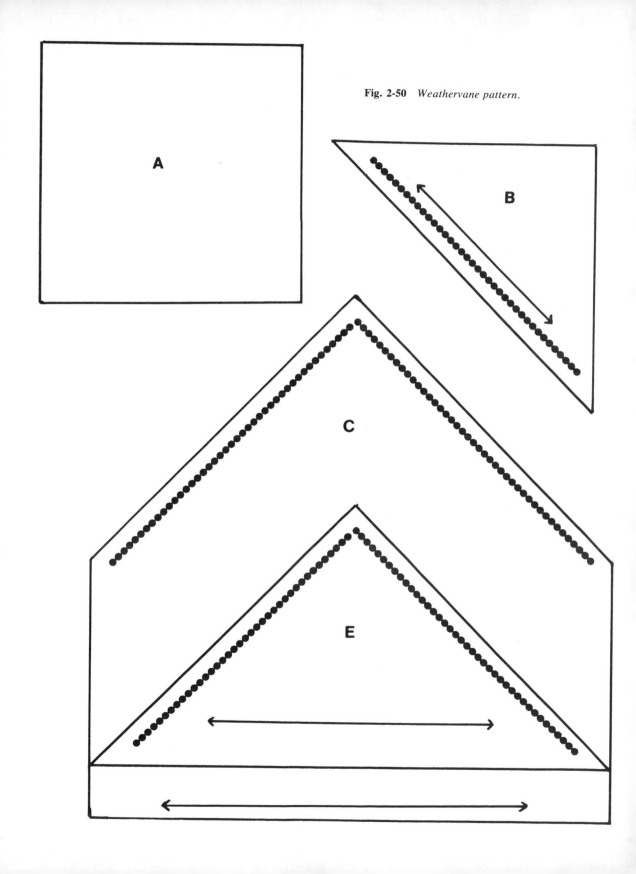

Fig. 2-50 *Weathervane pattern.*

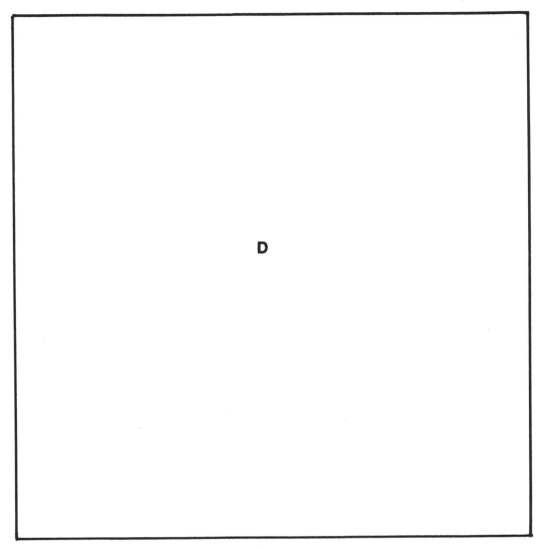

D

Fig. 2-50 *continued.*

original thirteen states against an oppressive form of government and also the catastrophic clash occurring in the Civil War. The word *Square* evokes a vision of the center of every small town in America. A place for marketing one's wares along with meeting and discussing the political and social events of the day. From Maine to California every year on May 30th, Americans turn out in the many town squares to pay homage to those who have helped preserve our Union and our freedom.

Fig. 2-51 *Union Square.*

A look at the block, with proper colorations, will lead the eye into the square. The center square should be a dominant color, flanked by a contrasting color or print in the four triangles around it. The outer four triangles with their sawtooth edges are a third contrast. The only background is the small square corners and half of the sawtooth perimeter edge.

Materials and Cutting

PATTERN A: Cut 1 strong color (solid preferred)

PATTERN B: Cut 4 second print or solid (contrast to A and C)

PATTERN C: Cut 4 third print or solid (contrast to A and B or same as A)

PATTERN D: Cut 4 background

PATTERN D or E: If hand piecing, cut 24 E same color as C and 24 E background

Alternate: If using the time-saving method, join colors C and background and cut 24 D.

Stitch only on marked seam line except around the perimeter (steps 4 and 5).

Assembly

1. Stitch two B's to *opposite* sides of A, press to the dark. Add the two remaining B's to the two remaining sides of A, press seam to the dark (Fig. 2-53a).

2. Along opposite sides of the diamond shape, add two C's. You'll be stitching along the bias cut edge formed by the B's. Press to the dark. Repeat with the two remaining C's on the two remaining edges (Fig. 2-53b).

3. If hand stitching, sew the bias edge of the background E to the bias edge of the print E until all 24 squares are made. Press to the dark.

Alternate: If using the time-saving method (Fig. 2-35), cut bias strips $2\frac{1}{2}$ inches

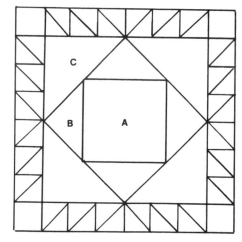

Fig. 2-52 *Union Square diagram.*

76

a   b

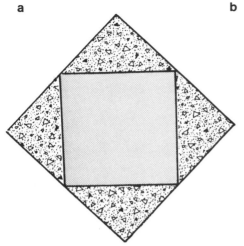 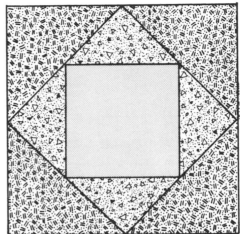

Fig. 2-53 *Union Square assembly of the center.*

wide from background and print. Stitch together and use pattern piece D to cut 24 bi-colored squares.

    4. Using Fig. 2-54a as a guide, stitch together six squares; note that the sawtooth pattern changes direction in the middle. Repeat for the other side and press. Stitch these two long strips to the left and right-hand portions of the partially assembled square. Press to the dark.

    5. Repeat step 4 but add a background D to each of the ends as

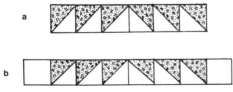

Fig. 2-54 *Union Square assembly of the outer rim.*

shown in Fig. 2-54b. Repeat a second strip; press to the dark. Stitch these two last strips to the top and bottom of partially finished block to complete; press to the dark.

    When using this block in a full quilt, it can be used one after the other or with bands running between blocks. Some quilters like to make the major portion of the bands the same color as the background. This pushes the basic blocks apart against a common ground but not so wide apart as to have a blank block between. The corners can be of a contrasting color. This gives a softer look to the sawtooth edge block, without diminishing its assertive design.

Quilting Suggestions

    Quilt $\frac{1}{4}$ inch within the seam line of pieces A and the four B's. Treat the C and the dark portions of the sawtooth edge as a complete element and quilt $\frac{1}{4}$ inch within

77

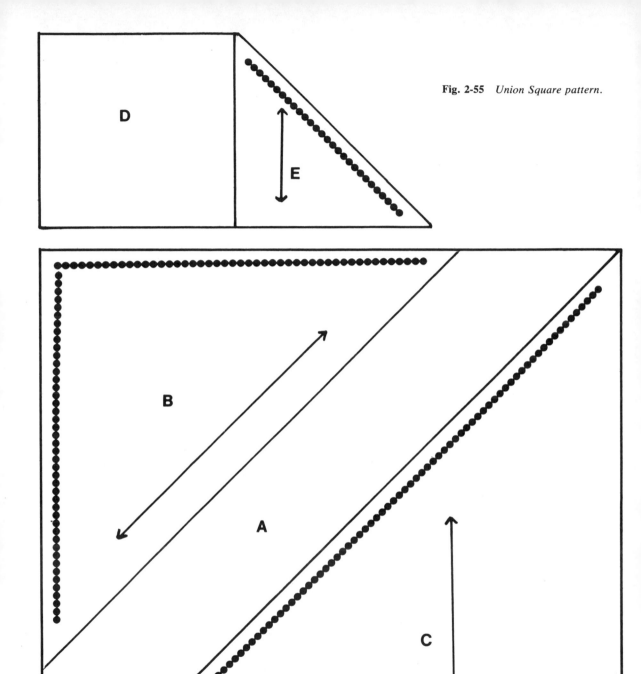

Fig. 2-55 *Union Square pattern.*

the seam line. Quilt ¼ inch off the edge of the remaining background pieces, quilting each unit separately.

AUTOGRAPH

A quilt is a handmade artifact. After the viewer takes in the scope of the quilt design, there is always a question about the maker or makers. This can be satisfied to some degree by adding this block to a sampler quilt (Fig. 2-56). The center is a rectangular piece suitable for signing the makers name either writing with indelible ink (used since the 1850s) or drawing the name on the fabric in pencil and then embroidering over it with floss.

The quilting bee has been in existence in America long before it was called America. When friends get together for the purpose of helping each other make quilts, we have a *quilting bee*. In the early days of rural America, this was also a social occasion. To commemorate one's friends be-

Fig. 2-57 *Autograph diagram.*

fore the popularity of photography, quilters would prepare entire quilts of this pattern at a quilting bee. Each friend would sign her work before it was put into the hostess' quilt. One's needlework and name were cherished momentos. An autograph quilt was often used as a gift for a bride-to-be. Today it is often used as a fund raiser and as a baby blanket if regraded to a smaller size. All kinds of names can be put into the blocks—from relatives to friends to classmates. With today's new laundry markers, it's an easy task. It's a good idea to sign the center rectangle (piece C) before it is cut out of the original fabric. If any mistakes are made, the piece can be redrawn and the mistake discarded. If an embroidered name is desired, it can be stitched before or after the blocks are made. Mark the block with a very light pencil line before stitching.

In a full quilt design where this block is repeated many times, bordering bands are sewn throughout the quilt. They should

Fig. 2-56 *Autograph.*

be equal in color value to the main portions of the block. The design can show the background in the center cross as well as around the perimeter of the block. It should look like ribbon woven in and out around the name.

Materials and Cutting

PATTERN A: Cut 2 print and 2 background (or second print)
PATTERN B: Cut 6 print
PATTERN C: Cut 2 print and 1 background (or second print)
PATTERN D: Cut 12 background
PATTERN E: Cut 4 background

Note carefully the marked grain line on the pattern pieces given. Adhere to the true bias of the fabric, matching up the bias grain markings on the pattern pieces. Stitch from raw edge to raw edge.

Assembly

1. On either side of the background C stitch two print B's, uniting the short ends (Fig. 2-58a). Add two background E's to either side, stitching the short ends of the B's to the bias cut end of E's. Press to the dark.

2. Stitch two print B's to either side of one background A and add two background D's to opposite ends of the print B's, joining the bias cut end of the D's to the narrow end of B's. Repeat for the other side (Fig. 2-58b).

3. Stitch the two strips made in Fig. 2-58b to either side of single strip made in Fig. 2-58a. Study Fig. 2-57. Press seam open.

4. Stitch the bias side of two D's to the short ends of one print C (Fig. 2-58c). Repeat for the other side. Press to the dark.

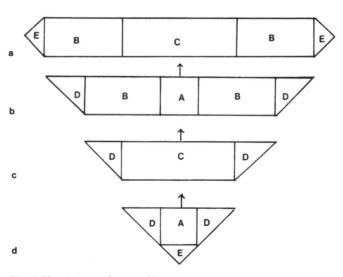

Fig. 2-58 *Autograph assembly.*

80

5. Stitch the two strips made in (Fig. 2-58c) to either side of the three strip center already completed. Press seams open. Study Fig. 2-57.

6. Using Fig. 2-58d as a guide, stitch two background D's to the bias cut edges of one A (Fig. 2-58d), keeping the straight of the grain toward the outside. Stitch one E to the short end of A to complete the triangle. Repeat for the other side. Press seams to the dark. Add to either side of block.

Quilting Suggestions

Quilt the center cross-like design $\frac{1}{4}$ inch off the edge. Treat as one piece. Treat the remaining dark area as one piece rather than small patches and quilt $\frac{1}{4}$ inch off on the inner and the outer portions. Just follow the step-like fashion of the design. Quilt the outer perimeter background D's and E's as separate little triangles.

Curved Seam Patchwork

Over time the straight line gave way to a variety of curved lines. There are soft lines with slight curves and there are strong tight curves. One of the most popular curved designs is made by drawing a quarter of a circle in a small square of any size. This will create two pattern elements, a partial square with a concave arc taken out (Fig. 2-61). The portion that comes out has two straight 90° edges and a third curved edge called a quadrant (Fig. 2-61, piece A). For great grandmother, this was an easy pattern to make since she could use a cup to make the round corner piece. When you copy patterns A and B (Fig. 2-61), add the seam allowance all the way around both

pieces. Mark the center of both the concave edge and the convex edge with a pencil line. This mark will be transferred to the seam allowance with the marking pencil used to outline the cutting edge and seam allowance. It is most important to include this mark but only in the seam allowance as it is used as a point of reference.

The design blocks that use these small two color patches are numerous; the most popular being Chinese Fan and Drunkard's Path. They use differing combinations of colors against the background. Most of the design blocks use sixteen of these small two-color combination patches; one portion is the color and the other is background. The colors or the background will change with the design block, see Chinese Fan and Drunkard's Path. When cutting the pattern pieces of the background, be sure to follow the grain line. The corners of each pattern piece will be on the lengthwise and crosswise grain. The concave and convex curves will be on the bias grain. It is best to try a sample first. To copy the pictures accompanying the text, cut quadrant A from the solid color and cut B (the square with the concave cutout) from a print. To assemble each patch, place the two pieces right sides together. Keep the quadrant piece on top, seam line facing you; curved edge up and point down (Fig. 2-60, top left). Match center markings and pin these two middle points. Place pin at a 90° angle to the line; the top of the pin going through the two lines and the bottom picking up only an $\frac{1}{8}$ inch of both fabrics. Pick up the quadrant on the left side first and line up the straight of the grain with that matching the piece behind. Place a pin exactly in the left corner of the seam line.

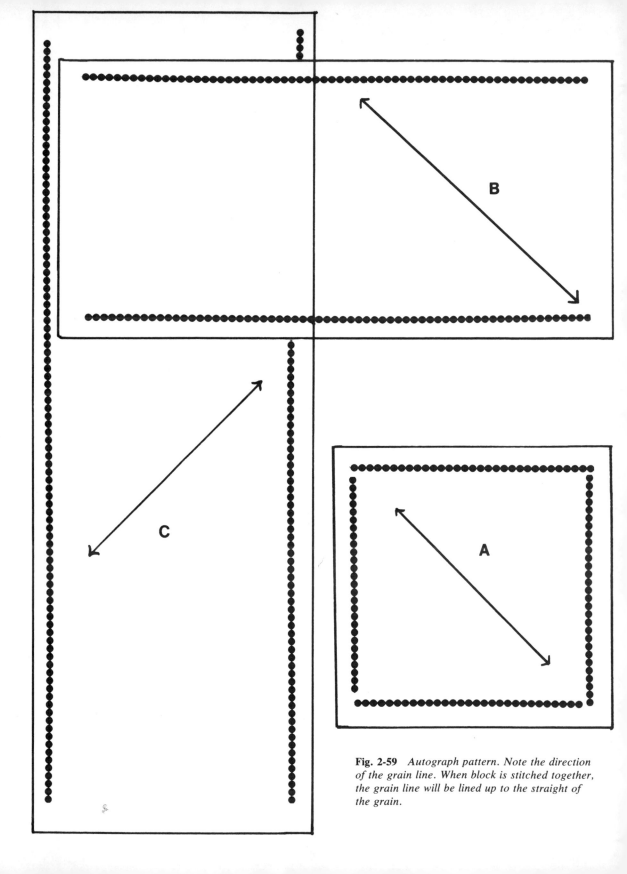

Fig. 2-59 *Autograph pattern. Note the direction of the grain line. When block is stitched together, the grain line will be lined up to the straight of the grain.*

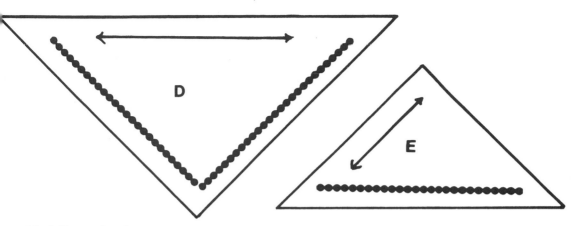

Fig. 2-59 *continued.*

This time pick up at least a ½ inch of both fabrics. This stabilizes the side (Fig. 2-60, top right); repeat for the right side. With both thumbs on top of the work and the rest of both hands behind the work, shape the curve of the quadrant against the curve of the piece behind.

Between the center pin and each side

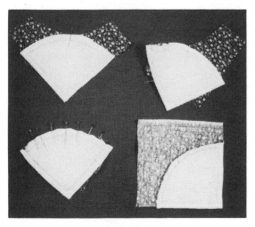

Fig. 2-60 *Curved line patch assembly. Hold work in your hand exactly as shown.*

pin place at least three more pins, picking up only an ⅛ inch of fabric in the pins (see Fig. 2-60, bottom left). This technique eliminates notching both seam allowances before hand. Stitch from seam line to seam line along the curved marking. Remove the pins and press to the dark. If necessary, clip in seam line to give fullness to the curve; place one clip at center and two others on either side about one inch from the center. The expert patchmaker will use a lot of pins to hold the curve; each pin on the curve picking up only a tiny amount of the fabric. The more curve to the seam line, the more interesting the pattern; and in the end the more valuable the work.

Assembly

Traditionally most blocks have sixteen patches and are generally assembled in rows. After teaching this for many years, I would urge the quilter to place the selected sixteen patches on the work surface. There will be four across and four down.

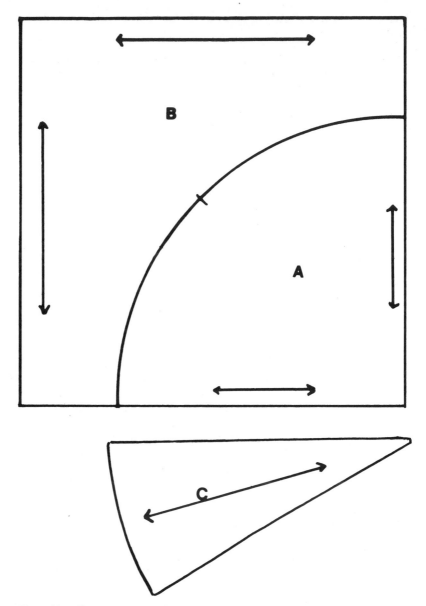

Fig. 2-61 *Chinese Fan, Drunkard's Path pattern
(A and B); Mohawk Trail pattern (B and C).*

Earthtones *by Dorothy Frager. (L to R) Row 1: Honey Bee, Aunt Sukey's Choice, Country Roads; Row 2: Clay's Choice, Stepping Stones, Orange Basket; Row 3: Union Square, Mohawk Trail, Autograph.*

Garden's Delight Wall Hanging *by Dorothy Frager. (L to R) Row 1: Butterfly, North Carolina Lily; Row 2: Reel and Oak Leaf, Dahlia.*

Indigo *(left) by Peg Harrison. (L to R)*
Row 1: Variable Star, Friendship Ring,
Duck and Ducklings; Row 2: Chinese
Fan, appliqued Le Moyne Star,
Crossed Tulip.

Potpourri *(opposite) by Carrie Link. (L to R) Row 1: Grandmother's Flower Garden, Duck and Ducklings, Le Moyne Star; Row 2: Crossed Tulip, Log Cabin, Drunkard's Path; Row 3: Eight-Point Star, Jack and Jill, Friendship Ring.*

Friendship Sampler *by Ginny Ruckert. (L to R) Row 1: Victorian Fan, Mohawk Trail, Friendship Ring; Row 2: President's Wreath, Bear's Paw, Bridal Wreath; Row 3: Turkey Tracks, Variation on Crossed Tulip, Oak Leaf and Reel; Row 4: North Carolina Lily, Eight-Point Star, Flower Basket.*

Calico Corners *by Gerri Schirmacher. (L to R) Row 1: Duck and Ducklings, Hearts All Round, Variation on Small Fans; Row 2: Reel and Oak Leaf, Blazing Star, Pineapples; Row 3: Drunkard's Path, Dutch Tulip, Friendship Ring; Row 4: Chinese Fan, Cat, Log Cabin.*

All American *by Joan Shaw. (L to R) Row 1: Reel, Jack and Jill, Crossed Tulips; Row 2: Butterfly, Eight-Point Star with Border, Friendship Ring; Row 3: Duck and Ducklings, Drunkard's Path, Bear's Paw; Row 4: Log Cabin, Pineapples, Chinese Fan.*

Album Quilt, *designed by Dorothy Frager. (L to R) Row 1: Oak Leaf Variation, Liberty Bell, New Jersey commemorative, Small Victorian Fan; Row 2: Man and His Horse, Le Moyne Applique, Two Brothers, Quilting Lady; Row 3: Rose Wreath, Pomegranates, Triple Tulip, Laurel Leaf; Row 4: R. R. Station, Hearts All Round, Bird in the Bush, The Old Homestead.*

Fall Spectrum *by Cheryl Todd. (L to R) Row 1: Windmill, Grandmother's Flower Garden, Log Cabin; Row 2: Le Moyne Star, Reel and Oak Leaf Variation, Wrench; Row 3: Variation on Water Wheel, Chinese Fan, Duck and Ducklings; Row 4: Crossed Tulip, Cornucopia—variation on Eight-Point Star, Friendship Ring.*

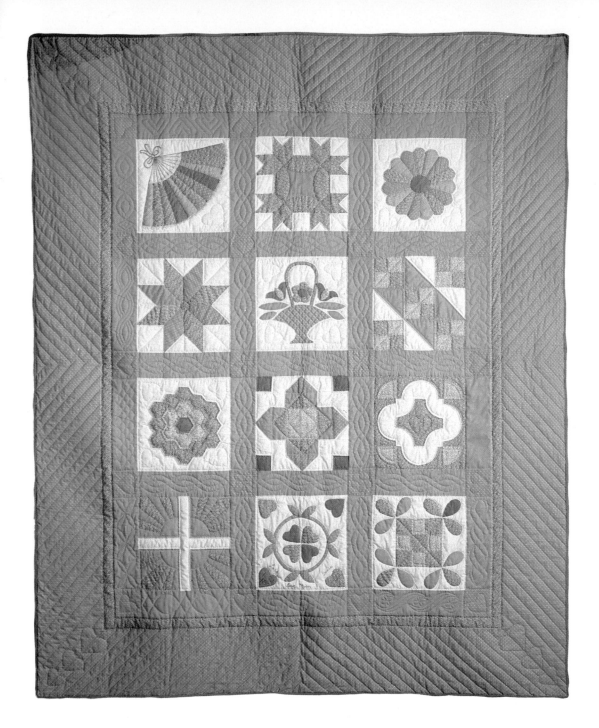

Forever Spring *by Ginny Ruckert. (L to R) Row 1: Victorian Fan, Crystal Star, Friendship Ring; Row 2: Eight-Point Star, Flower Basket, Jacob's Ladder; Row 3: Grandmother's Flower Garden, Aunt Sukey's Choice, Chinese Fan; Row 4: Variations on Small Fans, Wreath and Hearts, Honey Bee.*

Rhapsody *by Joan Dermond. (L to R) Row 1: Four-Patch Checkerboard, Honey Bee, Friendship Ring; Row 2: Duck and Ducklings, Gentle Turn, Drunkard's Path; Row 3: Le Moyne Star, Reel and Bud, Chinese Fan; Row 4: Grandmother's Flower Garden, Crossed Tulip, Log Cabin.*

Pascack Historical Society Quilt, *Dorothy Frager, quilt coordinator. (L to R) Row 1: Chair Factory, Octagon House, Farm Land, Seven Chimneys House; Row 2: Old Dutch Church, Wortendyke Barn, Bandstand, P.H.S. Museum; Row 3: Baylor Massacre Site, Garret Durie House, Sand Stone House, Canadian Geese; Row 4: Indian Heritage, Oldest Oak, Railroad Station, New Jersey Commemorative.*

The Putnam County Quilt *(opposite), designer and coordinator, Gladys Boalt. Photo by Marc Cohen. (Top to bottom, starting at the left) The Vulture Sloop used in Benedict Arnold's Escape, Distillery Bottles, Charcoal Burning, Carmel Raceway for Sulkies, Tilly Foster Mine, Dr. Adams, West Point Foundry, Phillips Crest, Hamilton Mine, Dog Churn, Hoop Pole Industry, Goose, Brook Trout; Row 2: Drummers, Sybil Ludington, Quaker Meeting House, Constitution Island, Ludington Mill, Warren's Tavern, Boyd's Reservoir, Stage Coach; Row 3: U.S. Seal, Enoch Crosby House, Putnam County Courthouse, Ludington's Store, Farmer's Mill, Fanny Crosby Home, Bible and Boscoble (in one panel), Wappinger's Indian Village; Row 4: Fifers, General Israel Putnam, Southeast Church, Beverly House, Red Mill, Smalley Inn, Chief Ninham and Fire Engine; Row 5: The DeWitt Clinton, Stoneware Crockery, Doanesburg School, Captain Kidd's Treasure, Ice Cutting, Oldest Oak, Gail Borden Milk Plant, Cow and Milk Can, Circus, Milestone, Great Swamp, Blacksmith, and Beaver, the N.Y. State Animal.* © Gladys Boalt 1976.

Everyone Has Eyelashes® *designed and made by De Ette Snider. Photo by Roy Hale.*

For the sake of accuracy, assemble four at a time into a patch grouping and work it just like a traditional four-patch (Fig. 2-1).

CHINESE FAN

Of all the curved line patterns, Chinese Fan is the simplest to understand. It gives a very circular effect, using quadrants of color against the squares with the concave cutout. It offers a great deal of freedom in the selection and arrangement of the quadrant colors which appear as fans. Novel effects can be made with the arrangement of the fans against the portion indicated as the background. All the fans (or quadrants) can be the same color against a common ground. (Study the color and black and white photos.)

Fig. 2-62 *Chinese Fan made by Joan Shaw.*

Materials and Cutting
PATTERN A: Cut 16 print or assorted colors
PATTERN B: Cut 16 background

Assembly
Using information given earlier under Curved Seam Patchwork, assemble 16 two-color patches. Use the patterns in Fig. 2-61 as a guide.

The Chinese Fan is generally used in a full quilt with bands between each block. It makes a dramatic design.

Quilting Suggestions
All quilting will be $\frac{1}{4}$ inch from the seam line. Treat the combined fans as one portion and quilt $\frac{1}{4}$ inch off the print on both inside and outside the circle of fans. For added definition, the center could have a novel design.

DRUNKARD'S PATH

This is a true diagonal pattern. The smartest of all the variations of this pattern is to use two bright colors going in opposite directions on a light background. The strength of color helps to exaggerate the uneven lines of the diagonals. The crossing colors should be of equal values and in good contrast to the background. It makes a sculptured looking full quilt and a unique block for a sampler quilt. In this sampler, it looks like bolts of lightning.

Materials and Cutting
PATTERN A: Cut 4 of one print, 4 different print, 8 background
PATTERN B: Cut 4 of one print, 4 different print, 8 background

Fig. 2-63 *Drunkard's Path made by Joan Shaw.*

Assembly

Using the information given earlier under Curved Seam Patchwork, assemble 16 two-color patches using patterns in Fig. 2-60, Fig. 2-61 and Fig. 2-63 as a guide.

Quilting Suggestions

Quilt $\frac{1}{4}$ inch from the seam line on the four background areas, treating each as one unit, even though the shape is odd. Quilt $\frac{1}{4}$ inch in from the seam line on each sculptured diagonal line.

This is an advanced stitching technique. The quilter will have to frequently refer to Fig. 2-63 to get the first 16 blocks together. The coloring must be chosen with the utmost care to assure a smart looking sampler block.

MOHAWK TRAIL

As the name suggests, Mohawk Trail has a mythical quality to it. It is done in me-

dium shades with a very dark color against a good contrast background. It is suggestive of the sunlight and shady spots along a twisting forest trail. It need not be executed in earthy colors to get this effect. It is best to stick to repeats of the same family of colors. Each quadrant has three triangular wedges, using pattern C in Fig. 2-61. When cutting the wedges, it is best to hold them on the straight of the grain.

Materials and Cutting

PATTERN C: Cut 48 assorted colors
PATTERN B: Cut 16 background

Assembly

Stitch three C's together, pressing the seams outward from the center. Be careful not to allow two of the same prints to be sewn side by side as this will give the effect of one large wedge and disrupt the symmetry of the small wedges. To assemble the three wedges together, sew only on the

Fig. 2-64 *Mohawk Trail.*

seam line; press and set aside until 16 three-piece quadrants are completed. Use the pattern piece A as a check for accuracy. Stitch quadrants into 16 background squares with concave corner cutouts (pattern piece B), press. Finish assembling as Chinese Fan. Be careful to match all corners and points. Stitch only on the seam lines.

In a full quilt, each block is placed side by side creating a very cheerful and animated quilt. The background areas are enlarged by adding a blank block between each design block. These are filled in with novelty quilting.

Quilting Suggestions

Treat the center portion background and the periphery portion of the background as solid units, disregarding the seam allowances. Quilt $\frac{1}{4}$ inch from the seam allowance off the colored portion. On either side of the center wedge in each quadrant, quilt on the seam line. That little bit of depression will help to make a big textural effect. A novelty design can be added to the center.

Eight-Point Stars

There is no doubt that one of the most spectacular designs of American folk art is the Eight-Point Star (Fig. 2-65). It is the epitome of the quilters art. It looks very complicated with all its bias seams. Indeed it was a mystery to me too, but a mystery I had to solve. It was well worth the effort because the solution is very simple indeed. Today's quilter could easily draft this pattern using an ordinary compass. Great grandmother did not have access to this

Fig. 2-65 *Eight-Point Star made by Ginny Ruckert.*

knowledge or tool but she did have paper and a quick mind to fold a perfect eight-point star. Once she had her correct diamond points, she could place it against a square background, and trace in the four square corners and four bias edge middle triangles to get her background pieces.

Here the work of pattern drafting has been accomplished for a 16 × 16-inch block. The art of this pattern is in the accurate marking, cutting and sewing of the pattern. Marking the outlines of the pattern pieces onto the fabric must be done very carefully so that the sewing line is exactly right on each diamond point. The points are placed with their longest length on the straight of the grain, giving the diamond four bias edges (Fig. 2-69). The background square (B) is placed on the straight of the grain (Fig. 2-70). The background triangle (C) is placed so the long edge is on the straight of the

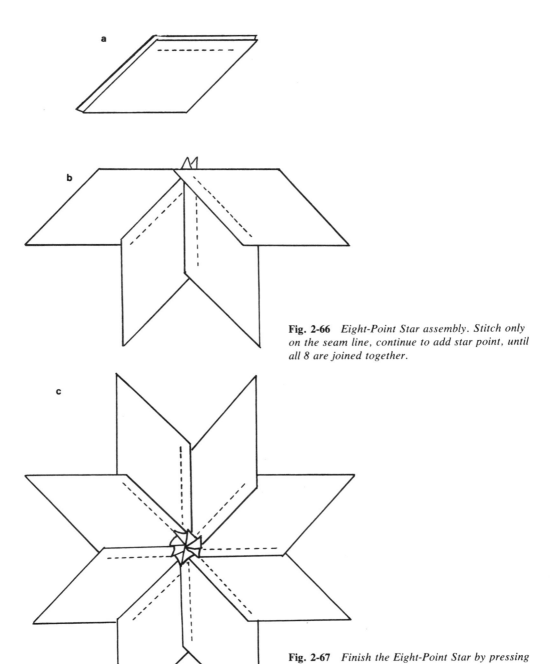

Fig. 2-66 *Eight-Point Star assembly. Stitch only on the seam line, continue to add star point, until all 8 are joined together.*

Fig. 2-67 *Finish the Eight-Point Star by pressing seams in one direction and the center in the opposite direction.*

88

grain, creating bias edges on the two other sides (Fig. 2-69).

EIGHT-POINT

Materials and Cutting
PATTERN A: Cut 8, using two contrasting colors (4 each) or all of one color
PATTERN B: Cut 4 background
PATTERN C: Cut 4 background (note grain line on piece C)

Assembly
1. To stitch the main portion of the star together, sew only on the marked line. Stitch one star point to the second, working from the outside toward the center. Stop stitching on the marked seam line and backstitch one (Fig. 2-66). Continue in this manner until all eight points are united in a circle (Fig. 2-67). The material at the center from the unused portion of the seam allowance will seem bulky. When all the points are united and before pressing, the center of the star must be secured. This is done by using a small needle and a 3-inch length of thread with a knot on one end. Slip the needle through the base of one of the star points, at the very point where the last stitch was made. Continue to slip the needle through each succeeding point at the same place until all eight have been joined in a circle of thread. Pull the thread tight, securing the center firmly. If you can push your finger through the center, it is too large and the pattern has to be checked.

2. Press the seams of the star in one direction, being careful not to stretch the bias edges. The center points will pop up

Fig. 2-68 *Fit the background into the Eight-Point Star. Made by Donna McGrath.*

almost naturally and use the tip of the iron to press these down, forming a pinwheel in the center (Fig. 2-67).

3. Fit in the four triangles first, uniting the two bias edges of the triangles to the bias edges of the star. Using the three corner seam shown earlier (Fig. 2-44), hold the triangle behind the star. Pin and stitch one side at a time. *Stitch on the seam line* to the point where the two star points are joined. Unpin the side just stitched and lift the other star point and second side of the triangle into place and pin. Slip the needle through the seam allowance and begin stitching on the seam line only. Turn to the dark and press; do not stretch.

4. Repeat the same procedure with the four corners but now *stitch to the raw edge*. This will close the seams

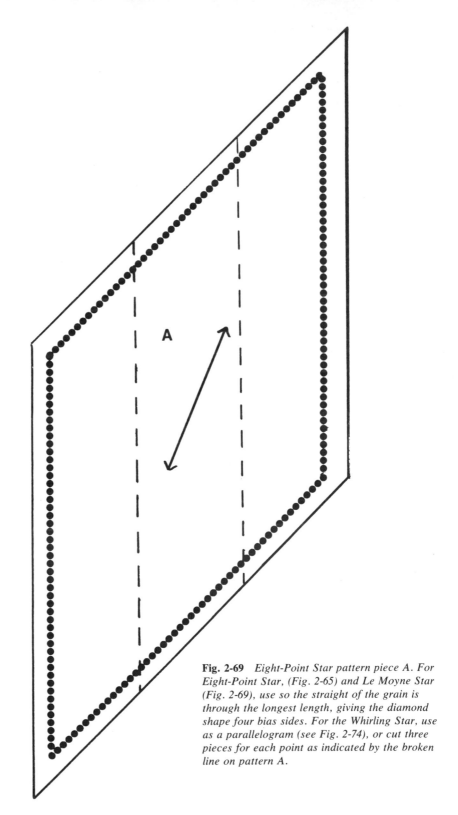

A

Fig. 2-69 *Eight-Point Star pattern piece A. For Eight-Point Star, (Fig. 2-65) and Le Moyne Star (Fig. 2-69), use so the straight of the grain is through the longest length, giving the diamond shape four bias sides. For the Whirling Star, use as a parallelogram (see Fig. 2-74), or cut three pieces for each point as indicated by the broken line on pattern A.*

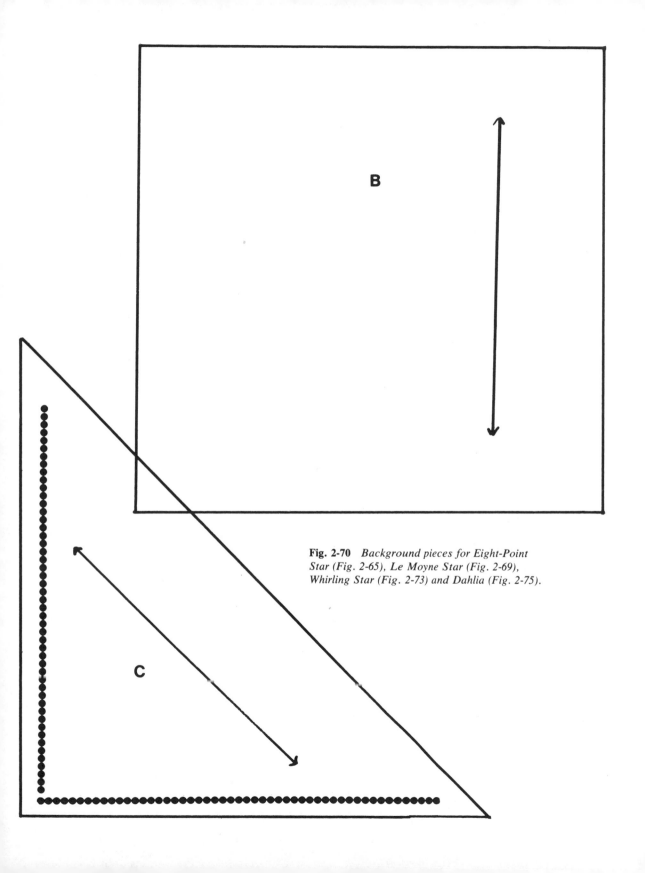

Fig. 2-70 *Background pieces for Eight-Point Star (Fig. 2-65), Le Moyne Star (Fig. 2-69), Whirling Star (Fig. 2-73) and Dahlia (Fig. 2-75).*

around the perimeter of the background, giving it strength. Press to the dark.

Color plays an important part in this star. While small stars look precious in solid colors, larger stars work better with alternating colors in the star points. It makes the design more dramatic and noticeable. Use opaque fabric in the star and a good contrast background.

LE MOYNE STAR

This star is renown for the quality of workmanship necessary to produce it (Fig. 2-71). It is a treasured heirloom displayed on the best occasions. Old quilt lore tells us this pattern was named to commemorate the founding of New Orleans by the Le Moyne brothers. As the pattern passed through the northern colonial states the name was simplified to Lemon Star. Nevertheless, it is simply an eight-point star with each diamond point cut down the middle (Fig. 2-69).

Materials and Cutting

PATTERN A: Cut 8, after seaming two strips together
PATTERN B: Cut 4 background
PATTERN C: Cut 4 background

Assembly

First a quilter must be able to stitch a standard eight-point star to perfection. If hand stitching completely, cut pattern A in half lengthwise (cut 8 each from two different colors). Place the center seam on the straight of the grain. Stitch from raw edge to raw edge. Press center seam open

Fig. 2-71 *Le Moyne Star made by Joan Dermond.*

and trim excess to the shape of the raw edge of a single diamond. Proceed with instructions for eight-point star.

For an even faster method that allows for more accuracy but less authenticity, cut strips of the two different colors to be used in the star. Cut them approximately half the width of star diamonds plus $\frac{1}{4}$ inch for seam allowance. For pattern piece A, Fig. 2-69, that would mean two strips each $2\frac{1}{4}$ inches wide. Seam them together on the machine with $\frac{1}{4}$ inch seam and press the seam open. Place the A shape template on the wrong side of this double strip, placing it so that the top and bottom points are exactly over the center seam (Fig. 2-72). Cut out eight solid diamond shapes using pattern A and proceed to assemble as an eight-point star.

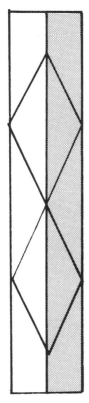

PATTERN B: Cut 4 background
PATTERN C: Cut 4 background

Assembly

1. Cut three strips of fabric, on the straight of the grain, which will equal the dimensions of the star when sewn together. (Hold the star pattern (Fig. 2-69) as a parallelogram as shown in Fig. 2-74.) In the case of pattern piece A (Fig. 2-69), it measures $3\frac{1}{4}$ inches. Since this cannot be divided evenly by three, cut two strips $1\frac{1}{16}$ inches and one strip $1\frac{2}{16}$ inches. This will equal $3\frac{1}{4}$ inches when sewn together. Add seam allowance to the suggested widths and seam together, stitching by machine using 10 to 12 stitches to the inch. Press to the dark.

2. Place the diamond template A over the strips on the wrong side (Fig. 2-74). Cut eight star points and treat each as a single diamond shape.

Fig. 2-72 *Le Moyne Star points (pattern A) may be cut as single units over two machine-stitched strips of fabric.*

WHIRLING STAR

If the Le Moyne Star is a double dose of color, the Whirling Star is a triple treat. The use of a striped star creates a dazzling movement of color. The colors carry the eye around in a circle. This looks very hard to make when actually the time saving methods suggested earlier will apply here.

Materials and Cutting

PATTERN A: Cut 8, after seaming three strips
together (Read step 1)

Fig. 2-73 *Whirling Star made by Gerri Schirmacher.*

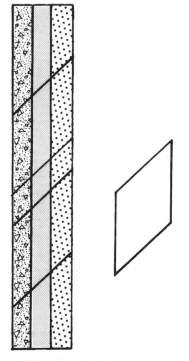

Fig. 2-74 *Whirling Star Points (pattern A) may be cut as single units over three machine-stitched strips of fabric. Place pattern as a parallelogram. Disregard grain line suggested earlier. See back of Whirling Star (Fig. 2-68).*

3. Assemble with pattern pieces B and C to complete the star. See wrong side of star Fig. 2-68. Study this star point in the color photo section in Calico Corners Quilt.

Alternate: If working by hand, the pattern piece A may be divided into three equal parts. Add seam allowance all the way around and cut eight each of three colors. Seam the colors together in the same order, press seams to the dark and proceed to unite as a standard eight-point star.

DAHLIA

Memories of a country garden are brought to mind with this variation on the basic star (Fig. 2-75). It's called a Dahlia and is usually made with two harmonizing colors toward the inside (pattern pieces A and D) with a contrast center, but anything goes in the world of flowers. This has a gathered center which is covered by a small round circle giving it a textural dimension. It uses the same pattern pieces for the background as the Eight-Point Star. (See Garden's Delight Wall Hanging.)

Materials and Cutting

PATTERN A: Cut 8 strong colors
PATTERN B: Cut 4 background
PATTERN C: Cut 4 background
PATTERN D: Cut 8 contrast to A
PATTERN E: Cut 1 contrast to A and D

Assembly

1. Stitch eight A's and eight D's alternately, placing the concave piece

Fig. 2-75 *Dahlia, a variation on an Eight-Point Star.*

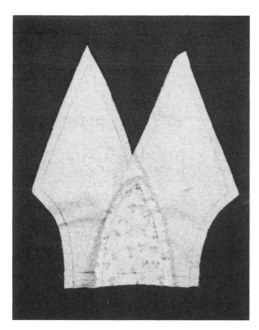

Fig. 2-76 *Dahlia's petals are stitched together one after the other.*

against the convex piece. Make small slashes in seam allowance of the concave piece A. Place it over the convex D piece. Start stitching with a knot at *point* of the D piece on the seam line. Finish the line of stitching at the raw edge and backstitch for strength (Fig. 2-76). Press to the dark.

2. When a full ring is completed, gather the center ¼ inch from raw edge. Pull the gather stitches until the center lays flat.

3. Turn the edges of the circle, pattern piece E, to the wrong side and baste over the gathered edges, hiding them completely. With a small running stitch, sew down the circle going through all layers. This center may be padded with a circle or two of batting before sewing, but this is optional.

4. Finish as the original Eight-Point Star, using pattern pieces B and C (Fig. 2-70).

The Eight-Point Star is such a favorite pattern that it is used in many variations. It can be appliqued to a background if the quilter wishes to have more of the background showing. Parts of the star can be used to create floral applique as shown in a pattern called North Carolina Lily (Fig. 4-46). A pattern called Cactus Rose uses four colored points for the blossom and two green points to look like leaves. The two lower points are removed to allow for a stem and leaves which are then appliqued to a background. The variations are endless.

Stars of any kind when put into a full quilt are found in every imaginable setting: star blocks, one after the other, star blocks alternating with blank blocks, star blocks intersected with bands of all kinds. Any arrangement the quilter decides upon will suit the star pattern, and that goes for the quilting. The quilt stitchery can go ¼ inch inside and outside each star point and or the background.

Log Cabin

Log Cabin holds a special place in the American quilt lover's heart. First it is a symbol of the log cabin which was so important to survival of the Colonial settlers. Each block encompasses a series of strips of fabric that quilters call *logs*. The block is split in half on the diagonal with dark and light logs. This represents the dark and light shadows of the sun as it travels around

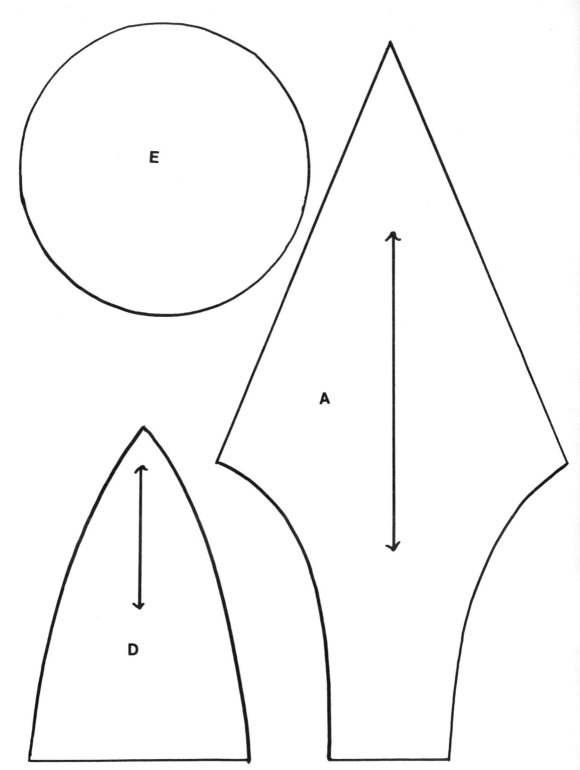

Fig. 2-77 *Dahlia center pattern pieces are completed with B and C from Fig. 2-70.*

the cabin. The square in the center has always been interpreted as the chimney and is shaded with a warm color (Fig. 2-78). This is one of the few designs that have names for the arrangement or setting of the blocks into a full quilt.

The most popular setting is Barn Raising. It begins with four common color portions of each block meeting in the center to form a diamond pattern. As blocks are added they form concentric diamond lines radiating from the center in darks and lights. This makes a very square quilt and must have an even number of blocks to right and left of the center (Fig. 2–78). This makes a great wall hanging as well as a full quilt.

The second most popular setting is called Straight Furrow. It creates dark and light diagonal lines across the quilt. With this setting, odd numbers of blocks across and down the quilt will not make any difference to its final appearance. See the color photo section for a quilt called Calico Corners. On the bottom right of this quilt appears an outlined Straight Furrow setting. Notice in Fig. 2–79, the lights and darks

Fig. 2-78 *Center of Log Cabin quilt in a Barn Raising Setting made by Gerri Schirmacher.*

Fig. 2-79 *Center of a Log Cabin quilt in a diamond setting made by Sonia Adams.*

are grouped in diamond-like patterns called a diamond setting. The second important aspect of this block is its construction technique. It is worked from the center out by building log strips in a concentric pattern around the chimney square.

LOG CABIN STRING QUILT

Up to this point in this text, selected squares, triangles and rectangles have been built upon

in very definite preselected arrangements. The Log Cabin departs from this technique. It moves into an area quilters call *string quilting* and it was used primarily to clean out the scrap bag. It works this way. Long, very narrow strips of fabric were cut from selected dark and light, new or scrap, yardage. Middle-grade colors are to be avoided. The strips or strings were rolled and divided into light and dark piles. The larger the assortment, the better. The narrower the log strips, the smaller the quilt block—and, if made well, the more intrinsically valuable. The logs may be cut in any proportions, from $\frac{1}{2}$ inch to 2 inches wide by as long as possible. A good rule of thumb which I have developed in making and teaching this block over the years is to make the chimney wider than the logs. The block can be any size the quilter wishes to make them in a given quilt.

Originally, when teaching the Log Cabin for a sampler quilt, I suggested that the students make it in the traditional manner. This left the quilters with a block with no background color showing and it made it look very heavy by comparison to other blocks. Later I discovered that the block is much easier to use in a sampler quilt if half the strips are made of assorted dark prints and the other half are made of the background fabric. Since this is a sample to learn the string technique, one print could be used for all the dark logs; and the background fabric which is common to all the other blocks could be used for the remainder of the light logs (Fig. 2-80). Cut the strips one inch wide, plus the seam allowance, by approximately 40 inches long for each set of logs (light and dark). Cut across the width of the goods or the length of the goods as long as the logs remain on the straight of the grain. Cut a contrast color for the chimney 2 inches square, plus the seam allowance. While it is authentic to use two sets of assorted prints and a common color chimney throughout a log cabin quilt, it is an asset to the sampler quilt as a whole to depart from this tradition. Study the color photos and you will see all kinds of renditions of this block.

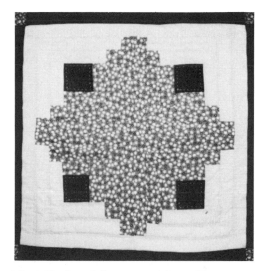

Fig. 2-80 *Log Cabin string quilt made by Joan Shaw.*

Assembly

1. Place the chimney on the work surface in front of you. Choose a *light* log of fabric. Place it against square chimney with right sides together. Pin in place and stitch from raw edge to raw edge (Fig. 2-81a).

2. Trim the log to be flush with the side of the square and open. Finger press the seam away from the chimney.

3. Turn the two pieces so the first log is to the right of the chimney. Place a second *light* log with right sides together across the top of the chimney and the first log. Pin, stitch and cut; open and finger press the seam away from the chimney (Fig. 2-81b).

4. Turn the patches to the right

again so that the second log is on the right. Now, add a third log that is *dark* across the top, right sides together. Pin, stitch and cut. Open and finger press seam allowance away from the chimney. Turn again to the right so that the third log is on the right (Fig. 2-81c).

5. Add a fourth *dark* log across the top of the first log, the chimney and the third log. Pin, stitch, cut and finger press to complete the first set of logs (Fig. 2-81d).

6. Repeat, alternately adding two

Fig. 2-82 *Log Cabin made of four 5½" blocks, with addition of outer border for background. This is more of a traditional use of assorted light and dark print logs. Made by Jane Emmer.*

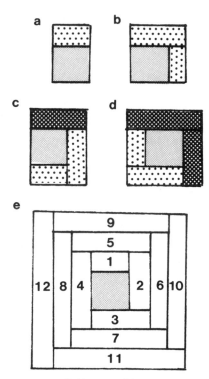

Fig. 2-81 *Log Cabin assembly.*

more light and then two more dark until the block is complete. This 8-inch block will have a chimney and twelve logs or thirteen pieces total. For the sampler, make three more 8-inch blocks. It is traditional to add another four logs around the outside to finish with sixteen logs and one chimney but it would not fit in this sampler quilt. Press all seams on the outside.

For those students who would like to try a true traditional rendition of the Log Cabin using assorted light and dark prints on each side, I have worked out a smaller version. This smaller version uses logs cut ¾ inches wide, plus seam allowance. Here the assorted fabrics can be used on both the light and dark side (Fig. 2-82). Cut the chimney one inch square plus seam allowance. Using assembly directions given above, proceed with steps one to six, using thirteen pieces for each Log Cabin patch. When four patches are completed, join the light centers together. When finished add four triangles that are of the common background fabric used throughout the quilt. Make a solid template pattern for the triangles $11\frac{3}{4} \times 8 \times 8$ inches, plus $\frac{1}{4}$ inch seam allowance. The $11\frac{3}{4}$-inch side is to be placed on the bias grain. This lightens the look of the design. The addition of the background material gives it a unified feeling with the other blocks in a sampler quilt. In a full quilt, there would be no triangular background showing.

Now it becomes easy to see the block may be any size, depending on the size of the chimney and number and width of logs. The chimneys are generally solid colors and always the same color through a full quilt. The smallest prints must be selected for the one inch or smaller logs. In this 16-inch square sampler block, try your hand with a limited pallet of color as suggested earlier. When considering making this for a wall hanging or full bed quilt, it is important to rid your mind of the rigid thinking of repeating each block exactly alike. If this is done, then each block would have exactly the same size and color logs on the outside edges. When placing these blocks together, the outside logs will appear as one log double the size, throwing the entire quilt design out of balance. To avoid this, use two to three times as many prints and/or solids as the number of logs on one side. Let us say that light blue and dark blue logs are chosen

for use with a red chimney. Choose at least eight light blues and eight dark blues. Start and finish the blocks with various prints to the outer edge.

I suggest to my classes they use the same print twice each time around. Referring to Fig. 2-81, log one and two are the same light print; log three and four are the same dark print; five and six are a second light print but different from one and two; seven and eight are a second dark print but different from three and four. This use of the same print twice helps to strengthen the appearance of the small print. Alternate the colors that finish around the outside as much as possible. This will allow you to join different print logs together when joining the blocks. It also uses up the yardage more effectively. This is the most valuable log cabin. Some quilters use the same prints on the first eight logs throughout the quilt but change the outside prints only (Fig. 2-78). If blocks are made exactly alike, then only a diamond setting pattern will be effective to finish a full quilt (Fig. 2-79). When finished making blocks, pile the blocks according to the outside log colors and assemble into a quilt, being sure not to have two of the same print logs on the outside touching each other.

It is always recommended to shop many places for new yardage of many different prints. Check what you might have in hand and take samples with you so you don't duplicate. Buy small yardages such as $\frac{1}{3}$ to $\frac{1}{2}$ yard of each. "More is better" is a good rule of thumb when selecting prints for this quilt. The greater the number of prints, the smaller the logs, the finer the stitchery the more valuable the quilt face.

Quilting Suggestions

Yesterday's quilter stitched around every rectangular shaped log and the chimney too. Today's quilter generally quilts this pattern on the seam line. This creates a depression, causing the log to puff up with batting as real logs do. This textural dimension helps to reinforce the log wall image created by the name Log Cabin.

3

PIECED APPLIQUE

Applique is the alternate needleart arrangement to decorate the quilt face for blanketmaking. *Patchwork* refers to stitching small pieces of fabric together, side by side; *applique* means to attach small pieces of fabric in an overlaying technique to a background fabric, generally to create a design of pictorial nature. Applique satisfies a need for softer curved lines that balance harmoniously in shape and color.

To bridge the gap from patchwork to applique, there exists a design area called *pieced applique*. This is a mixed media technique. It uses the workmanship principles of patchwork to create the major portion of a design that is appliqued to a background block. Besides learning some of these unique patterns on your own, it affords the sampler quilt maker the opportunity to try out a few of the most praised all-over patchwork designs in miniature (Tumbling Blocks and Grandmother's Flower Garden). At this point in the course, the patchwork techniques have been learned. It is now time to learn the basic principles for quality workmanship of applique. For each design shown, study them in the color photos. Sometimes there are slight variations to the patterns as they appear in the quilts. The Orange Basket shown here also appears in another quilt with tulips in the basket in place of oranges.

Fabrics for Applique

Both prints and solid colors combine happily together in applique. The smaller the pieces to be appliqued, the smaller the prints should be. The use of very small all-over prints help to give more depth to the colors. Widely spaced prints are not generally used. The most important prerequisite is the softness of the fabric. Material with hard crisp finishes do not lend themselves well to the curved lines of the patterns. Since applique is basically an overlaying technique, it is essential to use the most opaque fabrics that can be found.

Templates and Fabric Marking

Generally the solid type of template is used to mark the sewing line and the $\frac{1}{4}$ inch seam allowance is estimated by eye. If this is too difficult, by all means use two templates; one to mark the sewing and one to mark the cutting line. Place the larger one on the fabric first and center the smaller one within it. Mark the patterns on the *right* side of the fabric since all seam allowances are turned to the wrong side most of the actual work is concentrated on the right side of the fabric. Place the patterns on the straight of the grain where possible. Grain line is not as important in applique as in patchwork because the background fabric will keep the straight of the grain lengthwise and crosswise. This will reduce the tension of the individual pieces. When pieced applique designs call for a portion of the block to be made in the patchwork fashion, then adhere to the lessons learned earlier.

Wash all fabrics before using them as fabrics that bleed will have to be eliminated. Sometimes a fabric will have to be washed twice to get the extra dye out. Press all fabric and mark the patterns with a regular lead pencil used very lightly or a pastel used for the dark fabrics.

Working Order

First cut out the pieces that are needed, marking on the *right* side of the fabric. Then proceed to turn the seam allowance to the wrong side, using the marked sewing line as a guide, and baste in place. This is generally accomplished without the use of pins, working with a short needle and a rather short length of thread (12 to 15 inches). Place the knot on the *right* side of the fabric. Hold the applique piece with the wrong side facing you.

One mistake I often see when teaching this technique is students who sew *away* from themselves. Always sew *toward* yourself, supporting the work with the non-educated hand (Figure 3-1). Place four main fingers below the work, use the rotary motion of the thumb to turn the edge of the applique and hold it in place until it is stitched down. To create nice round edges on appliques, stitch all curved lines $\frac{1}{8}$ inch off the fold with very small stitches. The object of making a curve at all is to make it as defined as possible. *Do not press the appliques.* Do not turn the edges on areas of the applique that will be covered with another piece of applique, such as the top of a stem that will have a flower placed over it or the bottom of the oranges in the

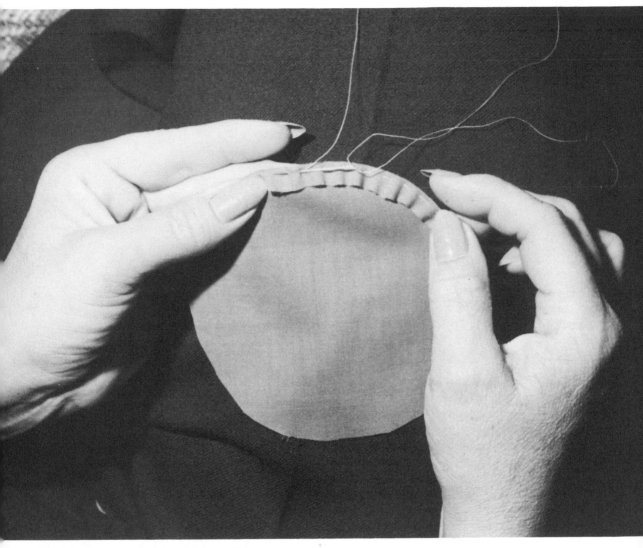

Fig. 3-1 *When basting edges on an applique, sew toward you and support the work underneath, using your thumb of support hand and needle in sewing hand to turn the edge.*

basket pattern where the fruit will be tucked inside the premade basket (Fig. 3-24). Only edges that will be permanently stitched will be turned.

Slashing and Mitering

In order to turn sharp corners, apply the mitering technique (Fig. 3-2). First turn the point in to the wrong side and then fold in the two remaining edges. On a perfect 90-degree angle, the two sides will meet. On the lesser angle, such as the end of a leaf in the basket pattern, the seam allowance may overlap (Fig. 3-2a and b). Sometimes, as in the case of a heart, to be able to turn the upper portion of the heart, a slash must be made into the deep V at the center of the heart. Just slash with a small scissor right up to the marked line. Turn the edges open so they lay flat (Fig. 3-2b). When basting these two open seam allow-ances, place a stitch over each raw edge, securing them down (see top of Fig. 3-2).

Using Opaque Fabric

Sometimes a lighter color fabric is needed to be placed over the darker one, but the darker one shows through. To create more opacity, place a piece of the same or any solid color fabric behind the applique. Cut this piece the same size as the sewing line without the addition of the seam allow-ance. Place this additional piece of fabric behind the applique before turning the seam allowance to the wrong side. When bast-ing, turn the seam allowance over it, catch-ing it in the basting stitches. If a color on hand is not dark enough, it can be made darker or warmer with the addition of an extra backing of fabric. Sometimes an ad-dition of an extra lining of batting behind

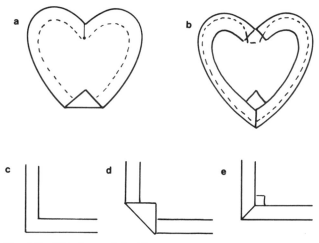

Fig. 3-2 *Mitering and slashing.*

Fig. 3-3 *To make appliques more opaque, add a lining of another fabric or batting.*

an applique, cut as above, can give more realistic dimensions to certain portions of an applique as well as give needed opacity (see Fig. 3-3). Only add this where you do not plan a lot of quilting as it is difficult to quilt through all these layers.

Basting the Appliques to the Background

Select a background square that will be at least one inch larger all the way around the applique's outer edges. The reason for this is that quilting may be placed around the outer edges of the applique. In the case of the blocks planned for this sampler quilt, the background block will measure 16 × 16 inches. Background is listed as 16 × 16 inches in materials list. Do not forget to add the seam allowance, cutting each $16\frac{1}{2}$ × $16\frac{1}{2}$ inches.

To find the placement of the appliques, quilters use the pre-folded square method. Take the background material and fold it in half and press. Fold in half again and press again. When opened, the folds will show the exact center and give four equal quadrants. If the pattern requires diagonal lines, this can be added by placing two folds on the diagonal and pressing as needed. It is easy to measure the remaining small details with a ruler and in the absence of a ruler, the hand will do (the width of two fingers or the length of the right pinkie). Great grandmother did not always have a ruler available.

Once all the applique pieces have been laid on the background square, then begin to pin in place. Check to see that the portions that are underneath another applique do not have more than the suggested $\frac{1}{4}$ inch seam allowance; if so, trim away. Baste all the appliques in place but *do not press.*

Hidden Slipstitch

Over the years many different kinds of stitches have been used to attach the appliques to the background: running stitch, buttonhole stitch and the smallest overcast. The best stitch to attach the appliques to the background is the hidden slipstitch. Use a short needle either a *between* or a *sharp,* threaded with the same color as the fabric to be appliqued and knotted at the end. Bring the knot up from the back of the background fabric and pass the needle through the fold of the piece to be appliqued. Now the needle and thread are on the face portion of the work. Slip the needle through the background, picking up a few of the threads, then back up and through the folded edge of the applique. Repeat going through a few threads of the background and tunnelling along a few threads of the fold. Then pull the thread through all the newly made stitches. Continue this

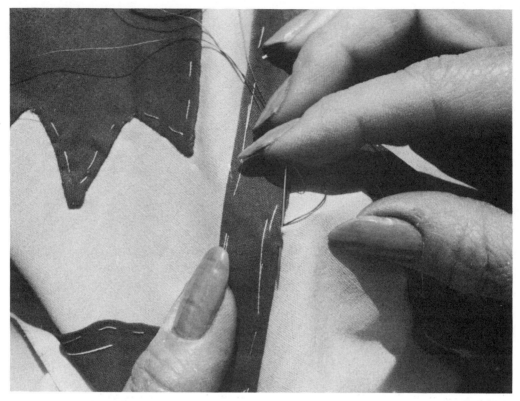

Fig. 3-4 *Hidden slipstitch used for applique.*
Note: All applique pieces have been basted down.

stitch. Pull it moderately firm, making the applique adhere tightly to the background fabric. Now, when making these small close stitches, you will understand why the instructions have recommended not to press the appliques after turning the seam allowance to the wrong side. This soft fold of the edge allows the needle to slip in and out of the edge of the applique easily. Soft fabric will also be appreciated at this point. Where there is less resistance to the needle passing through the fabric, the stitches can be made smaller. Try to make a minimum

of five to eight stitches to the inch, getting them evenly through the applique and the wrong side of the background fabric. To finish off a thread, bring it to the wrong side of the work in hand and secure it with several back stitches under the piece just appliqued. Clip the thread close. Use regular dressmakers thread with a color closely matched to the appliques (Fig. 3-4).

On an appliqued piece, the very sharp points, such as the base of a heart, have a tendency to wear. To prevent this, place one or two extra stitches at this point—

somewhat like little overcast stitches. These are called *whipstitches* and are said to whip the points down. They will not show as they are the same color thread as the applique. Another place to use the slipstitches is at any slash point such as in the center of the heart. If a few unruly threads have popped from the slashing, as often happens with blends of polyester and cotton, just push them back under the applique with the point of the needle and whipstitch over them. This whipstitch is done as you proceed with the slipstitch, not as an extra reinforcement.

Finishing the Applique

When all the slipstitches have been completed, clip all the threads, remove all the basting and press a final time.

Wedge Designs

The multi-wedge designs are a nostalgic step backward in time. Everyone loves this group of wedged patterns because they are easy to sew and they help to clean out the scrap bag. To make a really stunning looking block, the colors to be used have to be separated into effective looking groupings. First thing to note is the size of the wedges offered in the next three patterns. These small sized wedges need very small prints. All light and dark grounds should be separated. The dark ground prints should go on the light color background and the light color prints should go on a dark background. Then further select groups of colors that work well together or two to four shades

Fig. 3-5 *Friendship Ring, a circle of wedges made by Gerri Schirmacher.*

of one color that will assort best in the wedge design intended to be created. The effectiveness of the design depends on how well the quilter balances her colors and print sizes. Mark all the patterns on the wrong side as the stitching of the wedges will be treated just like patchwork.

To use these wedge designs in a full quilt, they may have intersecting bordering bands like on the Friendship Ring (Fig. 3-5) but the fan patterns generally are placed one after the other. They may be placed on the diamond so that they appear upright in the quilt and the edge may be filled in with triangles. This old circular pattern Friendship Ring (Fig. 3-5) is the most popular of all the wedge patterns and works beautifully in the sampler quilt. Anyone can fold this design with paper to any size and wedge proportions that please the quilter. Make a circle the desired finished size, fold in half and in half again and keep folding until the desired wedge size is found. Finish by cutting the center of the circle out after opening it. Use one of the folded wedges as a pattern. Trim outer edge to circular shape. The center of the circle of wedges may be left open with the background showing or the space may be used for additional applique design. The center may be covered with an additional circle of fabric that will be appliqued over the raw edges of the bottom of the wedges.

FRIENDSHIP RING

For convenience, a twenty-piece Friendship Ring has been prepared (Fig. 3-6, pattern piece A). Study the Friendship Rings in the color sections and on these pages. It is important to note that the colors are often repeated in these rings but they are not repeated haphazardly. When a ring has a specific number of wedges, the colors must be repeated in multiples. Find a number or numbers that will divide evenly into the number of total wedges. In the case of a 20-piece ring, 2, 4, 5 and 10 will all divide into 20, giving even number repeats so that 2 colors will be repeated 10 times, 4 will be repeated 5 times, 5 will be repeated 4 times and 10 will be repeated twice. This offers a great many differing combinations to put into the ring. The ring can also utilize a different print or color in each wedge.

As noted earlier, it is important to group compatible colors in the ring, and it is important to get a good conrast between the ring and the color of the background. If the background is light, avoid prints that have the same background color as the background fabric. I had a student who wanted to make each of her twenty wedges a different green print. She shoppped around and found nineteen different green ground prints and in desperation used an off-white ground print with small green print. When the rings were finished and placed on the off-white ground, it looked like a wedge was missing from each ring. The color selection and size of the print patterns do make a difference in bringing forth the beauty of the pattern.

The pattern gets its name from the practice of one quilter calling upon another quilter for small amounts of yardage to be placed in the rings. This helped to make the rings diverse and interesting.

Decide the number of repeats that would look appropriate in a Friendship Ring and decide if the center should be left open or if it should be covered with a coordinating color and contrast.

Materials and Cutting
PATTERN A: Cut 20 assorted wedges
PATTERN B: Cut 1 strong color circle, for covered center, cut one 16″ × 16″ background square (add seam allowance)

Assembly
1. Pin the first two wedges together and stitch only on the seam line. Continue to add the wedges one after the other until all twenty form a complete ring. The ring should lay perfectly flat when it is placed on the work surface. If either the center or the outside look too big and will not lay perfectly flat, go back and check the stitching and the pattern making. Make appropriate

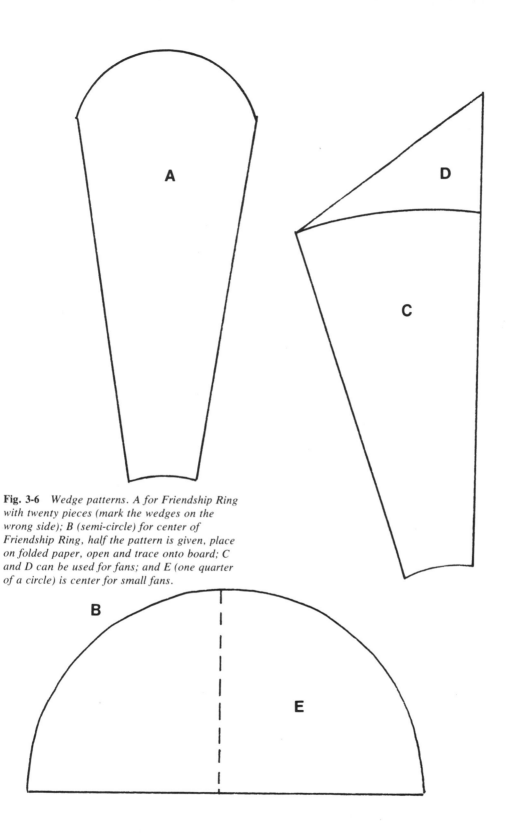

Fig. 3-6 *Wedge patterns. A for Friendship Ring with twenty pieces (mark the wedges on the wrong side); B (semi-circle) for center of Friendship Ring, half the pattern is given, place on folded paper, open and trace onto board; C and D can be used for fans; and E (one quarter of a circle) is center for small fans.*

adjustments to make the ring lay flat. Press seams in one direction or to the dark.

   2. Turn and baste the edges of the outer portion of the ring, keeping the curves of each wedge nice and round. (See discussion on applique and Fig. 3-2.) To get the curves round, place the small basting stitches close to the folded edge. Do not press.

   3. If the center of the ring is to be open, then turn and baste the raw edges of the center to the wrong side with $\frac{1}{4}$ inch seam allowance. If the center is to be covered, do not turn the raw edges of the ring back but cut out pattern piece B. Add the seam allowance, turn and baste to the wrong side of B. Set the B piece aside but do not press.

   4. Center the ring on the 16 × 16 inch background square (it will cut $16\frac{1}{2}$ × $16\frac{1}{2}$ inches). Baste in place all the way around the outside and on the inside. If the additional colored center is used, baste that over the raw edges of the center of the ring.

   5. Finish by using a small hidden slipstitch. If the overlayed center is used, then stitch through the three layers if possible. If it is too difficult to stitch through the three layers, then stitch the circle to the center edge of the ring. When work is totally finished, then press again.

SMALL FANS

Here is a very feminine pattern that is an offspring of the Friendship Ring (Fig. 3-7). It consists of five wedges of pattern A as used in the Friendship Ring or C which

Fig. 3-7 *Small fans, assorted small wedges made by Jane Emmer.*

has a smooth outer edge or the novel D (Fig. 3-6). They are all similar dimensions to the A piece, only the upper portion is different. The five wedges are stitched together in a random color order or a specific repeat or one color is placed in the middle and it is flanked with two repeating colors on either side. The center E, a quarter circle, is generally a good contrast color to the colors in the wedges or it may harmonize with it. If the wedges were all medium blue prints, then E could be a navy blue.

   These fans are basically one fourth of the Friendship Ring and therefore each would go on one fourth or an 8 × 8 inch section of the background.

Materials and Cutting
PATTERN A or C or D: Cut 20 pieces
PATTERN E: Cut 4 of a contrast color to
   above (E is half of pattern B)

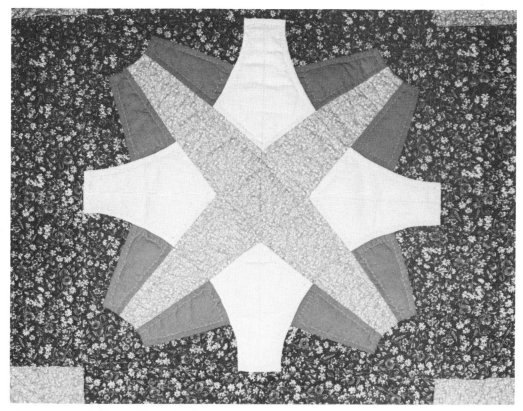

Fig. 3-8 *Position fan on 8½″ square of background so the seam allowance on the fan overlaps the seam allowance of the background square. The two raw edges will meet.*

Cut 4 background 8″ × 8″ (8½″ × 8½″ with seam allowance)

Assembly

1. Stitch five wedges together, sewing only on the seam line. Repeat for the other three fans (Fig. 3-7).

2. Turn the seam allowance at the top of the fan to the wrong side and baste down. Turn the *curved edge* of the E piece to the wrong side and baste down. Do not press either.

3. Position the fan over the corner of one piece of background material and baste the entire piece in place stitching all four edges. Then place the E piece in the corner, covering the raw edges of the bottom of the fan with the curved edge of E (Fig. 3-9) and baste down all three

113

Fig. 3-9 *A variation of basic fan made by extending the center onto a cross. (See color section on calico corners.) Made by Gerri Schirmacher.*

VICTORIAN FAN

The large romantic lace trimmed fan is a favorite for the sampler quilt (Fig. 3-10). Its edges may be trimmed with Cluny lace, Chantilly lace, eyelet or a self ruffle. The fan is further enhanced with a little back stitch embroidery and a bow. This big fan is actually very easy to make yet looks impressive. This can be made for the sampler quilt in calicoes and other cottons but it can also be made in satins and velvets for a very opulent, turn-of-the-century look. Sometimes these fan quilts were not used as bed coverings but as throws on pianos or couches.

Materials and Cutting
PATTERN F: Cut 12 assorted colors or specific 2, 3 or 4 combination repeats
1 yard of lace type trim

sides of E. Repeat for the other three fans.

    4. Hand stitch the curved edge of each fan and the curved edge of the base piece E with a slipstitch. Repeat for the other three pieces.

    5. Stitch the small fan patches together, using Fig. 3-7 as a guide. In Fig. 3-9, the center wedge has been extended to form a cross which helps to unite all four patches. This small 8 inch patch can be used in many ways. In a full quilt, the most traditional method is Fig. 3-7, haying all the fans on the diagonal. The fans made of scraps of various colors look very good when a common base (E) is used and a common background is used to sustain the variety of prints. The fan can be light in color and be placed on a dark ground.

Fig. 3-10 *Victorian Fan.*

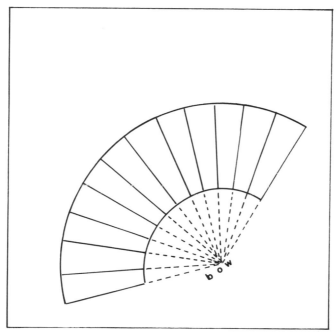

Fig. 3-11 *Center fan on background fabric. Draw in the lines for base of the fan and either embroider now or quilt in later. Cover end with bow. Placement will be determined by size of bow and width of additional lace.*

1 skein of embroidery floss, to match colors of F. Cut one 16″ × 16″ background square (add seam allowance)

Assembly

1. Stitch the twelve pieces of the fan together on the marked line only. Press and turn seams to the dark. Turn and baste all the edges of the fan to the wrong side.

2. If the lace is not pregathered, then gather at the lower edge and baste in place behind the top of the fan, turning the raw cut ends of the lace to the back. Repeat for the bottom of the fan.

3. Center the fan on the background (Fig. 3-11) so that the sides of the fan are approximately 2½ inches from the seam line. Baste the fan to the background fabric, stitching on the fabric portion only. Stitch down permanently with a hidden slipstitch and tack the edges of the lace to the background, securing the corners of the lace very firmly. This lace material is not to pop up from the background.

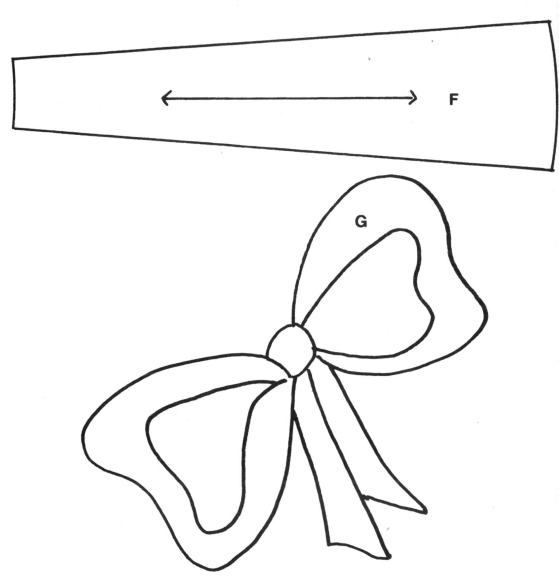

Fig. 3-12 *Victorian Fan pattern. G is optional embroidered bow.*

4. For an optional feature, very lightly draw lines from each edge of the fan until they intersect at a 90° angle. Add additional lines from each seam line to the point of intersection (Fig. 3-11). These may be embroidered or may be filled in with quilt stitching later. Add a bow made of additional material left over from the fan; embroider it in (see Fig. 3-12, pattern G), or add a ribbon bow. Keep it small and sew it to the background very carefully.

Quilting Suggestions

Each wedge may be outlined a ¼ inch from the edge or it may be quilted on the seam line, creating a depression between the seams which will cause the wedge to puff up. Outline quilting of each wedge design is practical as this will leave an open triangle shape in the corner above, which could be filled in with a novelty design; or the background could have a few concentric lines of quilting around the edge.

Parallelograms

TUMBLING BLOCKS

Tumbling Blocks, Fig. 3-13, is a study in three harmonizing colors which creates a blocklike shape in each three-piece patch. To execute the diminutive design in perfect balance, it is important to understand that this patch is to represent a block with light shining down from above and right (or left). When light shines on a block, the portion that receives the most light will be the lightest—in this case, the top portions. The secondary source will be a shade darker

Fig. 3-13 *Tumbling Blocks, a parallelogram pattern.*

and the portion receiving the least light will be the darkest. For this three-piece patch, light, medium and dark shades are to be selected. The contrasts have to be strong or the basic design will be lost. This is an all-over design used through an entire quilt. For the sampler quilt, a small version of seven blocks is prepared in a harmonizing shape. This is basically a patchwork pattern, but to enable the quilter to make a sampler block, it will be prepared as shown in Fig. 3-13 and appliqued to a 16 × 16 inch background square.

In order to prepare a good Tumbling Block patch, an understanding of the grain line is a must. As we have studied before, it is important to have the grain line running in lengthwise and crosswise direction where possible. There is one parallelogram shape given for the pattern. In teaching this patch, I suggest the students make two of

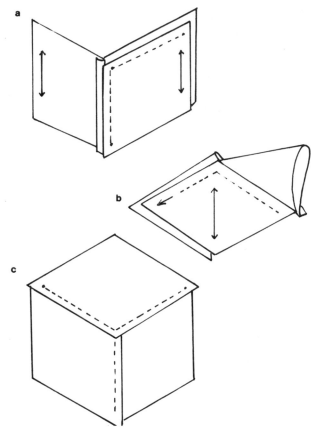

Fig. 3-14 *Tumbling Blocks assembly.*

the same template. One will be marked A. This will have the straight of the grain running in an upright direction across the shortest portion from point to point (Fig. 3-16). This is to be used for the lightest color, or the top, of the block. When cut, the A piece will have four bias sides. Template B is an exact replica of A, but the grain line is different. In the case of B, note that the straight of the grain is placed parallel to the two sides which will have

straight-of-grain threads. The top and bottom of B will have bias cut edges (Fig. 3-16b). To use pattern piece B effectively, shade one side slightly. To cut the medium color, place the pattern on the wrong side of the fabric, clean side up, and mark the pattern. To cut the darkest fabric, place the shaded side up on the wrong side of the fabric and mark. This will keep the grain lines all running in the same direction when the quilt is finished.

Materials and Cutting

PATTERN A: Cut 7 lightest color print or solid

PATTERN B: Cut 7 medium color print or solid and 7 darkest color print or solid. Cut one 16″ × 16″ background square (add seam allowance)

Assembly

1. Stitch a medium print to the dark print, lining up the two straight-of-grain edges. Sew only on the marked line, press to the left (Fig. 3-14a) center.

2. To complete the block, use Fig. 3-14 as a guide for this three-piece corner. Place the bias edge of A behind one of the B pieces. Pin and stitch on the marked line (do not get off the line). Take out the pins, slip the needle under the seam made in step one and repin the second side of A to the remaining B piece (Fig. 3-14b). Press the light A down against the two B's (Fig. 3-14c). Repeat until seven patches are finished. (Also refer to Fig. 2-44.)

3. First join three patches one next to the other, stitching on the marked line only (Fig. 3-15). Then add two more patches below and two above, using the same technique used in step 2.

4. Turn the seam allowances of the circle of blocks to the wrong side and baste down. Center on the background square and baste to the background. With a hidden slipstitch, sew to the background, then remove the basting and press.

To make this pattern in an all-over quilt, keep adding blocks until there are enough to cover the bed. The perimeter edge will not be straight; it will have a

Fig. 3-15 *Tumbling Blocks, joining patches together, then into a circle.*

geometric scalloped look. This look is left and the quilt is bound with this odd shaped border. When the quilt drops over the side of the bed, the shaped border adds an interesting touch. This is often made as a baby quilt in a small size in pastel colors.

Quilting Suggestions

Quilt each one of the parallelogram shapes $\frac{1}{4}$ inch off the seam line and around the outline of all seven blocks.

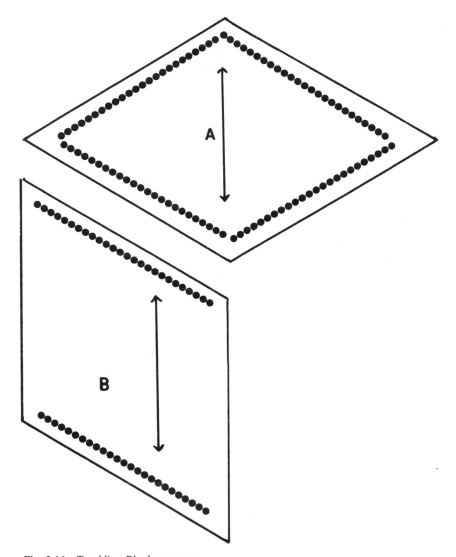

Fig. 3-16 *Tumbling Blocks pattern*

120

The Six-Sided Hexagon

GRANDMOTHER'S FLOWER GARDEN

This design is the epitome of technical excellence and is a real prize winner to make and own. Its name suggests the innocent

Fig. 3-17 *Grandmother's Flower Garden. A (top) is six-sided hexagon (19 pieces) made by Jane Emmer. B (using 32 pieces) is made by Joan Dermond. Both fit on a 16" background.*

charm of garden flowers. Each patch is comprised of nineteen hexagon-shaped pieces. The center hexagon represents the center of a flower. A warm color is suggested (often yellow). The two surrounding rows can be different colors. Sometimes the outer row is a darker tone of the inner row giving a one color look to the two circles surrounding the center. A full quilt of this type often helps to clean out the scrap bag, generally utilizing the pastels accumulated; but the quilt can have the flowerlet colors repeated exactly the same throughout the quilt. If the colors are not those of the garden but rather vibrant dark colors, the quilt is given the name of Mosaic. To sample this technique, make one patch and applique it to a larger background square. See full detail of a Grandmother's Flower Garden quilt in Fig. 3-18.

Materials and Cutting

PATTERN A: Cut 1 bright color for center (color 1); cut 6 of a second color for the second row (color 2); cut 12 of a third color for the third row (color 3) Cut one 16" × 16" background square

Assembly

1. Stitching on the marked line only, attach one of color 2 to one side of color 1 (Fig. 3-19a). Add a second color 2 to the side of the 2 already attached to the center, stitch only on the seam line from the outside to the inside (Fig. 3-19b). When arriving at the base of the seam, use the three-piece corner method shown earlier (Fig. 2-44). Pass the needle onto the center piece and proceed to lift and

Fig. 3-18 *Detail of Grandmother's Flower
Garden quilt made by Florence Kantor. This quilt
is made of one-inch hexagons and each hexagon
is quilted. This was made for a double bed.*

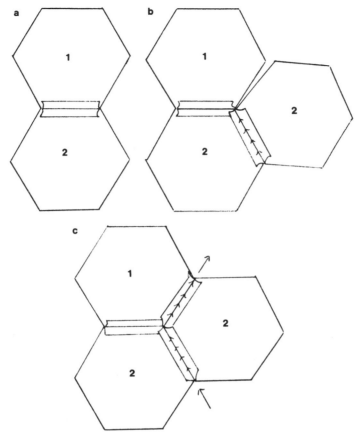

Fig. 3-19 *Grandmother's Flower Garden assembly.*

pin the rest of piece 2 against the center 1 (Fig. 3-19c). Finish stitching the 2's to the 1 and cut the thread at this point and repeat for the other four pieces of color 2. Press the side seams of the ring of the second color in one direction and the center piece outward.

2. Continue to use the three-piece corner method and add the twelve color 3 patches to form the third ring. Press all side seams in one direction and the

seams of the first ring out against the second ring.

3. Turn the seam allowance of the outer ring of patches to the wrong side and baste down, using Fig. 3-17 as guide.

4. Center the newly made flower against the background square and baste down. Applique with a hidden slipstitch to the background and press.

To use this in a single quilt as an all-

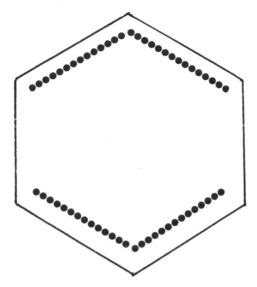

Fig. 3-20 *Grandmother's Flower Garden pattern.*

Quilting Suggestions

Each of the hexagons is quilted in a good rendition of this pattern. On the block for the sampler quilt, add some novelty quilting around the appliqued flower.

Patchwork Background with Applique on Top

HONEY BEE

This is a perfect blend of patchwork and applique used to create a picturesque block. As a teacher, I always turn to this block as the one that bridges the gap for a student who wants to do both a little patchwork and a little applique. The most important element of the design is to maintain the same color for the body of the bee and for the corners of the center nine patch. This corner appears as the head of the bee. The corners that touch the body of the bee and

over pattern, add an additional row of eighteen hexagons to the seventeen shown (Fig. 3-17). Add three background hexagons to the top and three to the bottom of one flower; add a flower above and below this. Continue in this manner until you have a length to accomodate the bed to be covered. On either side of this strip, add additional background hexagons. This will be the center of the quilt face. Make a second row of flower forms with the three hexagons between each. Fit this second row into the first and continue in this manner. Note that the edges of this finished quilt are scalloped; this is the charm of this quilt. It may be bound this way although some quilters prefer to applique a band of fabric around the perimeter to even out the scalloped edge and then bind it.

Fig. 3-21 *Honey Bee applique on top of patchwork.*

the center of the nine-patch will set up a strong diagonal effect in the quilt. It is important to select opaque fabric when planning this block.

Materials and Cutting

PATTERN A: Cut 5 dark print and 4 background or very small print
PATTERN B: Cut 4 background
PATTERN C: Cut 4 background
PATTERN D: Cut 8 solid or very small print for wing
PATTERN E: Cut 4 dark print as used in A (body)

Mark A, B and C on the wrong side and mark E and D on right side.

Assembly

1. Using the nine small A pieces, assemble a checkerboard nine patch, keeping the dark square on the corners and in center (Fig. 3-22a). Press to the dark.

2. Attach two of the B's to either side of one C; repeat for the other side to form the right and left sides of the block. Press. Attach two of the remaining C's above and below the nine patch made in step 1. When completed, this should measure $16\frac{1}{2} \times 16\frac{1}{2}$ inches, including the seam allowance (Fig. 3-22b).

3. Turn the seam allowance to the wrong side on pieces D and E and baste, mitering the corners Fig. 3-2. Do not press. Pin the bees in position on the corners, using Fig. 3-22c as a guide. Baste in place and finish off by appliqueing with a slipstitch, using Fig. 3-4 as a guide. To use this size block in

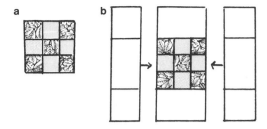

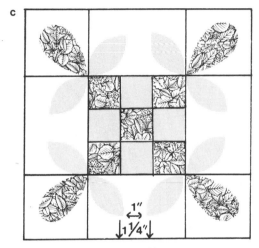

Fig. 3-22 *Honey Bee assembly.*

an overall quilt, place the blocks one after the other. If using in a smaller quilt, the size of the block can be reduced and the blocks can be alternated with a blank block. A nice wide outer border can be added around the outside of the quilt with random bees added as decoration.

Quilting Suggestions

Outline each of the small center squares $\frac{1}{4}$ inch off the seam line. Outline each portion of the bee $\frac{1}{4}$ inch off the edge of the applique.

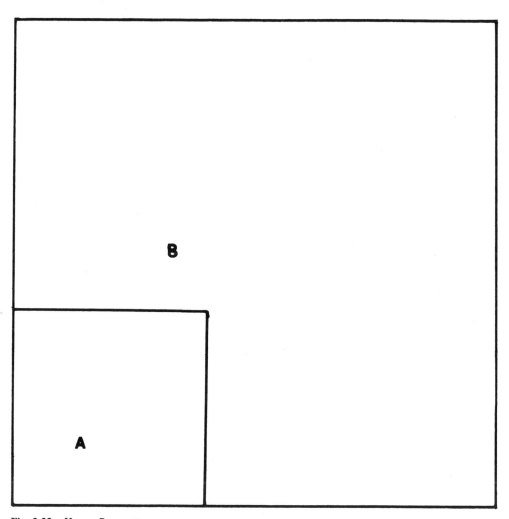

Fig. 3-23 *Honey Bee pattern.*

126

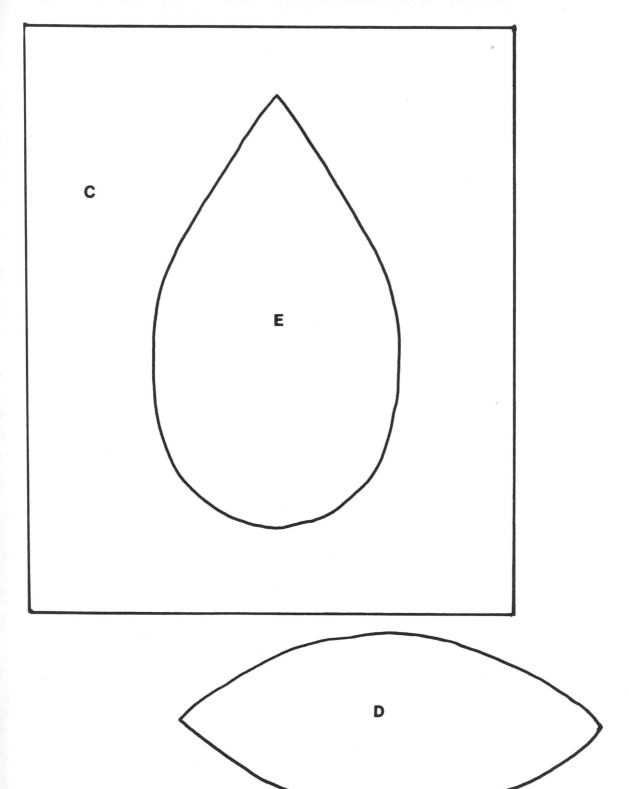

Fig. 3-23 *continued.*

Fig. 3-24 *Orange Basket patchwork basket filled with applique.*

Patchwork Basket Plus Applique

ORANGE BASKET

The basket in folk art is always associated with abundance. The patchwork basket has been a favorite for many years. It is simple

to make and goes very quickly. Here it combines oranges in the basket, but it could have any fruit or flowers. It brings together small piece patchwork and small, very curvy applique pieces (Fig. 3-25 and 3-26). It again brings the best of two worlds together.

Materials and Cutting

PATTERN A: Cut 11 dark print, 5 light print for basket
PATTERN B: Cut 1 light print as above
PATTERN C: Cut 1 dark orange
PATTERN D: Cut 2 light orange
PATTERN E: Cut 2 dark orange, same as C
PATTERN F: Cut 9 green leaves
PATTERN H: Cut 1 dark print, same as A for handle

Cut one 16″ × 16″ background square (add seam allowance). Mark A and B on the wrong side, all the rest on right side.

Assembly

1. Stitch a row of dark and light A's together, using 4 darks and 3 lights.

Fig. 3-25 *Orange Basket assembly.*

128

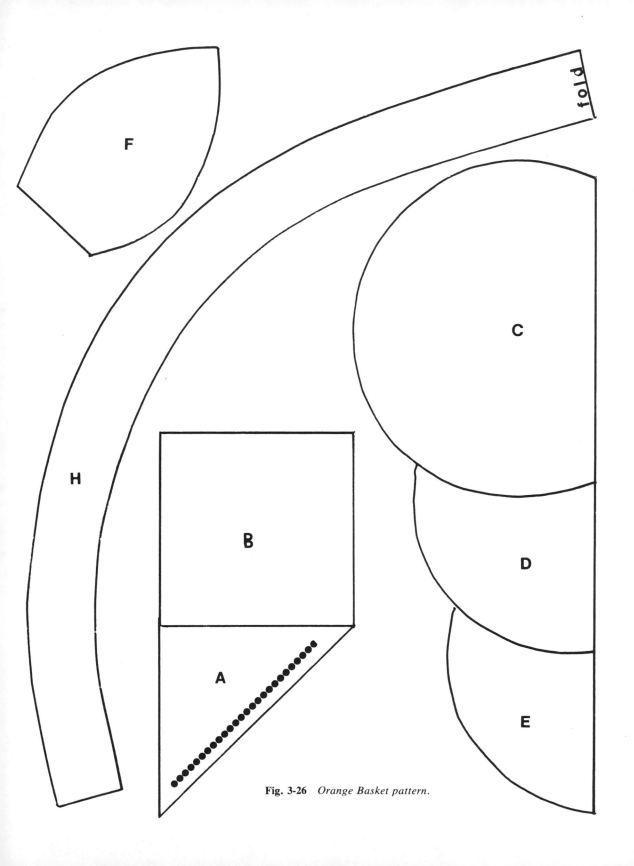

Fig. 3-26 *Orange Basket pattern.*

Stitch a second row of A's, 3 darks and 2 lights (see Fig. 3-25). Stitch the four remaining dark A's to the outer edges of the single B. Press seams to the dark and assemble into the basket shape, press. Turn and baste the seam allowance around the basket to the wrong side. Do not press and set aside.

    2. Turn the seam allowance on all the *curved* edges of pieces C, D, E, F and H. Do not press.

    3. Place the basket near the bottom of the background square on the diagonal and tuck in the oranges and leaves and handle, using Fig. 3-24 as a guide. Pin first then baste everything in place and finish with a hidden slipstitch.

Quilting Suggestions

    Quilt on each of the pieces of the basket, outlining the basket and its handle $\frac{1}{4}$ inch off the outer edges and the fruit $\frac{1}{4}$ inch off the edges. The leaves can have some outlining stitches to indicate the veins. The background may have some fill-in stitching.

4

APPLIQUE

Applique was used as early as the Crusades as trimmings for clothing, banners and flags. It was a craft that was brought along with many other needleart forms to the Colonies. The English had a flourishing trade in printed Chintz cotton goods which were in strong demand in the new Colonies. Today in our restoration sites, we can see entire rooms decorated in these prints. The designs fascinated our foremothers so much that they would cut out portions of the designs and applique them to background cloth of white wool or heavy linen to make bed covers. These were unquilted and show the skillfulness of using parts of these all-over designs to accommodate the need for decorating the bed. Up to now,

all this fabric was hand screen printed with rather large designs. When copper plate printing was invented, it lead the way to other printing designs such as calicoes which were more suitable to clothing. The American Colonies were quick to establish textile mills in the north which first relied on imported cotton and later on the development of cotton as a home grown crop. With more fabric to work with, the applique needlecrafters turned to making representations of objects around them. The need for the decorative bed coverings was an ideal place for this needleart to grow. Being part of a new social order without the restrictions of preconceived forms of design; applique was able to take off in new

131

directions and meet the needs of the people at a new time.

This line of historic knowledge supports the idea that applique was a very well established needleart in the Colonies from its earliest days. Applique was primarily attributed to the reading class; not only Bible readers but those that had access to newspapers and books. The reader conjures pictures consciously or unconsciously. It was their active minds, their need to express themselves, the availability of materials and the acquired skill that fused together at this point in time to make the American applique quilt so unique in needleart history. The opportunity to create pictures with fabric commemorates life and ultimately that person's mark on civilization. So we are left with an exquisite form of commemorative needleart. These quilts were always revered. Some say because of the quality, time and workmanship needed to be put into the quilts, they were considered best quilts. I believe it was a reverence for the preservation of the self—an integral part of each quilt. Try it and see how you feel about your pictorial art.

Start with the large, soft, gentle curves and the efficient mitered corners. Then keep working these shapes into smaller pieces with greater definition in each concave and convex curve. Add to this your growing knowledge of how to use color and fabric effectively. Keep in mind there are no hard and fast rules. If you like smallish picture motifs on open large background or large pictures covering most of the background block, change the proportions to suit yourself.

For these reasons, you have more flexibility in using the patterns in this chapter. They are grouped in general categories. The techniques do require time and patience, but many of the areas that appear difficult can be made easy with a few tricks of the trade.

The open background behind the appliques opens up another dimension for the quilter—that is background quilting. This is the textural element that is added to color and design. Very often the larger floral blocks are placed one after the other with no bands separating the designs. This open space is then filled with beautiful and imaginative quilt stitchery. The quality of this stitching and the intricacy of the pattern stitches help determine the intrinsic value of the quilt. In this sampler quilt, the designs are caught in a frame of borders. It offers an opportunity for the quilter to try differing forms of background or novelty stitching.

Applique for the Sampler Quilt

The patterns in this section offer the widest use of shape, from the large gentle curves to the very strong tight scallops. From an historic point of view, the most often used shapes have been included. All the patterns are graded to fit the 16 × 16 inch finished background block with room to spare for quilting around the appliques. Applique patterns are very easy to make in any size with a sharp pair of paper cutting scissors. If you see a pattern or a shape that you would like to use in a design, draw it and then cut it out from paper. Adjust to size and recut as necessary until you get the shape, size and definition that you feel will create the most effective design. One of the most common shortcomings of students who are new to applique is the fear of creating strong curve lines. This results in appliques that lack definition. Keep in mind that designs means the use of lines and if the lines are flat and dull, the work is not very distinguished. Generally the shapes are repeated, four tulips or twelve hearts, and with paper cutting the proportions can quickly be duplicated, placed on a background paper or fabric and adjusted to please. At this point the pieces of paper may be colored to see what the design will look like when finished or they may be cut from colored construction paper and pinned to a background. This will help to eliminate mistakes.

Review the instructions given in Chapter 3, Pieced Applique, on basic techniques of mitering, slashing and sewing curves. As the design blocks proceed in this chapter, more sophisticated techniques will be added to your repertoire of skills.

Solid templates are generally preferred for this medium. Mark all the fabric on the *right* side as that is the side where most of the work is concentrated. Mark the sewing line and estimate the seam allowance by eye. If you are having trouble with this, then use the double template method suggested earlier (Fig. 1-9). Accurate marking of the seam line is again stressed so that all the repeating forms will be exact replicas of each other, offering balance and symmetry to the block.

Cut all the applique pattern pieces out for each block selected, turn and baste the edges to the wrong side. *Do not press appliques*. Press the appropriate folds in the background square that is cut $16\frac{1}{2} \times 16\frac{1}{2}$ inches, including the seam allowance. Pin the pieces in place, checking to see that there are no excessive overlaps and baste to background. Using matching color thread, applique the pieces to the background permanently with a hidden slip-stitch or the smallest possible overcast stitch. After the work has been completed, take out the basting and press.

Crossed Diagonal Designs

The use of selected design shapes on the crossed diagonal in a quilt pattern offers a relief from the vertical-horizontal lines most often found in quilts. The curves of the appliques offer a wide departure from the linear lines of patchwork. The crossed tulip type is the most popular and has the greatest opportunity for variation. The main portions of the designs are definitely on the diagonal but the leaves offer a secondary direction of north, east, south and west. The leaves are generally a strong color because they are small. If they are to carry any weight to the design, the strength of color is important. The leaves and the stems of the flowers need not be the same. Study the interesting uses of color as shown in the color photo section. Leaves need not be attached, remember that you are not making an accurate reproduction but a design rendition for a needlecraft medium. Another thing to remember is that if you don't like tulips you may change the flower on the end of the stem to any one that pleases your fancy—roses, lilies, Irish bells or even a cluster of small flowers.

CROSSED TULIP AND DUTCH TULIP

Both these gay tulip designs lend themselves to bright prints as well as solids. The center shape A of the Crossed Tulip (Fig. 4-1) may be changed to a teardrop or oval and placed on the surface of the main body of the tulip. To add definition to the work make strong deep slashes in the tulip (B) and sharp miters on the points. The leaf on the Crossed Tulip has a small S-shaped curve to it and it may be necessary to pre-notch these seam allowances so that they turn back easily. Both design blocks are put together the same way; use Fig. 4-3 or Fig. 4-4 as a guide for patterns.

Fig. 4-1 *Crossed Tulip made by Joan Shaw. (See color section, All American.)*

Fig. 4-2 *Dutch Tulip made by Gerri Schirmacher. (See color section, Calico Corners.)*

Materials and Cutting

PATTERN A: Cut 4 bright print or solid
PATTERN B: Cut 4 bright print or solid in contrast to A
PATTERN C: Cut 4 strong color print or solid
PATTERN D: Cut 2 strong color print or solid
    Cut one 16″ × 16″ background square (add seam allowance)

Assembly

Baste all the seam allowances to the wrong side and fold the background square on the diagonal twice.

1. Center the B with the A behind it on the pre-folded diagonal lines of the background; pin in place.

2. Pin the two D stems in a cross fashion on the pre-folded diagonal lines. Tuck the raw edge of the stems under the tulips and be sure to trim off any excess under the tulip portion.

134

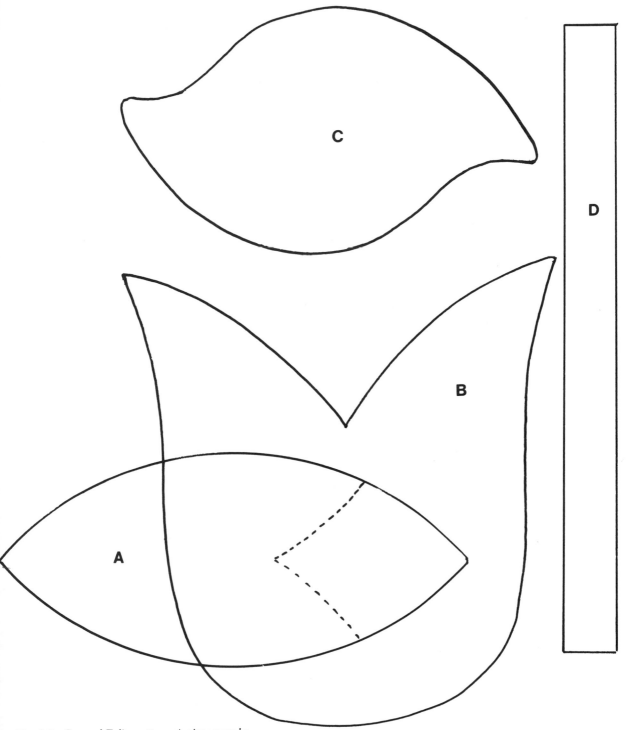

Fig. 4-3 *Crossed Tulip pattern. A piece may be tucked behind the B tulip; if so, cut off at dotted line or it may be overlaid on top. If a light color is required as an overlay, then back it with additional fabric so the color of tulip A does not show through.*

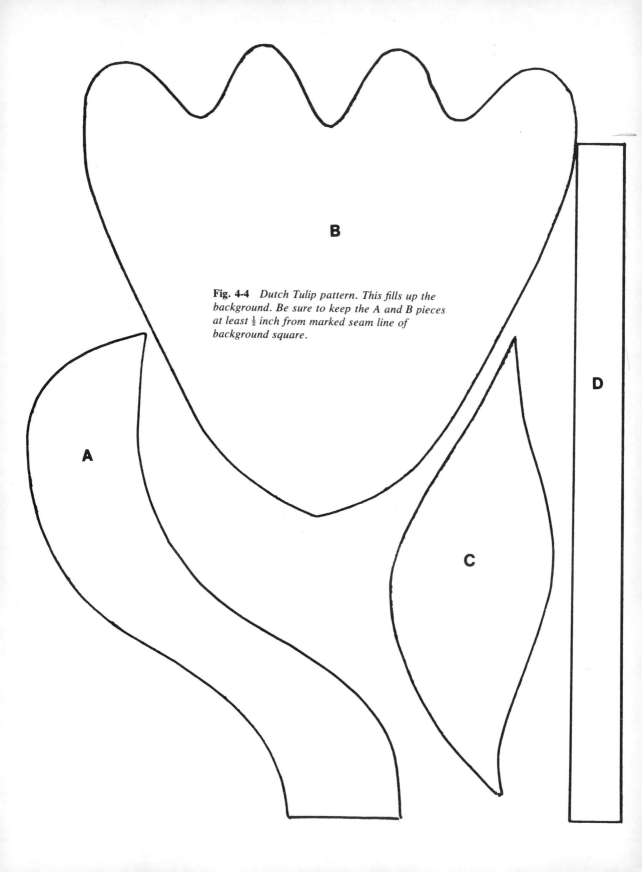

Fig. 4-4 *Dutch Tulip pattern. This fills up the background. Be sure to keep the A and B pieces at least ½ inch from marked seam line of background square.*

A

B

C

D

3. Pin the leaves in the center lengthwise and crosswise, using Fig. 4-1 or Fig. 4-2 as a guide.

4. Baste all the pieces in place; stitch down permanently; remove the basting stitches and press.

Quilting Suggestions

There is not much space allowed for novelty quilting so just outline the combined elements. The leaves may have an S-curved line defining the center.

To use the tulip patterns in a full quilt design, it is not necessary to have bordering bands in-between. It makes a very easy quilt to put together, placing one block after another.

TURKEY TRACKS

This authentic provincial pattern could only have its roots in early American quilt records. The three-pronged print of the wild

Fig. 4-5 *Turkey Tracks made by Sally Rowe.*

turkey left in the snow or mud assured the early settlers that dinner was not far off. It can be worked as a silhouette all in one color (see color photos) or with assorted, very small calicoes (Fig. 4-6). It is an elegantly sleek pattern of deeply curved pieces. It keeps the eye moving across the quilt on a diagonal line. The branching of the corner tracks expands the movement in several directions at once. While the corners are filled, they are not dominated with a large single unit such as a flower. The concave lines of the center balances the convex lines of the foot track. The art in making this pattern is to make well defined curves that end in sharp points. One of the tricks to very sharp points is that sometimes when mitering the point, a bit of the second fold of the miter sticks out beyond the applique. Do not fuss with this when basting. When sewing it down permanently, just push it back under the applique with the point of the needle and hold it with your thumb until stitched in place.

Materials and Cutting
PATTERN A: Cut 1 strong color
PATTERN B: Cut 4 strong color, matching or contrasting with A
PATTERN C: Cut 8 same color as B
Cut one 16″ × 16″ background square (add seam allowance)

Assembly
Fold the background square on the diagonal twice; baste all the seam allowances on A, B and C pieces. The A piece may need some clipping into the seam allowance to make a strong curve.

1. Pin the A piece to the center, lining up its points on the diagonal folds.

Fig. 4-6 *Turkey Tracks in a full quilt alternated with a blank block that echoes the design in dark quilt thread. Made by Sally Rowe.*

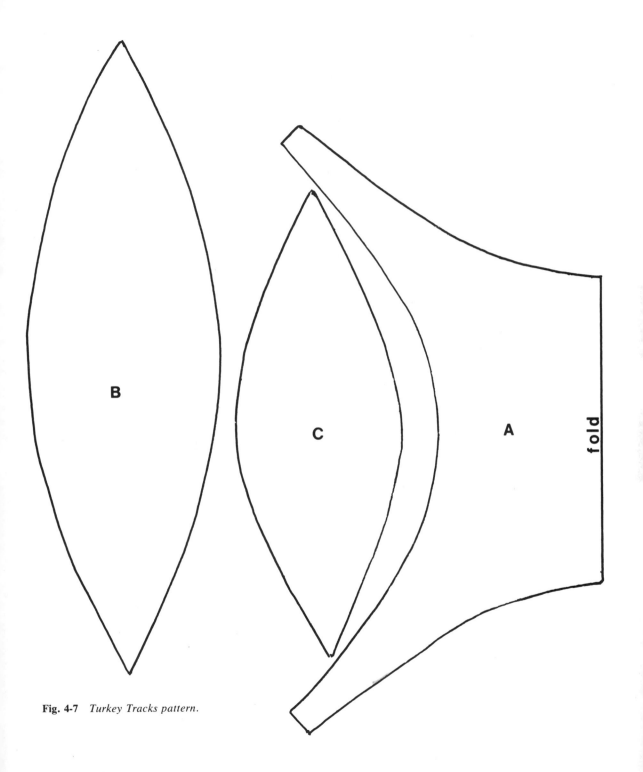

Fig. 4-7 *Turkey Tracks pattern.*

2. Pin the B pieces, covering the ends of the A, lining up the B's on the fold.

3. Place the remaining C pieces to the right and left of the B's. The base of the B's and C's will come evenly together. Baste all the pieces down; stitch permanently; remove the basting and press.

Quilting Suggestions

This pattern provides a lot of open space to try some novelty quilting between the foot tracks. Outline the entire applique first.

To use this pattern in a full quilt, it is best to leave out the bordering bands. Place one block after each other or alternate each with a blank block (Fig. 4-6).

Common Center Designs

There are many designs in which the center is the focal point of the block. The Pineapples radiate from the center but form diagonal lines also. The Hearts All Round has a solid center and the hearts form a ring around the center, giving a circular feeling. The use of the common center creates a harmonizing effect that works particularly well in a sampler quilt.

PINEAPPLES

This is a design that has a long and happy history in Early American design (Fig. 4-8). It is known as a sign of welcome. I suspect that because the fruit was not a home grown item, the offering of imported fruit to guests was a show of great honor. The pineapple is found in folk art painting

Fig. 4-8 *Pineapples made by Joan Shaw.*

and in wallpaper prints, is carved on furniture and is a favorite of quilters. It may appear as a single pineapple in silhouette form or in a cluster with a common center as shown here. The main body of the pineapple is quilted with stitchery to simulate the diamond shape cross-hatching on the real fruit. The A piece may be padded with additional batting to give it more definition or to intensify the color.

Materials and Cutting
PATTERN A: Cut 4 light print or solid
PATTERN B: Cut 4 darker color to simulate leaves
PATTERN C: Cut same as B

Cut 16″ × 16″ background square (add seam allowance)

Assembly
1. With right sides together, place the B's straight edge against the straight cut edge of the A and stitch across with

140

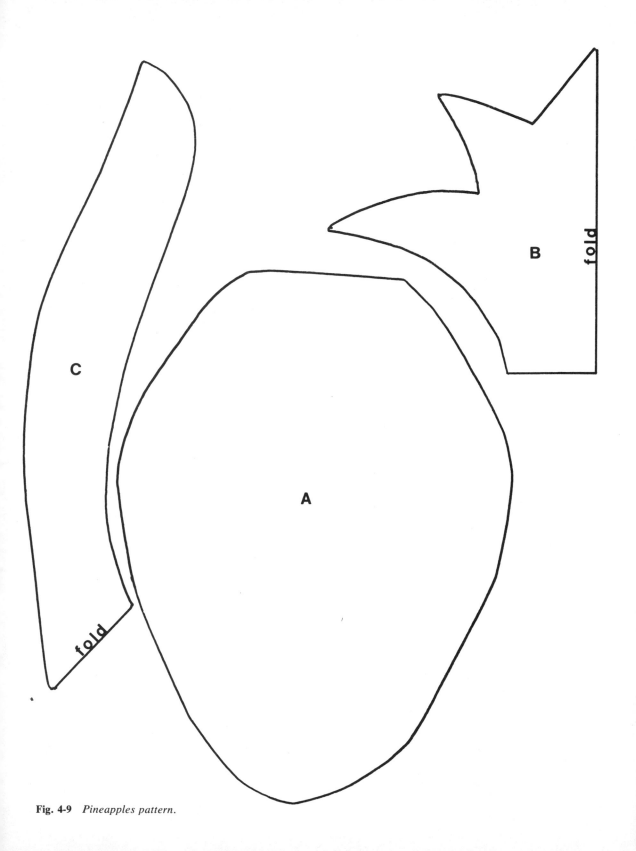

Fig. 4-9 *Pineapples pattern.*

a hand running stitch on the marked seam line only. Press this seam allowance to the dark and baste the seam allowance of the combined pieces to the wrong side. Repeat for the other three pineapples.

2. Turn the seam allowance to the wrong side of the C pieces.

3. Fold the background square on the diagonal twice and press. Pin the four C pieces in place, using Fig. 4-8 as a guide, and add the four pineapples, tucking them under the C portion slightly. Baste in place; stitch down permanently; remove the basting and press.

Quilting Suggestions

Quilt the Pineapples with a diamond pattern about $\frac{1}{2}$ inch apart. Quilt lines on the B portion to simulate leaf separation and quilt $\frac{1}{4}$ inch off the edge of the entire applique.

To use this design in a full quilt, separate with bordering bands and use strong colors. This design also makes a lovely wall hanging for a kitchen or a den.

HEARTS ALL ROUND

Hearts in any form are associated with bridal and baby quilts. They have become a symbol of affection. Because of their shape, they are often used to fill in small open spaces. Hearts need not be red; they can be any color. Many quilters use this pattern to unite several colors used in the sampler quilt. The hearts must be made very carefully, getting full round curves at the top and sharp points at the bottom. Each

Fig. 4-10 *Hearts All Round made by Gerri Schirmacher.*

heart point touches a corresponding point of the center (Fig. 4-10).

Materials and Cutting
PATTERN A: Cut 1 center in strong color
PATTERN B: Cut 12 assorted colors or one single shade
    Cut one 16″ × 16″ background square (add seam alowance)

Assembly
Baste all the seam allowances to the wrong side and fold the background in four even folds horizontally and vertically.

1. Fold the A piece in four even folds horizontally and vertically. Center this piece on the background, matching the folds, and baste.

2. Center four hearts over the four exposed fold lines; pin in place. Add the remaining hearts, making sure they do

142

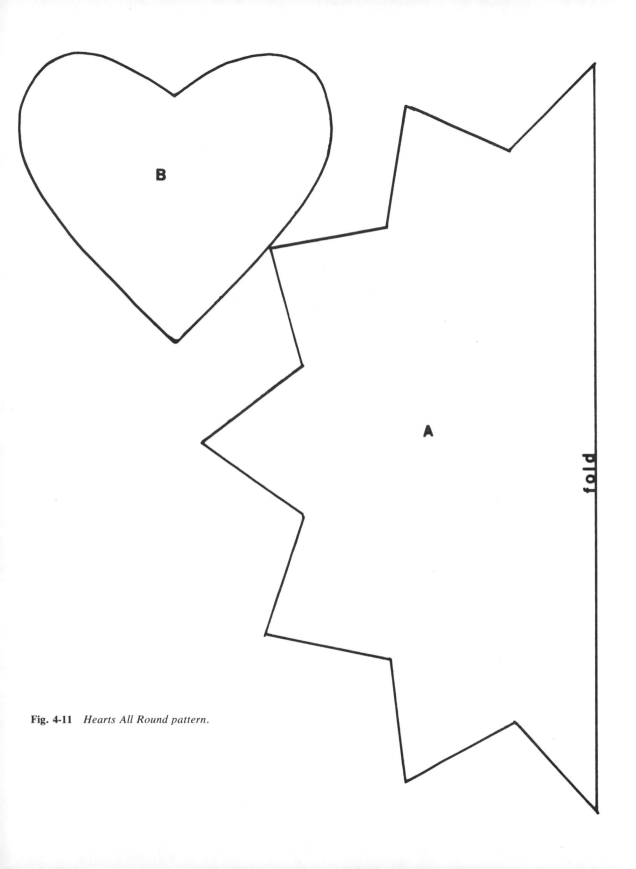

Fig. 4-11 *Hearts All Round pattern.*

not overlap. Baste; stitch down permanently, remove the basting and press.

Quilting Suggestions

Quilt the center with a sunburst pattern and quilt the perimeter of the hearts. Add a novelty design in the corners, such as a little flower or butterfly or rows of concentric lines. This design may be used in a full quilt with or without bordering bands.

The Reel Designs

These old patterns get their names from the lively dance popular in Early American times. The pattern should give the feeling of endless motion, never letting the eye settle in one place. The design is basically a circle that has been intersected with four convex quarter crescents. The corners are decorated with buds and leaves (Fig. 4-12

Fig. 4-12 *Reel and Bud made by Joan Shaw.*

and Fig. 4-14). The colors are always contrasts of strong lively colors. These patterns look very well made up in very large sizes. While they are both circular at the center, the corner trims create diagonal lines through the quilt. (Study the color photos for variations.)

REEL AND BUDS

This is the simplest of the Reels made with full round lines throughout. The corners are adorned with two leaves and a bud or three leaves (Fig. 4-12). The background shows through the center.

Materials and Cutting
PATTERN A: Cut 4 of a strong solid or print
PATTERN B: Cut 4 of a contrast to A and C
PATTERN C: Cut 8 bright solid or print for the leaves
Cut one 16″ × 16″ background square (add seam allowance)

Assembly

Fold the background square on the diagonal twice. Baste all the seam allowances to the wrong side of the applique.

1. Using Fig. 4-12 as a guide, pin the A pieces in the vertical and horizontal positions so their points touch on the folded lines and baste in place.

2. Pin the B's so they face out of the block and are centered on the diagonal lines. Pin 2 C's on either side of each B. They may overlay slightly. Baste in place; stitch permanently; remove basting and press.

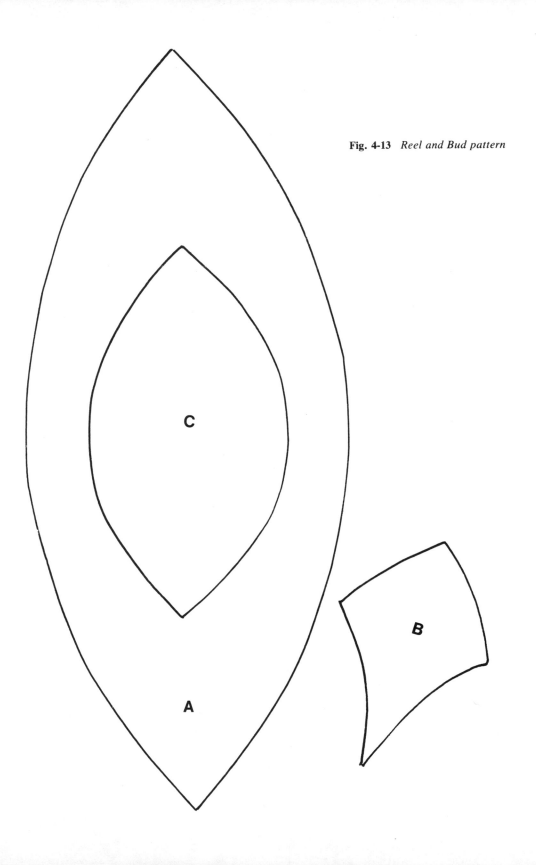

Fig. 4-13 *Reel and Bud pattern*

Quilting Suggestions

Outline both the inside and the outside of the entire applique $\frac{1}{4}$ inch from the applique pieces. The center of the reel is a good spot for some novelty, show-off quilting.

To use this pattern in a full quilt, it may be used with or without the bordering bands. It should always be made of bright, cheerful colors.

OAK LEAF AND REEL

Here the center is a more complex form of the reel (Fig. 4-14). Its concave center is augmented with four shaped crescents. It is the shape of the crescents that makes this pattern so interesting. Look carefully and note that the outside curve of the crescent is deeper than the inside curve. The pattern sets up a strong circular movement at the center of the block and the leaves

Fig. 4-14 *Oak Leaf and Reel made by Gerri Schirmacher.*

create a crossed diagonal direction. The oak leaf with its long shapely leaves creates the most interesting of all the leaf patterns, although the pattern can be made with other leaf motifs. Use very soft, pliable fabric for the leaves.

Materials and Cutting

PATTERN A: Cut 1 strong color
PATTERN B: Cut 4 contrasting color to A and C (leaves)
PATTERN C: Cut 4 matching A
Cut one 16″ × 16″ background square (add seam allowance)

Assembly

Fold the background square on the diagonal twice.

1. With right sides together, place the narrow end of each leaf B against each of the narrow ends of the A piece. Pin in place and then stitch from raw edge to raw edge on the marked seamline. Press the seam open. Turn the seam allowance on the entire piece, slashing into the deep scallop shape of the leaves. If the scallop shape of the leaves seem hard to make with definition, run a small row of tiny basting stitches in the seam allowance at the highest point of the curve. Pull the stitches together slightly and it will cup the end of each scalloped edge. Then baste to the wrong side. After completing the basting, set this portion aside. Do not press.

2. Turn the seam allowance on all the C pieces.

3. Center the large piece made in Step 1 to the background square, using the diagonal folds and Fig. 4-14 as a

146

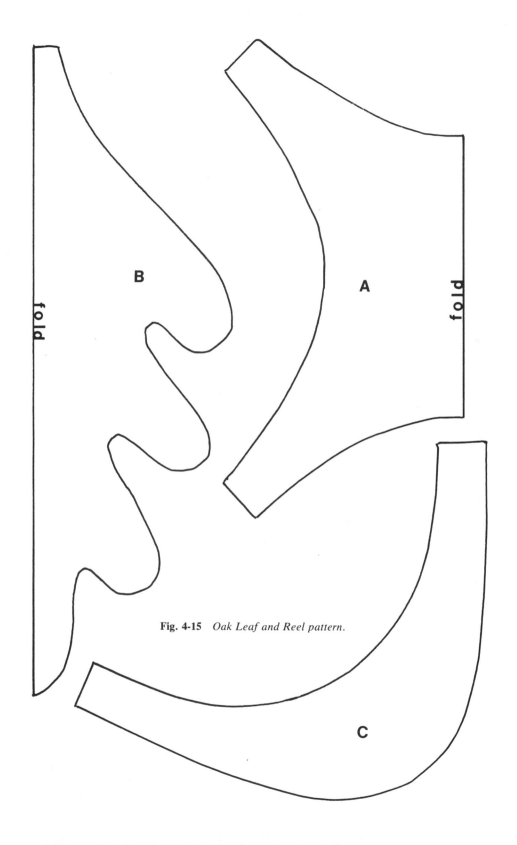

Fig. 4-15 *Oak Leaf and Reel pattern.*

fold

fold

B

A

C

guide. Pin in place and arrange the C pieces in their corresponding positions, tucking the pointed ends under the seam of the A/B piece. Baste all the appliques to the background; stitch permanently; remove the basting and press.

Quilting Suggestions

Outline the entire pattern $\frac{1}{4}$ inch off the edges, both on the outside and the inside of the reel. Add a second row of stitches $\frac{3}{4}$ inch off the first one around the outline.

The most popular rendition of this pattern in a full quilt is to place one block next to another without any bands. This sets up a very interesting looking quilt. Many times the leaves almost touch each other with just a little space between for quilting.

Single Motifs

The single motif is generally pictorial in nature and needs very little explanation as they fill the need to portray every day life. Butterflies have always been popular with quilters as they offer an opportunity to utilize lovely pastel scraps. They may be silhouettes of the entire figure, or they may use several colors. Animal motifs are seen most often in the quilts of the 1800s; the cat is by far the favorite.

BUTTERFLY

This design offers the challenge of overlaying one color on another color. Only half of the pattern appears here (Fig. 4-17). Cut the four pieces for the wings separately. Many quilters will not choose to overlay the wings and will use the entire

Fig. 4-16 *Butterfly.*

pattern as a silhouette. The instructions are given so that the overlay is used. When making the pattern, make a complete right and left side, using two A's and two B's (Fig. 4-16). The pattern will be split in the middle. This will be covered by the body of the buttefly. The entire butterfly may have a layer of additional batting placed behind to give a raised feeling.

Materials and Cutting

PATTERN A: Cut 2 strong color for the main part of wings
PATTERN B: Cut 2 contrast color to A
PATTERN C: Cut 1 for the body, another contrast
Cut one 16″ × 16″ background square (add seam allowance)

Assembly

1. Cut out the A and B portions and turn the seam allowances to the wrong side (Fig. 4-17). Arrange on the

148

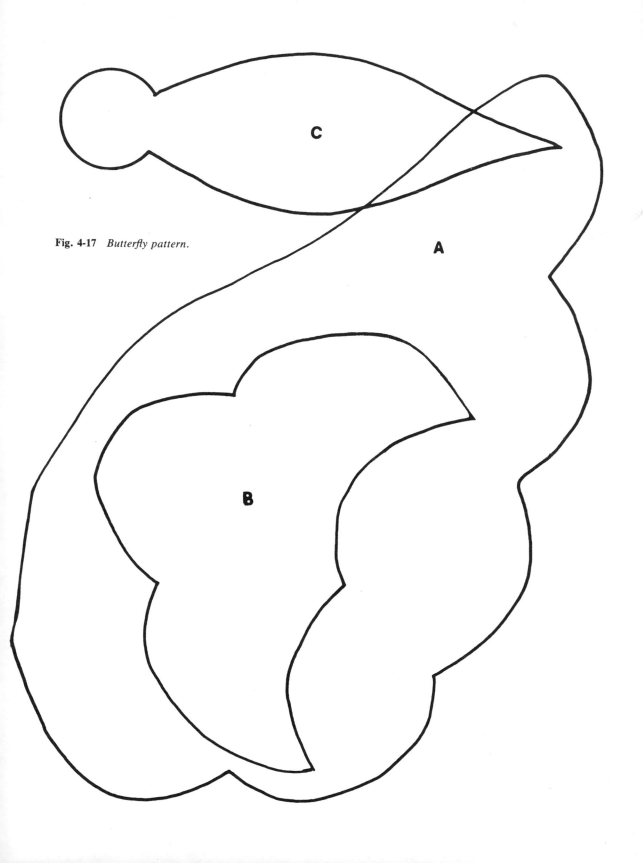

Fig. 4-17 *Butterfly pattern.*

background fabric, using Fig. 4-16 as a guide. It should be placed on a slight angle as it would look too static if placed upright. Baste in place.

2. Turn the seam allowance to the wrong side on the C piece and center over the middle of the butterfly. Baste in place; stitch permanently; remove all basting and press.

Quilting Suggestions

Fill the background portions with flower motifs or additional butterfly stitchery. On the actual butterfly, trace in some interesting teardrop-shaped lines with the quilt stitches on the wings.

To use this in a full quilt, place each butterfly going in the same direction and use the bordering bands between; or place four blocks together so that the butterflies face toward the center and repeat this group of four blocks without any bands in-between.

THE CAT

Over the years, cats have established a nostalgic place in American art. They appear on hooked rugs, old quilts, pottery, in tole art and in both fine and folk art painting. The napping cat offers a simple and harmonious shape that is easy to copy. The closed eyes are a big plus since two accurate eyes need not be attempted. The cat napping on the hearth rug anchors this cat in the sampler quilt block. It will need a little embroidery stitchery to make the face come to life. Select an opaque small print or solid color. The head of the cat may be padded with additional batting or it may be lined with additional fabric.

Fig. 4-18 *The Cat made by Gerri Schirmacher.*

Materials and Cutting

PATTERN A: Cut 1 (body) print or solid
PATTERN B: Cut 1 (head) to match A
PATTERN C: Cut 2 contrast to A and B, for ear shadow
PATTERN D: Cut 1 contrast to A, B and C to mark nose
PATTERN E: Optional, cut 1 rug, contrast to all above
Cut one 16″ × 16″ background square (add seam allowance)
One skein of embroidery floss

Assembly

1. Trace B (head portions) onto the selected fabric but do not cut. Trace on the features and embroider over tracing with a backstitch and three strands of floss. (A hoop is suggested for all embroidery.) Turn the edges on the C and D pieces and applique in place. Now cut out B and turn the seam allowance to the wrong side.

2. Outline the A piece on the

150

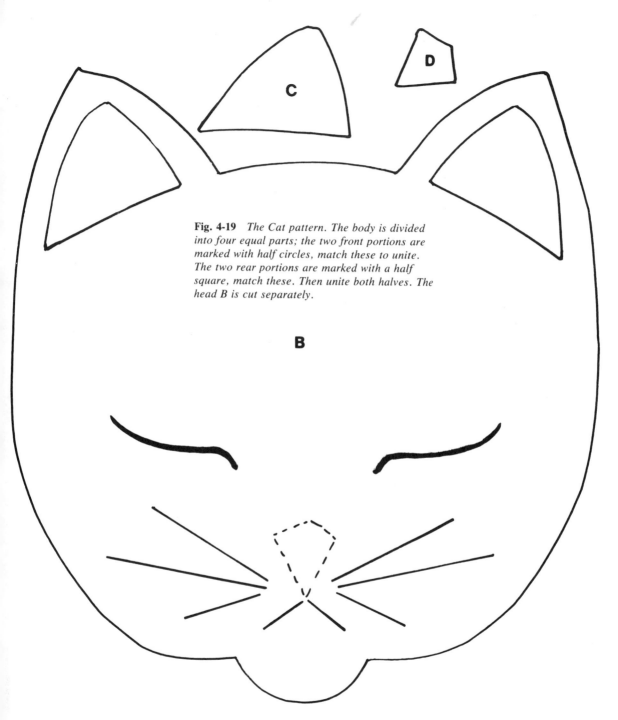

Fig. 4-19 *The Cat pattern. The body is divided into four equal parts; the two front portions are marked with half circles, match these to unite. The two rear portions are marked with a half square, match these. Then unite both halves. The head B is cut separately.*

C

D

B

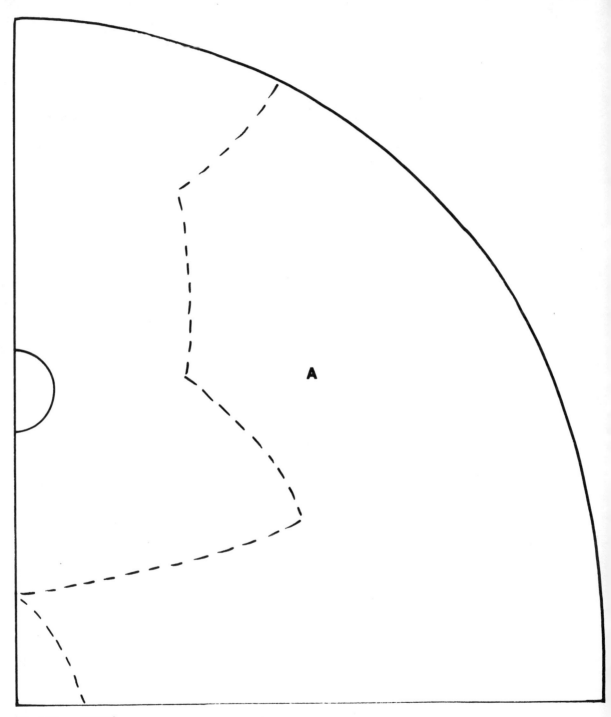

Fig. 4-19 *continued.*

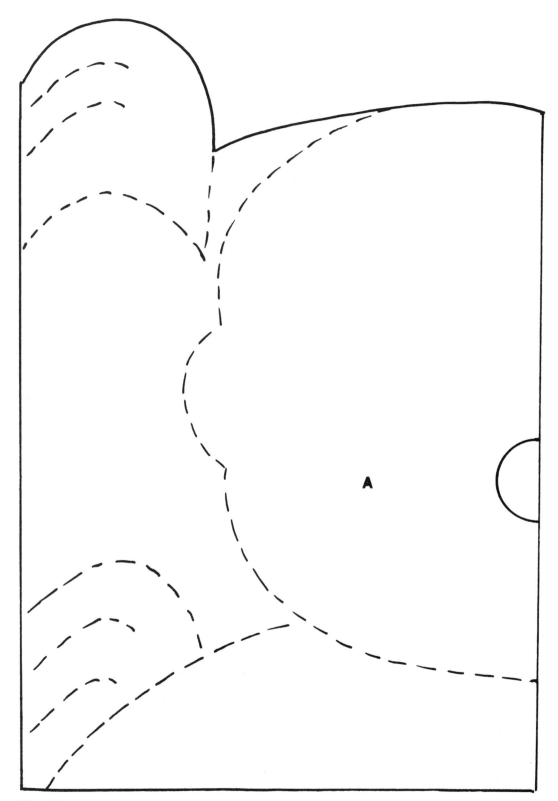

Fig. 4-19 *continued.*

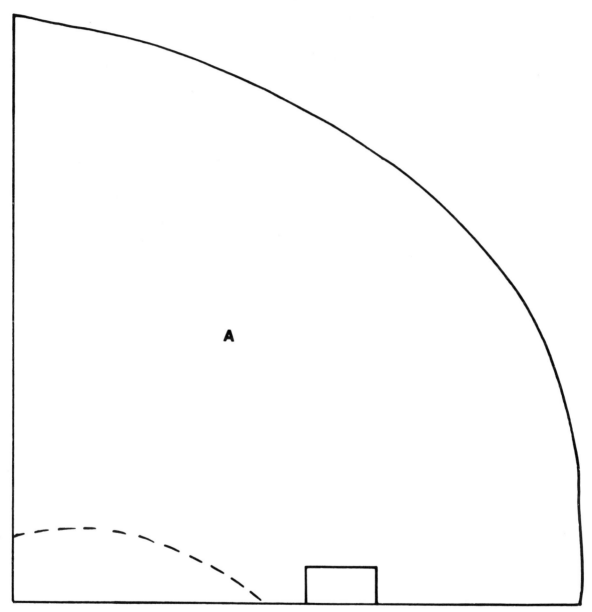

Fig. 4-19 *continued.*

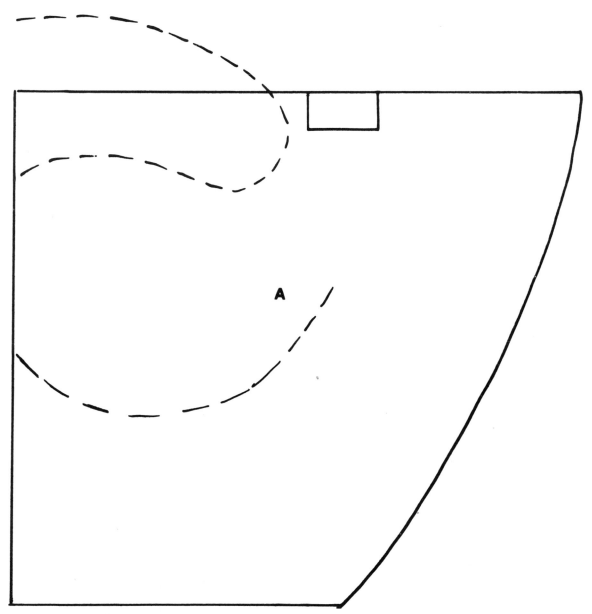

Fig. 4-19 *continued*.

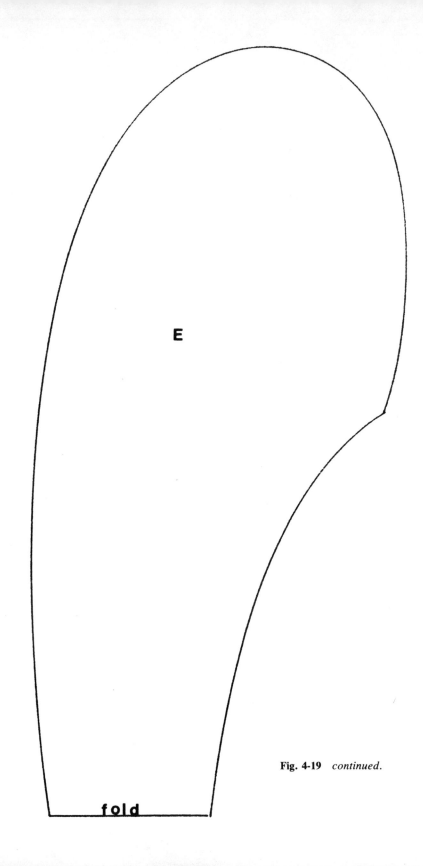

E

fold

Fig. 4-19 *continued.*

selected fabric and trace in the tail and paw definition. Embroider the tracings and then cut and turn the seam allowance to the wrong side. Cut out E and turn only convex portions of the seam allowances as the concave will be under the cat.

3. Using Fig. 4-18 as a guide, center the body of the cat on the rug E and the head B, overlapping the left side of the body A. Pin all pieces in place first; then baste down and stitch permanently. When stitching the head of the cat, be sure to stitch through all layers to the background fabric to give the head definition. Remove the basting stitches and press.

Quilting Suggestions

Quilt some curved lines on the back of the cat and on the rug to give it the look of ridges. If you are very ambitious, quilt the rug to look like a braided rug. Quilt around the entire outline of the cat $\frac{1}{4}$ inch from the edge.

This is rarely used as an all-over pattern for a quilt except by great cat lovers. But it makes an excellent piece for a sampler quilt, a baby quilt, a wallhanging or a pillow.

Wreaths

The single pattern motif that has endless variations is the wreath. While they are found in all sizes, they are generally made large to accommodate four flowers and many leaves. The circle itself evokes thoughts of the continuation of life and the flowers symbolize the regeneration of life.

One of the reasons so many old wreath quilts do exist today is because the are made of opaque fabric and they do require a great deal of work, thus taking on the status of a "best" quilt. These were always treated with care.

The materials may vary but the technique for assembling the wreaths is the same.

Basic Wreath Assembly

1. Study the accompanying figures with the pattern and study the color photo section. Fold the background square as necessary to help center and line up the assorted pieces.

2. Study the photos to see where the pieces overlap. Turn all the necessary seam allowances to the wrong side.

3. Using the folds as a guide, pin and then baste the pieces in place. Remember to keep the outer edges of the appliques at least $\frac{3}{4}$ to 1 inch away from the sewing line edge of the background square. While the background is cut $16\frac{1}{2}'' \times 16\frac{1}{2}''$, remember its marked sewing line is $16'' \times 16''$. This will allow ample space for quilt stitching. Baste all the pieces down and stitch permanently; remove the basting and press. Make sure that when tucking the leaves and the connecting rings behind the flowers there is no more than $\frac{1}{4}$ inch underneath. Trim out any excess.

ROSE WREATH

This wreath features four large, scallop-edged roses with small leaves peeking out behind (Fig. 4-21).

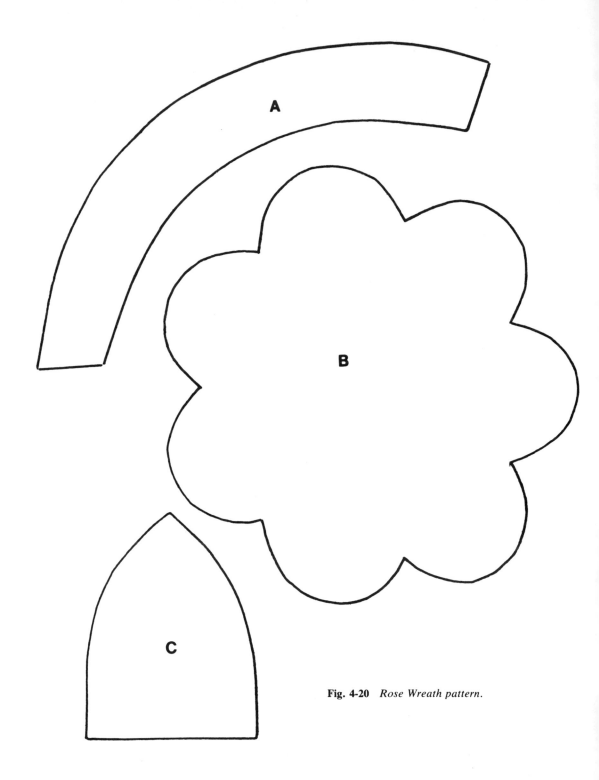

Fig. 4-20 *Rose Wreath pattern.*

Fig. 4-21 *Rose Wreath.*

Fig. 4-22 *Bridal Wreath made by Ginny Ruckert.*

Materials and Cutting
PATTERN A: Cut 4 dark strong colors
PATTERN B: Cut 4 small print or solid
PATTERN C: Cut 12 small print or solid
    Cut one 16″ × 16″ background square
    (add seam allowance)

Turn the seam allowance on the long curved edges of the A pieces; do not turn the short ends. Turn the curved edges of the C pieces, not the flat edge, as it will be tucked under the flowers. Use Fig. 3-2 as a guide for slashing into scalloped edges of flower B. Use Fig. 4-21 as a guide to arrange the pieces.

BRIDAL WREATH

This wreath dramatizes the use of diminutive pieces for the applique (Fig. 4-22). It is the most delicate of all the wreaths. The flowers are small but must have strong, well-defined scalloped edges; the connecting vine must be a strong color but a thin and light shape. Above all the leaves must be evenly made and evenly placed so that there is plenty of background showing between leaves.

Materials and Cutting
PATTERN A: Cut 4 medium to strong solid
    color
PATTERN B: Cut 4 contrast to A and C in
    solid or very small print
PATTERN C: Cut 20 solid color to match A
    Cut one 16″ × 16″ background square
    (add seam allowance)

Turn the seam allowance on the curved edges of the A, getting it as thin as possible and clipping where necessary into seam allowance. Turn the leaves, C, keeping the edges nice and round and the points sharp. The flowers should have as strong a scalloped edge as possible. Fold the background square twice on the diagonal. Use Fig. 4-22 as a guide to arrange the pieces,

Fig. 4-23 *Bridal Wreath pattern.*

160

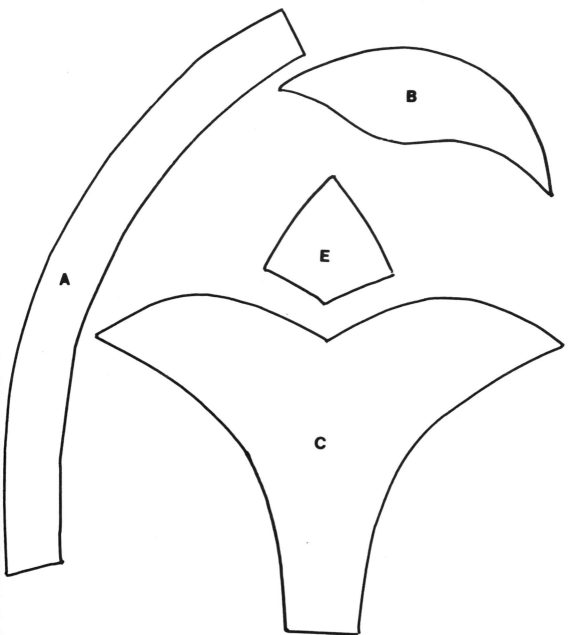

Fig. 4-24 *President's Wreath pattern. For pattern piece D, use Fig. 4-23 piece B.*

Fig. 4-25 *President's Wreath. Made by Ginny Ruckert.*

Fig. 4-26 *Laurel Leaf Wreath. Made by Ann Chas.*

but do not crowd the pieces. The flowers are placed about 4 inches from the center, measuring along the diagonal fold line of background fabric.

PRESIDENT'S WREATH

This legendary wreath dedicated to a past president is unique because it has a horizontal and vertical movement as well as a diagonal movement. It is shown in the color section in the Friendship Sampler quilt with sedate colors. It would look just as good in bright calicoes. There are so many pieces to this design that it is a treasury of shapes to experiment with.

Materials and Cutting
PATTERN A: Cut 4 strong color
PATTERN B: Cut 8 leaves, same as A
PATTERN C: Cut 4 same as A and B
PATTERN D: Cut 4 flowers of strong color or small print, using pattern B, Fig. 4-23
PATTERN E: Cut 8 same as D
Cut one 16″ × 16″ background square (add seam allowance)

Turn all the seam allowances on the applique pieces except the flat ends of A, C and E. The object is to get as much curve to the small pieces as possible. Fold the background square twice on the diagonal and twice through the center so that four folds appear when finished. Use Fig. 4-25 as a guide to arrange the pieces. Leave sufficient space around the pieces to give an airy feeling to the block. In some places around the perimeter, there will be less than one inch space to the edge.

LAUREL LEAF WREATH

This is traditionally the winner's crown and so it will be for any quiltmaker. It is generally made in greens but any of the fall color calicoes will do as well to give a cheerful effect. This wreath has been included for the special way that the full circle is achieved.

By looking at Fig. 4-26, you may think that a full circle was cut out of a single fabric about $\frac{1}{4}$ inch wide. This is one way that the circle could be made; however, due to the need to conserve fabric in quiltmaking years ago, our forebears found a better way.

First lightly pencil in the circle wanted and measure the circumference. In this case, the circle is 10 inches across. Make a strip of bias material (like bias binding) 36 inches long and $\frac{3}{4}$ inches wide. Turn the $\frac{1}{4}$ inch seam allowance one entire length to the wrong side and press. Mark the seam allowance on the other raw side.

With right sides together, place the raw edge bias against the background and baste the two penciled lines together. Keep the pressed edge toward the inside of the circle (Fig. 4-27). Overlap the narrow ends, crossing one over the other with a bias fold on the raw end. Stitch down permanently.

Lift the bias then press to the outer perimeter of the background so the right side shows. Stretch the outer edge with the iron and baste in place. Stitch down permanently. Very little material has been used and a beautiful ring has been stitched.

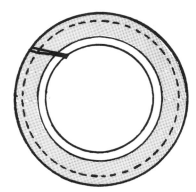

Fig. 4-27 *Bias circle. Stitch down the inner portion of the bias edge. Overlapping bias folded edge of narrow end. Then turn to outside, away from center and stitch.*

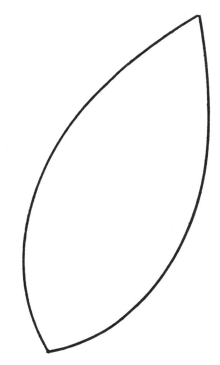

Fig. 4-28 *Laurel Leaf Wreath pattern.*

Materials and Cutting

PATTERN A: Cut 12 leaves in calico or solid fabric

> Cut one length of bias cut fabric $\frac{3}{4}'' \times$ 36", matching or contrast to A
> Cut one 16" × 16" background square (add seam allowance)

Make the 10-inch circle as suggested above. Turn the seam allowance on the leaves. Fold background square twice through center. Use Fig. 4-26 as a guide for arrangement of the leaves. Sometimes small hearts are also added to the center of the circle, or four green heart shapes are added plus an embroidered stem to create a four-leaf clover for good luck.

Quilting Suggestions

Quilt $\frac{1}{4}$ inch off both the inside and outside edge of the appliques. Then use the center for some novelty quilting.

To use the wreath patterns in an all-over quilt, place them one after the other, without intersecting bands. This gives a very expansive feeling to the circles.

Upright Patterns

There are a few patterns that are decidedly upright. They fill a need in a quilt. They are generally placed in the middle of a sampler quilt to fall on the main portion of the bed with the other patterns circling around them. This gives a focal point to the center of the overall design. (See the photo of the Album Sampler Quilt.) They also may be used on the portion that covers the pillows. Note the Liberty Bell and the silhouette of New Jersey over the silhouette U.S.A. Once an upright pattern is planned into a quilt, it can never be used upside down like a patchwork design or many appliques.

These upright patterns are used most effectively in a full quilt top with borders around them. They need to be separated from the next one and stand as pictures by themselves. Other than the Pomegranate which we know as a red fruit, the others may use a wide variety of assorted colors

in each block. If working with scraps, always keep one element in the design the same or very similar pattern or color to create a unifying effect, such as the hats on the Jack and Jill.

JACK AND JILL

This is the most well-known and popular of all the upright designs. It is most often used in children's quilts with either one or both figures in a single block. It is filled with innocent charm and memories of lovely picture books. In the classes I teach, there is rarely a student who does not enjoy the challenge of recreating these storybook figures. Study Fig. 4-29 and Fig. 4-30 and quilts in the color photo section.

Materials and Cutting
FOR JILL: Cut one each A to E
FOR JACK: Cut one each G to K
PATTERN F: Cut as directed, using a piece of fabric 4″ × 3″

Assembly

The most important point to remember in dealing with figures such as these is the center of gravity. The figure must stand upright and the head must be directly over the feet. The rest of the figure can be stylized. Each of the pattern pieces in Fig. 4-31 and 4-32 has a broken line down the center indicating the center of gravity. After the pieces have had seam allowances turned back, place them back on the paper patterns. On the wrong side, indicate where this center of gravity should be. When lining up the pieces on the background, match the centers of gravity so that the figure will look balanced. The dress and sleeve are generally made of calico and the apron can be a solid color, another print, a sheer or

Fig. 4-29   *Jack and Jill made by Jane Emmer.*

an eyelet. The back of the apron can have a little tie or ribbon as there is a pinch in the back of the dress to accommodate this. The apron may be trimmed with $\frac{1}{4}$ inch sheer lace. Turn the seam allowances on the two sides and bottom of the apron. Baste the lace behind the side (or apron back) and bottom seam allowances, placing a few gathers at the corner. Do not place lace up the front of the apron. At the top, the apron will not be turned back because it will be placed under the hat. Turn seam allowances on all the applique pieces to the wrong side except for the hand. Pin on the background material, lining up the center of gravity marks. Pin the dress first, then apron with feet tucked under the dress and hat over the top of the dress and apron. A ribbon or trim may be added on the hat. Pin in place first, then baste.

The hand is far too small to turn as a single unit. Fold in half a 4-inch wide piece of pinkish fabric to be used for the hand.

Trace the sewing line of the hand on it, keeping the wrist portion at the double raw edge and the fingers facing the fold. Stitch on the machine, using 12 to 15 stitches to the inch, exactly on the marked line. Slash between the thumb and index finger (Fig. 4-36). Turn the seam to the inside. It will look like a mitten on the right side. The lightweight fabric will be lined and at the same time all the seam allowances will be quickly and easily turned. Tuck the hand under the sleeve and treat as one piece. Baste all the pieces down and stitch permanently; remove the basting stitches and press. Additional embroidery may be added at this time—a few flowers in the hand or a flower on the hat. The lazy daisy stitch is suggested for the flowers.

The boy needs the same careful layering as the girl; but his shirt (Fig. 4-35, pattern H) will be placed on the background first. Only its front and back seam allowances must be turned. Turn the seam allowances on the rest of the pieces except the top of the overalls and shoes. Next pin

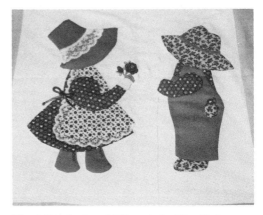

Fig. 4-30   *Jack and Jill made by Kim Aiello.*

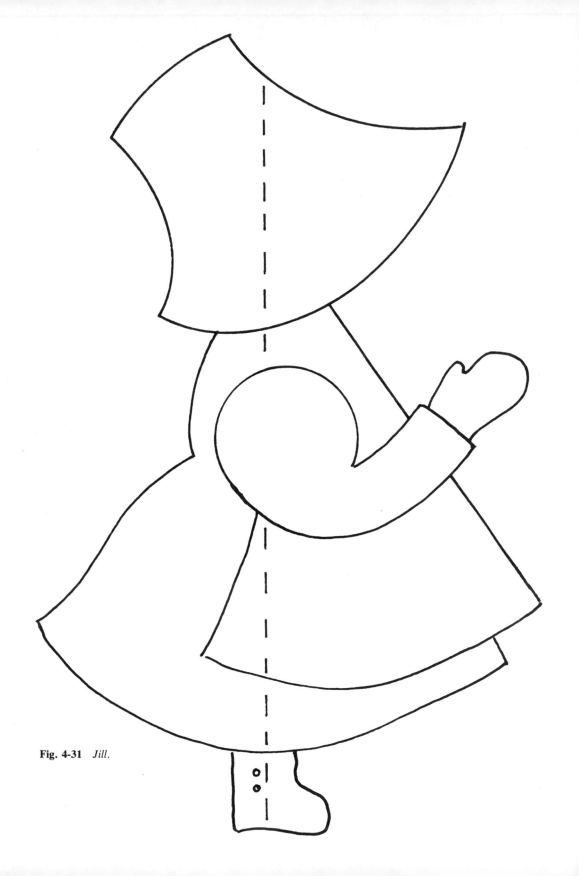

Fig. 4-31 *Jill.*

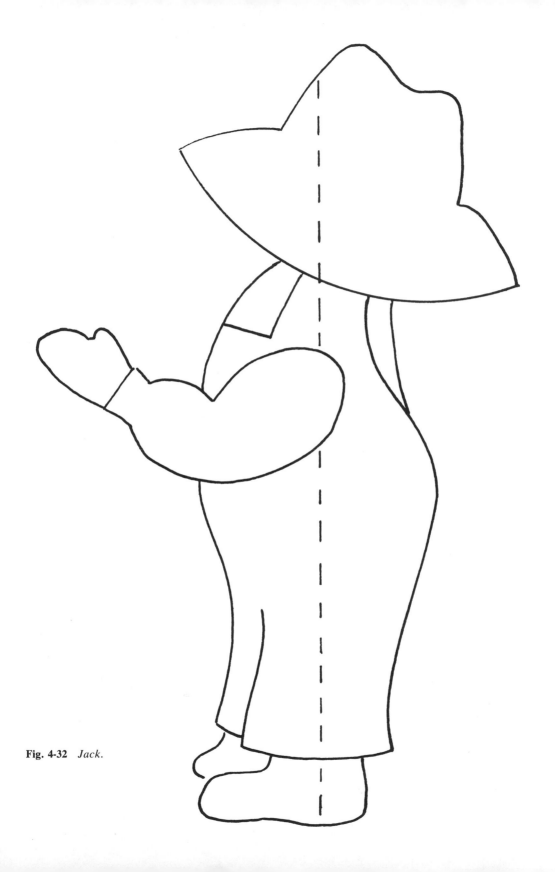

Fig. 4-32 *Jack.*

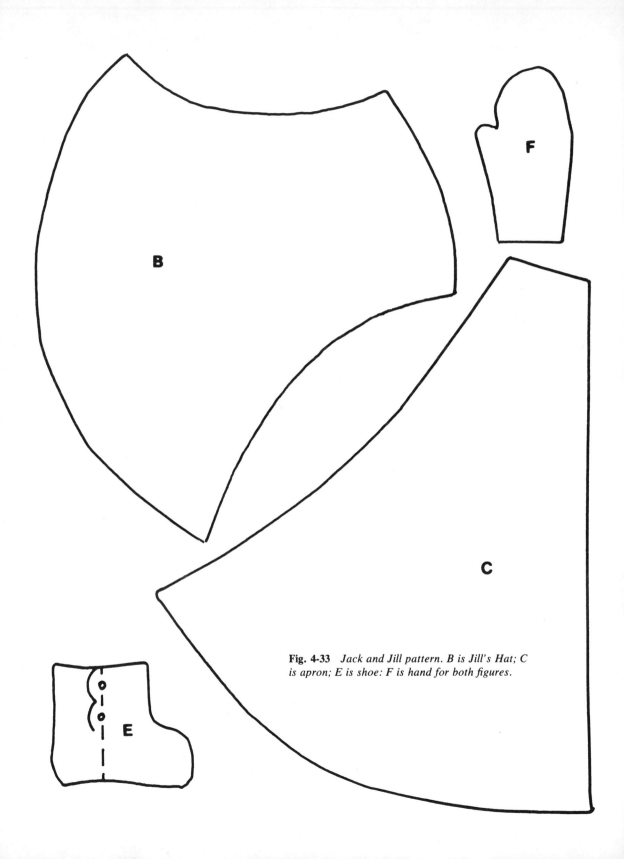

Fig. 4-33 *Jack and Jill pattern. B is Jill's Hat; C is apron; E is shoe: F is hand for both figures.*

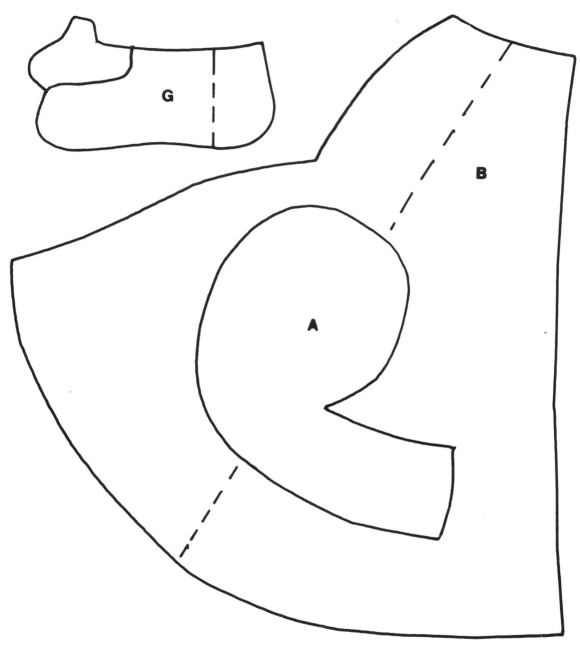

Fig. 4-34 *Jack and Jill pattern. A is Jill's sleeve; B is dress; G is Jack's shoes.*

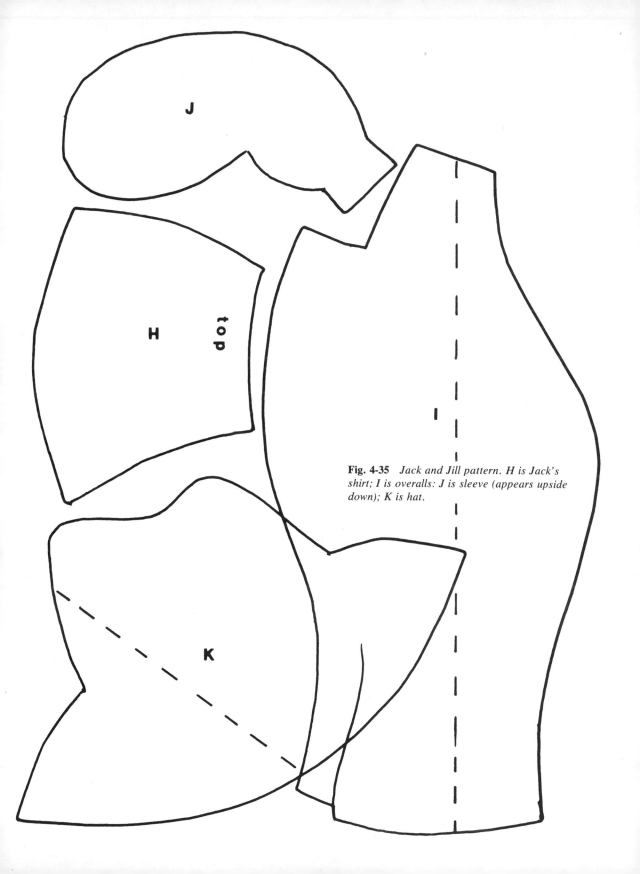

J

H

t o p

I

K

Fig. 4-35 *Jack and Jill pattern. H is Jack's shirt; I is overalls: J is sleeve (appears upside down); K is hat.*

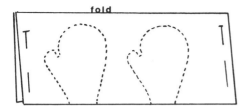

Fig. 4-36 *Turning of the hand.*

the overall over the shirt, tuck the top of the shoes under the overall, position the sleeve over the overall and then tuck the hand (made as suggested above) under the sleeve end. Finish off with the hat over the top of the shirt and overalls. Remember to line up all center of gravity markings. A small pocket may be added to the back of the overalls and a colorful hankerchief may be added. He may have any kind of farm implement embroidered in his hand but the favorite is the fishing pole. To indicate two pants legs, use embroidery or quilting stitches.

TRIPLE TULIP

This is a very typical rendition of an upright tulip combined with hearts, buds and leaves. The tulip shape itself is uniquely Pennsylvania Dutch, with its center pieces flanked by two additional side pieces. A variety of prints and solids can be used. It is particularly good to use this in the middle of a nine-patch design. The side tulips may face up or down.

Materials and Cutting
PATTERN A: Cut 1 small print or solid
PATTERN AA: Cut 1 contrast to A
PATTERN B: Cut 1 solid to harmonize with A

PATTERN BB: Cut 2 same as AA
PATTERN C: Cut 1 dark strong solid
PATTERN D: Cut 1 contrast to C
PATTERN E: Cut 1 dark stem
PATTERN F: Cut 2 same as E
PATTERN G: Cut 2 same as E or harmonizing shade to E and F
Cut one 16″ × 16″ background square (add seam allowance)

Assembly
Turn all the seam allowances where necessary. Remember the inside curve of A will be tucked under the AA. Fold the background square in half once and use this as the guide. Pin on the pieces using Fig. 4-37 and the color photo in the Album quilt as a guide. Make sure that the measurement below the heart and above the large tulip is the same. Baste in place, stitch permanently, remove the basting and press.

Fig. 4-37 *Triple Tulip. Made by Ann Smith.*

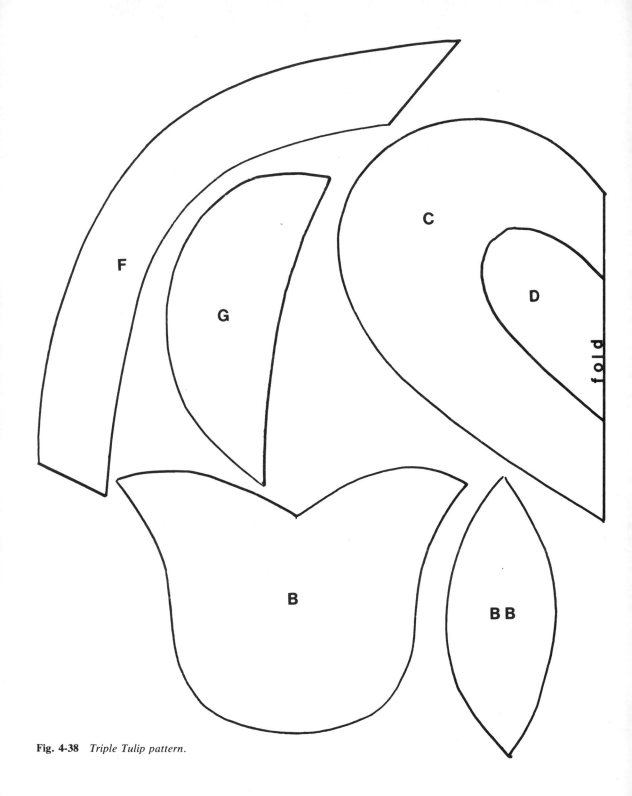

Fig. 4-38 *Triple Tulip pattern.*

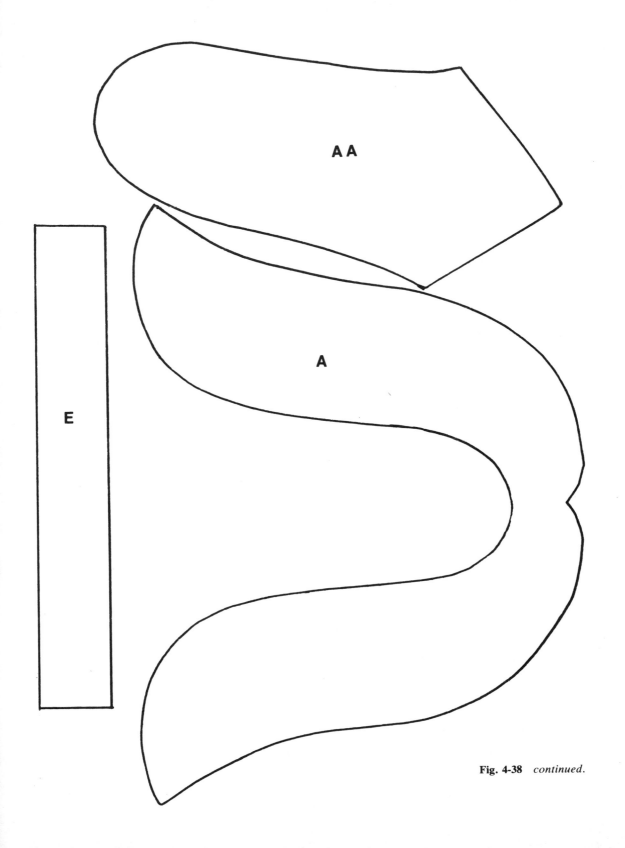

AA

A

E

Fig. 4-38 *continued*.

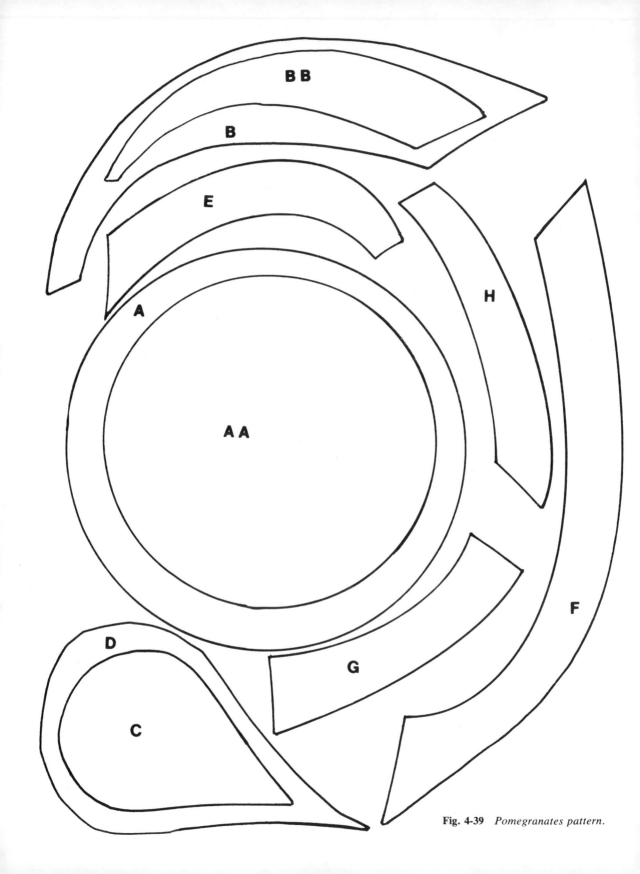

Fig. 4-39 *Pomegranates pattern.*

Fig. 4-40 *Pomegranates.*

POMEGRANATES

This small branch of the Pomegranate tree with its four fruits offers a lovely upright design, but one that is not static (Fig. 4-40). There are two sized fruits on this branch and they are made of a solid and print combined. The shape of the branches and the heart-shaped leaves gives a very free-form look.

Materials and Cutting

PATTERNS A and AA: Cut 2 each solid color
PATTERNS B and BB: Cut 4 each matching print of a lighter shade
PATTERN C: Cut 4 strong leaf color
PATTERN D: Cut 2 strong leaf color
PATTERNS E and F: Cut 2 each as above
PATTERNS G and H: Cut 1 each as above
    Cut one 16″ × 16″ background square (add seam allowance)

Assembly

Turn the seam allowances to the wrong side on the flower and leaf pieces (A to D). Turn only the long curved edges on the stems (E to H). Using Fig. 4-40 and the color photo of the Album quilt, place the stems, leaves, A and AA portions of the flowers on the background. Pin in place and baste. Arrange the B and BB print portions over the large solid A and AA pieces. Baste the B's and BB's and stitch permanently. Remove the basting and press.

BIRD IN THE BUSH

This is a very old Pennsylvania Dutch pattern that comes in all forms and shapes; only the concept of a bird surrounded by foliage remains the same. This type of pattern can use a variety of materials, such as many colors for the leaves and flowers.

Fig. 4-41 *Bird in the Bush.*

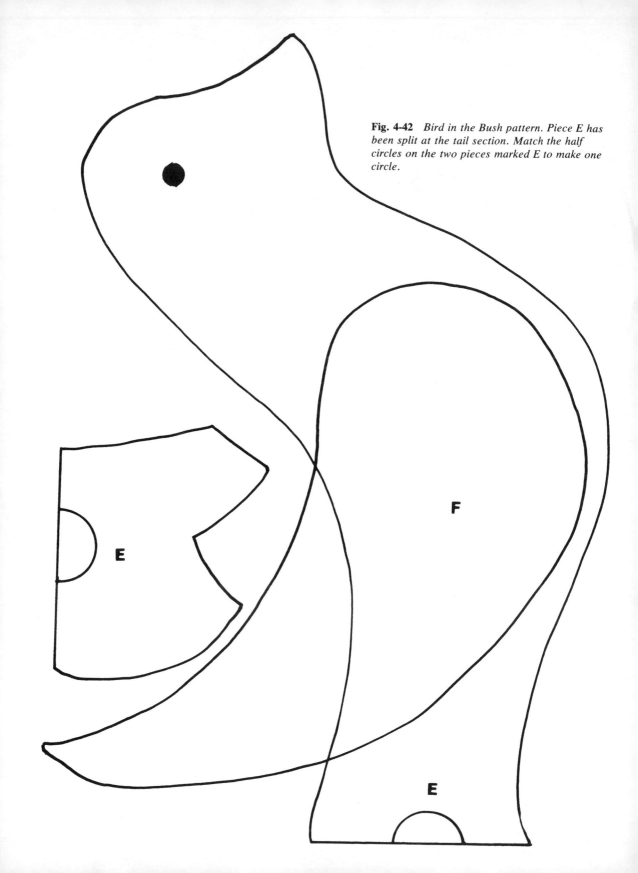

Fig. 4-42 *Bird in the Bush pattern. Piece E has been split at the tail section. Match the half circles on the two pieces marked E to make one circle.*

E

F

E

Fig. 4-42 *continued.*

Materials and Cutting

PATTERNS A, B, C: Cut 1 each of a leaf-like color

PATTERN D: Cut 8 in floral color

PATTERN E: Cut 1 in strong color for the body of the bird

PATTERN F: Cut 1 contrast to above for the wing

Cut one 16" × 16" background square (add seam alowance)

Assembly

Turn all the seam allowances to the wrong side on all the pieces. Center and pin to the background, using Fig. 4-41 and the color photo in the Album quilt as a guide. Overlap the centers of the flower petals. Baste in place, stitch permanently, remove the basting and press.

Upright patterns are used on the top of a full quilt. Because they are a bit static, they are generally reproduced in a variety of colors. This offers a good opportunity to clean out the scrap bag. This works very well for the Bird in the Bush. The shape remains the same, but the colors vary to add the variety. Border bands are always used.

Quilting Suggestions

Outline the perimeter of each large applique and choose some portions of the main part of the applique to quilt, such as the bird, the tulip or the inside portions on the Pomegranates. The leaves would benefit from some outline stitching.

The Central Floral

These are the most stunning of all the antique quilts we have today. The most effectual designs have great curved stems and vines that emerge from behind an elaborate center of a many-layered flower. The simplest ones have rather straight-lined stems extending from behind the central floral. The variations are limitless. They were made in rather large sizes and stitched one after the other into a quilt with no bordering bands. This gives an all-over effect of flowers intermingling.

WHIG ROSE

This is a pattern with legend. The Whig Rose was named for the political party of the mid 1800s. This is the prize of all the central floral patterns. It is very interesting with its scalloped edge center which is enhanced by four pointed motifs called combs. They generally appear in green. The most important portions of the design are the V-shaped stems that jut out from between the combs. As the V-stem splits, each branch forms another circle with a floral end. The curved stems seem to interact with the stems from the surrounding blocks. They entwine in full quilts and form large round circles that appear to intersect the center floral combination. This is not a beginner pattern but is well worth the effort.

Fig. 4-43 *Whig Rose.*

178

Fig. 4-44 *Whig Rose pattern. Cut A as a solid piece, but cut B with the center circle cut out.*

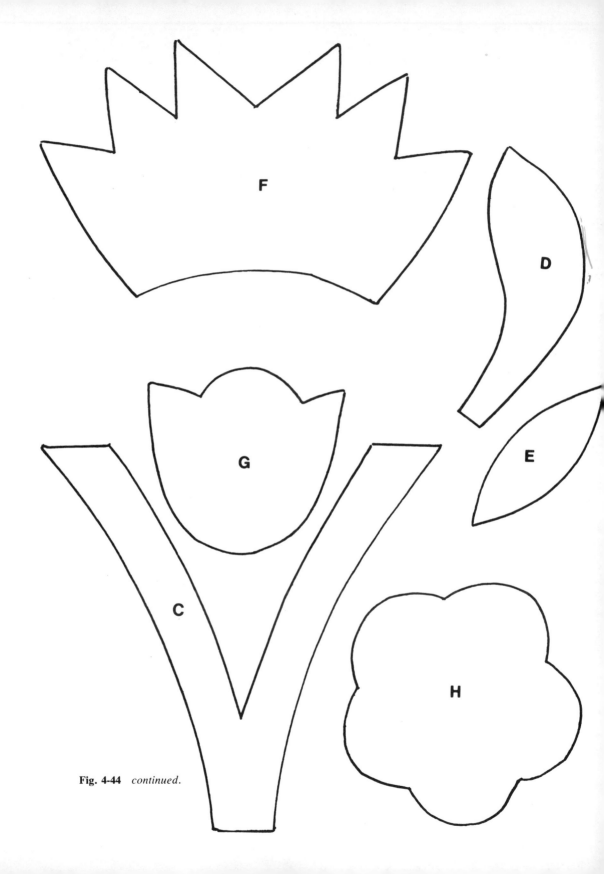

Fig. 4-44 *continued.*

Materials and Cutting

PATTERN A: Cut 1 strong dark color

PATTERN B: Cut 1 print or solid contrast to A

PATTERN C: Cut 4 in leafy color

PATTERN D: Cut 4 dark strong solid color

PATTERN E: Cut 12 same as D

PATTERN F: Cut 4 same as D

PATTERN G: Cut 4 solid or print suggested to match A

PATTERN H: Cut 4 solid or print suggested to match A

Cut one 16″ × 16″ background square (add seam allowance)

Fold background square twice on the diagonal.

If this pattern is used in a full-quilt face, it can be used this size or may be graded larger by adding $\frac{1}{4}$ inch to all the seam allowances. The floral design looks best if it is on the top portion of the bed and the outer border has a horizontal applique of a vine-like design circling round it.

Assembly

Turn all seam allowances. Use Fig. 4-43 as a guide for placement of pieces. All the leaves are not the same; four of them seem to have a sharp curved shape (piece D). This one is placed on the left-hand branch, going in a circular motion around the central floral. Arrange the first V-shaped stem and its companion leaves and flowers and use it as a model for the other three. Use all opaque fabric.

Quilting Suggestions

A floral of this nature should be outlined first and maybe the comb and some of the leaves accented with additional

quilting. The remaining background should be filled in with background quilting; and if one wishes to get very ornate, combine background quilting and additional quilt motifs.

Effective Use of Diagonal Designs

No text would be complete without patterns that are made to fit the background square on the diagonal. In the sampler quilt, they can be used on the diagonal very adequately. They can be placed in the bottom

Fig. 4-45 *Placing a pattern on the diamond so it appears upright to the bottom of the quilt. The sides are filled with the same background fabric or a contrast. An additional border may be added in contrast or the background color.*

Fig. 4-46 *North Carolina Lily. Made by Sally Rowe.*

corners as in the Friendship Sampler (see color photo). In full quilts, they are used on what quilters term the diamond. That means the patterns are presented to the viewer upright. Instead of assembling a series of squares, the quilter assembles a series of even-sided diamond blocks. This leaves the sides of the quilt with a saw-tooth looking edge. This is then filled in with half a diamond to even out the sides (see Fig. 4-45).

THE NORTH CAROLINA LILY

This pattern is arranged and sewn on the background square on the diagonal and it uses several lessons worked on earlier (Fig. 4-46). It is not a beginner's pattern but it is worth the effort to make correctly. The floral portion is half of an eight-point star and to that a triangle B (Fig. 4-47) is added. Join the triangle and the half star just like a piece of patchwork. Press the seam to the dark. The stems (C and D) are made

of two pieces of narrow bias fabric (Fig. 4-48). The bias fabric of the D piece curves to accommodate the two sides of flowers. It stretches on the outer curves and contracts on the inner portions of the curves. The edges are basted to the wrong side and then it is basted to the background (Fig. 4-48). Do the stem first. Overlap the flowers on the ends after they have had their seam allowances turned to the wrong side. The base of the three flower stems can be made in any design that pleases you. Some quilters use leaves, some use just a triangle, others use a shape that appears to be a pot holding the flowers (Fig. 4-47e) and the Friendship Sampler quilt in the color section.

Materials and Cutting
PATTERN A: Cut 12 solid or print
PATTERN B: Cut 3 green
PATTERN C: Cut 1 green bias strip, 8"
PATTERN D: Cut 1 green bias strip, 14" long
PATTERN E: Optional base
    Cut one background square 16" × 16" (add seam allowance)

Assembly
1. Stitch together four star points (A) and add one B across the bottom of the combined points. Repeat for the other two flowers. Baste the seam allowance to the wrong side on each flower.

2. Turn the seam allowances to the wrong side on stem pieces C and D. Fold the background once on the diagonal. Pin C over the fold beginning 6 inches from the bottom. Using Fig. 4-48 as a guide, arrange piece D behind the C piece, intersecting it approximately 2 inches from the bottom. If this seems

182

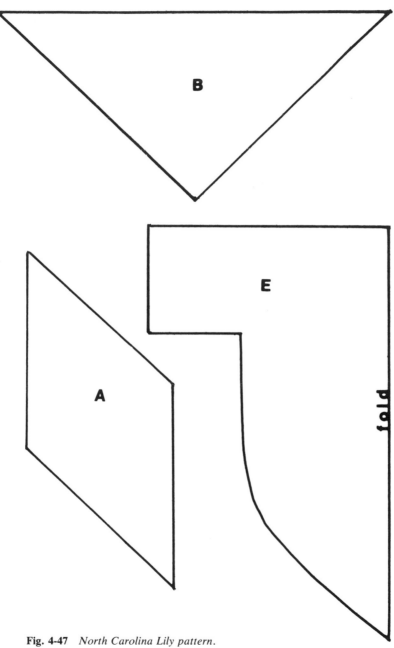

Fig. 4-47 *North Carolina Lily pattern.*

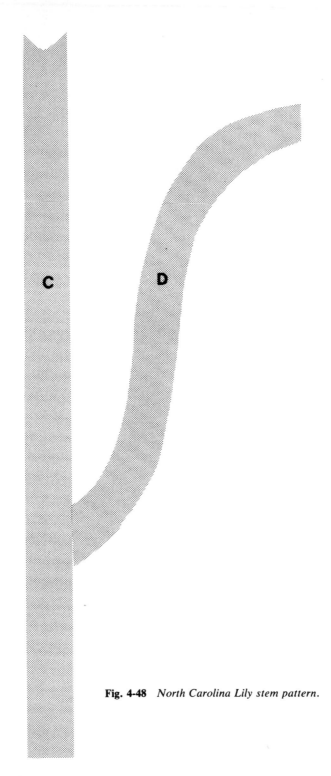

Fig. 4-48 *North Carolina Lily stem pattern.*

bulky when it passes under the stem (C), then notch out bulk and pin in place. Cover the tops of the C and D pieces with the flowers. Baste in place.

3. Turn the seam allowance on the E piece and place so it covers the base of the center stem (C).

4. Stitch down permanently, remove basting and press.

Pictorial Applique Designs

In each quilter's heart, there is a desire to commemorate ourselves in a multi-design quilt. If a quilt is composed of designs that all represent special occasions or are of a pictorial nature, then it's called an *album* quilt. If you look carefully at the Album quilt in the color photo section, you will note that many of the designs which are traditional have initials near them. These are pattern blocks that I designed. Each has special significance to me. As a special remembrance, the makers signed the blocks. As you may have guessed, the seated woman with the quilt frame is me and the man on the horse is my husband. These block designs are offered to help you get started in pictorial design. Study the Pascack Valley Historical Society and the Putnam County Quilt.

Most novice quilters cry they are not artists and cannot draw. Well, remember the type of work that will appear in a picture quilt block is folk art in nature. Fabric does not lend itself to the fine detail of paint but embroidery floss will help compensate for the fine lines needed such as the features on the faces.

For the person who can draw a fairly good representation, this medium in quilt-ing is a small challenge; but to the rest of us who claim we cannot draw, there are some special ways to compensate.

Decide What You Want to Represent

Loved ones, an historical building, your home, nature scenes, historical sites, the town hall or park bandstand, historical people (George and Martha Washington), a boat (your racing skiff or the Half Moon of Henry Hudson), a car (your first model T)—all make wonderful subjects. The list is endless. There are many ways to approach the original drawing, called the cartoon by artists.

What Size Drawing is Needed?

The blocks in this quilt are 16 × 16 inches when finished. We know quilting must be added around the outer perimeter of the appliqued material. Set the picture material at least one inch within this 16-inch square, thus the space to be filled will be 15 × 15 inches. Sometimes a tree or a stream will have to lead out of the picture.

People

Large size children's storybooks and coloring books offer basic forms and simple outlines for starting a figure. The dress can be changed to fit whatever you are trying to depict. There is another way to approach this. Find a figure you want to use, say a football player in action in a sports magazine, and grade it to size. If the figure is too small, trace it onto $\frac{1}{4}$ inch graph paper. Then get the next size larger graph paper and copy the picture duplicating where the lines intersect each of the squares. Keep repeating this trick until the picture is large enought to fit the space allotted.

Fig. 4-49 *The Quilter.*

Fig. 4-50 *Man and His Horse.*

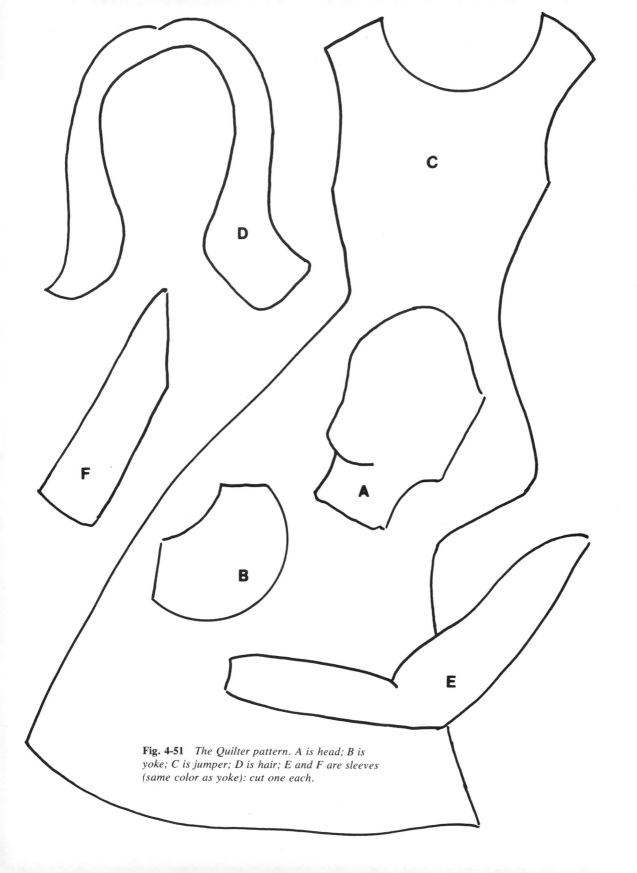

Fig. 4-51 *The Quilter pattern. A is head; B is yoke; C is jumper; D is hair; E and F are sleeves (same color as yoke): cut one each.*

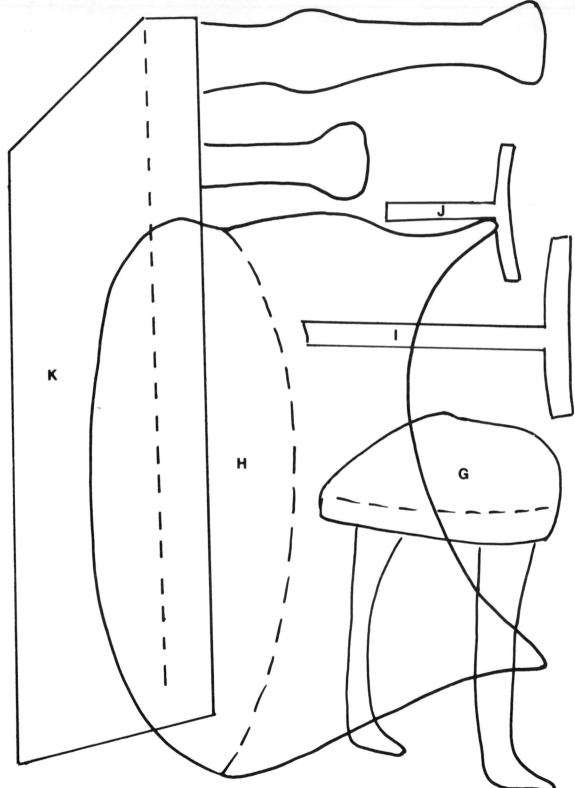

Fig. 4-52 *Background for the Quilter. G is stool;*
H is quilt on an oval frame; I and J are legs to
the frame; K is table; cut one each.

Fig. 4-53 *Man and His Horse. A is jacket; B is ascot; C is head; D is hand; E is leg: F is boot; G is blanket; H is horse head to overlap HH front half of horse. Place double lines of HH over double lines of HH to add rear of horse. Cut one each. See pages 195-197.*

E

C

H

F

G

Fig. 4-53 *continued.*

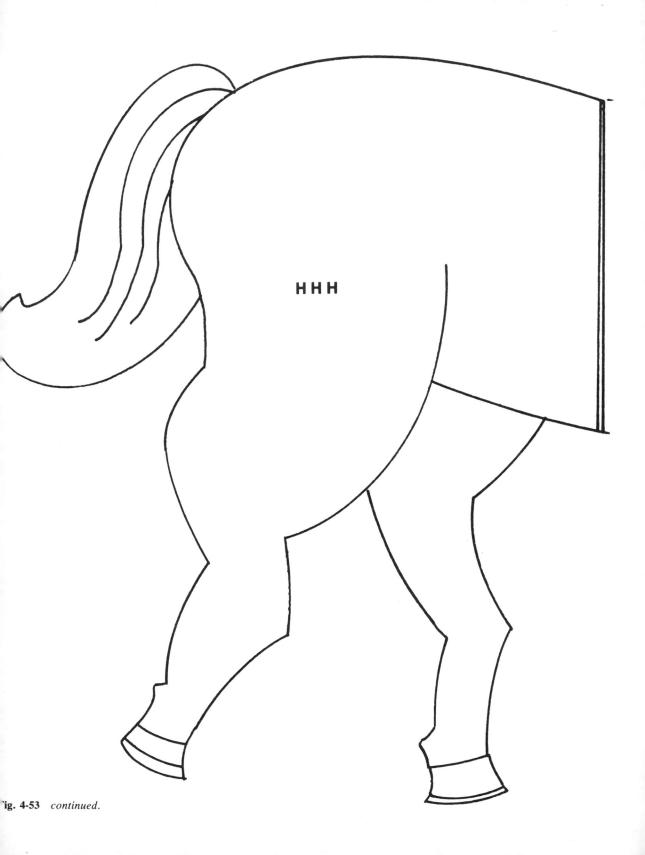

HHH

Fig. 4-53 continued.

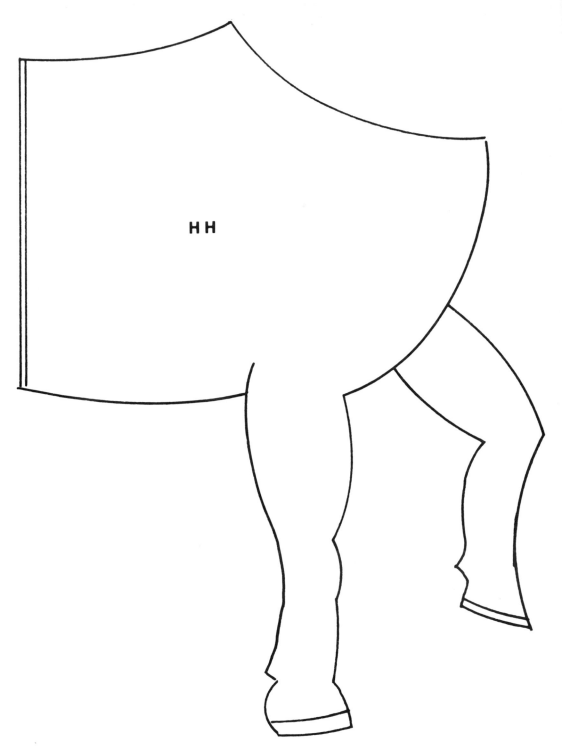

HH

Fig. 4-53 *continued*.

Facial Features

There are two types of features. The easiest is the cartoon type—a few stitches for nose and mouth and two french knots for eyes with embroidery floss (Fig. 4-50). The second type calls for more defined features and for this the skills of the embroiderer are needed. To get the features right on a face, grade the figure to the right size and then watch the newspapers for a line drawing of a similar face in the right position: full face, side view or three-quarter view. Trace the features onto sheer paper then onto the fabric after it has been appliqued onto the background (Fig. 4-49 and Fig. 4-50).

Buildings

These are easier than figures. To do your own house in applique, take a picture of the house and enlarge it as big as possible. Then put it on ¼ inch graph paper and start to grade it up to the size you need. This will help to keep the proportions. Embroidery can be used to indicate window and door trim, siding, shingles and flowers on the bushes. The one thing to leave out is the driveway. First of all it is generally not a complementary color to the quilt and secondly it leads the eye out of the picture. The window areas will have to be lighter and they will have to have embroidery to indicate the structure of the panes of glass. A white sheer over a blue or green gives a good glass look. Windows are not as easy to make as doors. Doors are just appliqued on top of the facade of the building. Some windows need an inset feeling. These may have the window shape cut out of the facade of the building and the seam allowance turned to the wrong

side on the facade piece. Another color fabric is then slipped behind the window opening. This is generally done for old churches and other heavy stone buildings. Add smoke to your chimney of the homestead: this indicates warmth within. Try to keep the trees within the picture if possible and use several colors and small green prints on the trees and shrubs.

Historic buildings are sometimes easier than your own home because libraries, newspapers, local and county historical societies have photographs and line drawings of historical sites. Such buildings may have been painted several colors over the years and you may have to do some research. In the color photo of the Album sampler quilt, I added the Victorian train station which is in the middle of our town. In our town hall, I found a large painting of our Victorian train station (found bottom left in the quilt) done in greens with reddish doors and window trim and a dark roof. I checked with the artist; his research revealed that it had indeed been painted these colors once and they fit into my quilt very nicely (even though today the building is an entirely different color). You can, of course, take artistic liberties with the colors.

Placement

So far one of the few unifying factors in this multicolored pictorial sampler quilt is the background. Do not disturb this in order to create a more realistic picture. Simply set your rendering on the common ground of the quilt. If a quilt is made up entirely of pictorial blocks, then a more accurate rendering can be obtained by creating a horizon line—the line between the sky and land. Never place this in the middle of the picture, always above or below the middle. The sky is generally light blue, but it may be dark to indicate night. A nighttime historical event would have a dark blue sky—Paul Revere saw the lamp in the church tower and subsequently rode at night.

Assembly

After the cartoon is completed, trace each individual element onto transparent paper and glue to firmer board. Mark exactly what the pieces are and how many are to be cut. Baste on the main portions of the facade and roof. Add the windows, doors and shrubbery on top. For the entire project of this nature, it is important to have opaque fabric. It you need to use a color that is not opaque, then back it with another fabric to make it opaque.

The placement of pictorial blocks in a quilt is important. In checking the photo of the Album sampler quilt, note that the four pictorial blocks are placed on the four corners of the main section of the bed. They may be grouped in the middle or lined up across the pillows. Be careful not to intersperse them with the other assorted appliques.

To help you get started here, patterns for the seated woman at the quilt frame and the man on the horse are offered in Figs. 4-51 to Fig. 4-53. Use Fig. 4-49 and Fig. 4-50 as a guide in developing these blocks. Cut one piece each from the pattern pieces given in Fig. 4-51 to Fig. 4-53. Be mindful of the pieces that have to be put down first; baste only the portions that will not be covered by another piece of applique. Pin the pieces carefully to the background and then baste in place. Stitch down permanently, then remove the basting. Place quilt stitching around the main design elements.

PASCACK VALLEY HISTORICAL SOCIETY QUILT

In my original contact with the Pascack Valley Historical Society of New Jersey, the initial intent was to create a quilt as a fund raiser. When I showed these earnest and determined women what they could do in a quilt, they immediately gravitated to the pictorial quilt. Although the group was bursting with enthusiasm and ideas, I found that I had only one person experienced at applique. Many were good needlecrafters and sewers, but a little more strength was needed. I called on four of my quilt companions. One was Ginny Ruckert of the Friendship Sampler (see color photo section). Together with patient instruction, a lot of zeal and a few laughs, we created a beautiful quilt. The quilters were so taken with the project that they could not bear to part with this needleart history of Northeastern New Jersey—an area truly rich in history due to the area's proximity to the original settling of New York (or New Amsterdam). The quilt is taken to lectures and brought out at special events. It may have failed in its original intent as a fund raiser, but it has enriched a lot of lives with its ingenious rendition of a way to teach history with one panoramic view.

I was the coordinator for the Pascack Valley Quilt. Bicentennial quilters of the Pascack Historical Society who worked on this quilt were Ginny Ruckert, Mary Lou Della Bella, Ann Chas, JoAnn Schawm, Mary Petrakakis, Joan Winkelhoff, Doris Stockel, B. Beaumont, Jane Milliagna, Carol Caputo, Julia Farrel, Frances Ciminelle, Nan Ward, Muriel W. Wassmann, Dorothy Dawson.

Fig. 4-54 *Putnam County Quilt. Stage Coach designed and made by Gladys Boalt. Photograph by Charlotte Brooks.*

Fig. 4-55 *Putnam County Quilt. Ludington Mill designed by Gladys Boalt; made by Ella Townsend. Photograph by Charlotte Brooks.*

Fig. 4-56 *Putnam County Quilt. General Israel
Putnam. Designed and made by Gladys Boalt.
Photograph by Charlotte Brooks.*

THE PUTNAM COUNTY QUILT

To honor Putnam County for the Bicentennial Year, this quilt was designed by Gladys Boalt and was executed by nineteen women in one year, from 1975 to 1976. It includes some fifty pictorial representations of the past 200 years of county history. It is hand appliqued and quilted with millions of stitches applied with caring hands. The design of the quilt is totally unique. It did away with the block and band format and created an open background. The pictures are delineated with flora and funda expertly woven throughout so as not to take away from the importance of the pictures. I feel it is the finest needlecraft article to come from all the commemorative needlework produced for the Bicentennial.

It includes historical events dating from the Revolution. It commemorates important people who lived, worked, fought and risked their lives in and for Putnam County, its land and its people's liberty. The original inhabitants, the Indians, are honored. The institutions of learning, schools and churches are remembered, as well as the power of the horse and the great mills that served the farmers. Industries, large and small, are remembered from New York's first steam train to the racing sulky to the first forty-quart milk can. Fabled stories that have been handed down over the years, such as the one about the pirate Captain Kidd who left a treasure on the banks of the Hudson River, are added for amusement.

There have been both bad and good times that has left a rich legacy in Putnam County. These representations are gathered together under the great seal of the United States and a slice of time has been captured for all to see. If we wonder about the contributions that we as good citizens make each day in our own ways, a look at the history represented in this quilt will remind us our good works count for something in the long history of man.

Here are the quilters who worked on this: Gladys Boalt, quilt designer and co-ordinator, Harriet Shelton, Ann Boalt, Karen Oehlschlager, Inta Dravnicks, Beverly Schappach, Betty Hatfield, Lorraine Cheney, Madeline Moger, Nancy Greenwood, Etna Matchett, Thelma Boutz, Ella Townsen, Dolly Bouton, Kate Mitchel, Betty Crumley, Lou Belle Porter, and Jean Irwin.

FACES AND FASHION QUILT

De Ette Snider of Paradise, California, is one of the most imaginative quilters working today. The wide range of her subject matter is amazing. She has taken quilt crafting and made it into a medium for fine art expression. Everyone Has Eyelashes, shown in the color section, won the Los Angeles County Fair in 1976. This rendition of storybook characters will make everyone smile. At the other end of the spectrum is Faces and Fashion (Fig. 4-57). It combines fine line embroidery with applique to produce a sophisticated quilt.

Fig. 4-57 *Faces and Fashion designed and made by De Ette Snider. Photograph by Ray Hale. Many quilters like to portray their own life or that of a son or daughter in a quilt wallhanging.*

5

QUILTING AND FINISHING

There are several necessary steps between making the face of the quilt and the finished product. First, the three layers—face, batting and backing—are basted together. Then the three layers are put into a frame to hold it taut for quilting. The quilting stitch designs are chosen and stitching through the three layers is accomplished with a running stitch. The quilt is removed from the frame and the edges bound. The procedure is a logical one. Each step is explained in sequence in this chapter; I have included the most popular variations used today, with illustrations and photos.

Assembling the Face, Batting and Backing

A completely finished face is required at this point. All outer borders are added, the entire face is pressed and any loose threads are trimmed. The face is measured and a backing is chosen. This may be a print to match or complement the prints in the face. It may be a muslin or broadcloth. The muslin is less expensive and a special consideration when a lot of yardage is needed. A bed sheet is not suggested as it is so tightly woven that it is hard to quilt through. Select a weight for the backing that will match the face and try to get as high a cotton content as possible. New quilters particularly like the print backings as they are cheerful and the irregularities of the beginner's quilting are not noticed. As dexterity and skill increases, a dark, solid-color backing can be enjoyed. The backing should be at least one inch larger than the perimeter of the face. This will mean that two to three widths of 45-inch material may have to be stripped together with $\frac{1}{4}$-inch to $\frac{1}{2}$-inch seams to accommodate the measurements of the face. When stripping two 45-inch widths together, you will get a 90-inch width. If the face is only 64 or 84 inches wide, there will be some waste. Select the backing, wash it to reduce shrinkage, press the fabric and press the joining seam to one side. Do not trim to match the face until you are ready to work with it.

Selecting the batting is a relatively easy task as the batting is plentiful and comes in finished sheet sizes. The fibers are held together with a sized finish that makes this material easy to handle. It is purchased in sizes to accommodate most normal bed cover sizes, starting with the crib size 45 × 60 inches and going up to 96 × 108 inches. If a quilt is made 108 × 108 inches, then purchase one 96 × 108 inches and one crib size and butt the extra batting together where needed. Never sew it together or overlay it between the face and backing as it will cause uneven lumps. Most of the batting sold today is polyester. It is soft and easy to quilt through. Polyester batting has played a large role in the revived interest in quilting today. What the quilter is actually doing when uniting the three layers together is pocketing the batting in a small space. The polyester batting

can be pocketed in areas up to 8 × 8 inches without loss of fluffiness. Cotton batting is available (see resource list), but should be quilted in pockets no larger than 2 × 2 inches. Cotton has a tendency to ball up into a corner of the stitched quilt pocket, while the polyester will fluff up and refill the space after washing and drying.

Batting has no right or wrong side. Do *not* wash or iron before use. Just roll it out and place between the face and backing. Batting is sold by size and weight so it is easy to compare one product to the next. Ask for batting that is meant for hand quilting. There are thicker battings that are used in comforters but it is not meant to be hand quilted.

Place the backing wrong side up on a work surface that is large enough to accommodate the entire quilt. Place the batting over backing. It is good to have a few extra hands to help with this process as it will make the work go faster. If the batting is not large enough to accommodate the size of the quilt, then cut batting needed from additional roll of batting and place it next to the larger batting. This is called butting the batting together. Make sure that the backing is laying flat and the batting is smooth over it. Do not stretch the batting. Place the face on top of the batting with the right side up and the wrong side to the batting. Batting and backing may extend an inch or two beyond the face, but trim away any excesses beyond that.

Using a long needle (darning or milliner's), baste the three layers together in a sunburst pattern (Fig. 5-1 and Fig. 5-2). Start the knots at the center and work out to the edge. After getting the first horizontal and vertical stitches in the quilt, raise the three layers from the work surface and check the backing to be sure it does not have any folds sewn into it. Replace on the table (Fig. 5-3). Put in the diagonal stitches to the corners, lift and check the backing again. If there are any folds in the backing, then take out the basting and re-baste the layers.

The next consideration is the frame. If the quilt is to go into a traditional frame, then do not baste the edges; but if a round lap or oval floor frame is to be used, baste around the edges to prevent the batting from fraying out.

The Frame

All good needleart work is done in a frame. The purpose is to hold the threads of the fabric straight and keep the fabric taut so that the stitches which are placed through the layers can be pulled with the same degree of tension. This way all the stitches will be even. Another reason for using a frame is to hold the work in a stationary position, thus having both hands free to work above and below the quilt.

The traditional American quilt frame is made of wood; old ones are usually made from oak and chestnut (very heavy), and today's of pine (rather light). There are two long boards called *rails* that the top and bottom of the quilt are attached to (Fig. 5-4). To make a standard frame for personal use, use 1 × 2-inch lumber that has been *kiln dried* (green lumber will leak sap onto your quilt). If this is to be quilted by a group where many people will work on the frame at one time, then use 2 × 2-inch lumber for the rails (see Fig. 5-5). The short

boards at the ends are called the *stretcher bars* and they separate the two long rails holding the quilt taut. The frame does not have any legs as it may be placed on the back of two chairs, two card tables or two stools. When not in use, the quilt may remain in the frame and be stood against the wall or tucked under a bed. Many people fashion legs for frames, such as saw horses.

The stretcher bar is attached in two ways today, with small C-clamps found in the hardware store or by drilling holes through the 2-inch side of the rails and bars to accommodate a nut and bolt combination. In both cases, place the rail below the bar and have the rough end of the screw

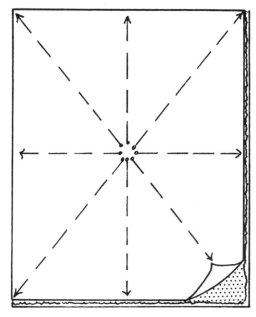

Fig. 5-1 *Baste the three layers together in a sunburst pattern, starting with a knotted thread at the center for each line of stitching.*

Fig. 5-2 *Basting a nine-block quilt together, note small amount of batting and backing showing around edge. Made by Karen Deer.*

or clamp facing upward to the ceiling (Fig. 5-4).

Study the photographs throughout this chapter. These are quilts being worked on by a fall class at Pascack Valley Regional High School Adult Education Department, Hillsdale, N.J. There is no one quilt pictured in sequence. Many different quilts are used to demonstrate the points being made.

The traditional frame for quilting a large size bed cover will have rails that will match the width of the quilt plus 10 inches. Each rail has a 2-inch wide width of unhemmed

sturdy fabric stapled or tacked to it so that the fabric hangs off the wood at least one inch (Fig. 5-6). Mark the center of each rail. The basted quilt will be stitched to the fabric. Line up the center of the basted quilt with the middle of the frame. Place the raw edges of the basted quilt top against the fabric extending from the rail. Working from the center out, pin first then stitch the quilt to the fabric attached to the rail. Since you will be working from the center to the sides, keep the pin heads facing to center and the points to the outside. If you can get someone to pull the three layers

Fig. 5-3 *Basting a twelve-block quilt together, note that basting will go through the large outer border. Made by Irene Holm.*

tightly as you stitch to the outer edges, it helps the work go faster (Fig. 5-7). If a little of the backing and batting overlaps the rail, that is all right. It helps to raise the rails by placing a few books under each end (Fig. 5-8). That way it is easy to slip your hand around the rail to hold the quilt in place. Withdraw the pins as you proceed with the basting. Stitch out past the face, catching the extending batting and backing onto the rail. Repeat the process, attaching the bottom of the quilt to the remaining

rail. This is called, by many quilters, laying the quilt into the frame.

The next process is to roll the quilt to the back on each rail. This is where a few extra hands are appreciated. With one person or a few heavy books positioned on the bottom end of the quilt to hold it stationary, begin to roll the top of the quilt backwards onto the rail. Keep the fabrics feeding onto the rail evenly and smoothly. It helps to have a person stationed at either side of quilt holding the fabric taut as it

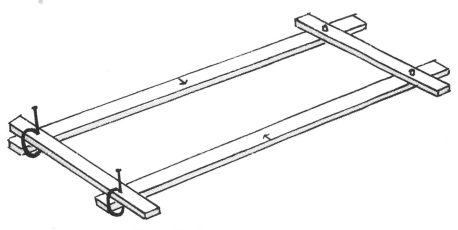

Fig. 5-4 *The long bars of the quilting frame are called rails. The center is marked with an arrow. The short bars are called stretcher bars. At the left side, the units are held together with C clamps. On the left side, the units are held with nuts and bolts. Either is correct.*

feeds onto the rail. Figure 5-9 shows a nine-block quilt and Fig. 5-10 shows a larger twelve-block quilt with large outer borders being rolled. In the latter case, the quilt and rails become quite heavy and the helping hands support the quilt as it's rolled. Keep smoothing out fabric as it feeds on the rail to avoid wrinkles. You can do this yourself, it just takes a little longer.

Roll the top end toward the center. In a nine-block quilt, the center will be the middle row across. In a larger quilt with four or five rows of blocks down, choose one to act as center and roll the quilt to the border just above the middle row. Stop the rolling at that point. Repeat the rolling process from the other end, stopping at the border just below the middle block (Fig. 5-11).

The Stretcher Bars

This short bar of wood (matching or unmatched in size to the rails) serves the exact purpose of its name. It stretches the two rails as far apart as they can be stretched. The length of the stretcher bar should be such that at least all, or almost all, of one row of blocks shows. For a 16-inch block, the stretcher bar should be about 18 to 20 inches (Fig. 5-11). This allows several blocks to be worked on at one time. The size of the stretcher bar may be large enough to accommodate two rows of blocks; this is important for a group project such as a club or a quilting bee (Fig. 5-5).

The stretcher bars are attached in two ways, either by nuts and bolts with holes drilled through both the rails and bars or

Fig. 5-5 *Working on a standard frame. Here the stretcher bars and rails are 2″ × 1″ lumber. The frame rests on a sawhorse frame. This Eight-Point Star quilt was designed and is owned by Phyllis Shane, seated at the right front. Other quilters are Sonia Adams, Marge Beucler and me.*

with C-clamps placed with the screw turned upward. First attach the two stretcher bars to the top rail. Then pull the bottom rail as far as it will stretch and secure the bottom rail. It's very helpful to have a second person help with this but when I am alone, I place my thigh against the top rail and use my hands to push the bottom rail away

and to clamp it. Repeat for the rail at the other end.

After the quilting has been accomplished on the exposed blocks, remove the stretcher bars and reroll to a new unquilted area for quilting. Quilting proceeds from the center out. All of the exposed area is quilted, even the exposed outer borders.

Fig. 5-6 *Each rail has a 2″ width of unhemmed sturdy fabric stapled to it.*

Fig. 5-8 *Stitch from the center out to either side. Working alone, support the rails on a few books so that hands can work above and below the frame with freedom. Stitch to the end of the backing, removing pins as you go along.*

The quilt patterns are selected before quilting is started and are marked very lightly with a regular pencil on the light color portions or with a white dressmarker pencil on the darker portions. This is done as the work proceeds. This is the most popular way to work; however, occasionally a quilt will be completely marked before it is put in the frame. I find that the pencil markings must be very dark so that they do not rub off in handling and consequently they do not wash out either. The white marking will rub off completely when handled too

much. So it is far better to mark quilt patterns on each area as it is exposed on the top of the quilt frame.

Strapping the Quilt

In a frame of this type, the center of the quilt is very taut but the ends are unsupported and would be hard to work on in this way. As in other needlearts, the ends are strapped. This means taking 2-inch wide strips of even-weave fabrics such as muslin that are cut as long as possible (Fig. 5-12). First, tie one end to the intersection of the rail and stretcher bar. Bring the length of the fabric up to the quilt and place two pins in the edge of the quilt. Fold the strip back toward the stretcher bar and wind around the top coming up again around the bottom and pull tightly. Return the strip back to the quilt and pin again; repeat winding the strapping material between the

Fig. 5-7 *Pin the quilt to fabric attached to the rail. Here one quilter helps another quilter support the work as pinning is accomplished.*

Fig. 5-9 *The nine-block quilt of Karen Deer being rolled. Note another quilter holding opposite end firmly in place. Also see stretcher bar to be used on this quilt laying on the table in the foreground.*

Fig. 5-10 *The twelve-block quilt of Irene Holm. As the quilt rolls onto the rail, support on either side will help prevent folds in the quilt. The object is to get it on the rails smoothly.*

quilt. These frames or reasonable facsimiles can be purchased from mail-order houses and quilt shops. It is not uncommon for quilters to have two sets of rails; one set about 80 inches long will accommodate crib size up to twin size quilts and another set 105 to 110 inches long will accommodate up to king size quilts.

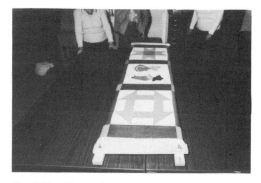

Fig. 5-11 *The quilt rolled from either side to the center. The stretcher bars are secured with nuts and bolts. Note how tight the frame keeps the work.*

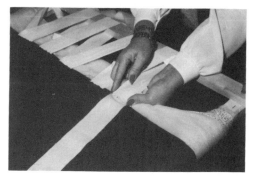

Fig. 5-12 *Strapping the side edges of the quilt to the stretcher bar to create tension across the width of the frame.*

quilt and the bar, each time making the end of the quilt as taut as possible. Repeat for the other end.

A quilt frame to most quilters is like a pot to most cooks—something to be used for a utilitarian purpose. When not in use, it is unassembled and stored for the next

Round and Oval Frames

The alternate to the traditional rail and bar frame described above are the round or oval frames. The most popular is the round lap frame. The three layers of the quilt are basted together and the outer edges are basted closed. The lap frame is like a giant embroidery hoop. It is 16 or 18 inches across and about one inch thick. At the top of the outer hoop is a screw to adjust the tension. The lower hoop is placed under the center of the quilt and the upper hoop with the adjustment screw is placed on top so that a small section of the quilt is worked on at a time (Fig. 5-13). After the quilting is completed in the center, the frame is moved to a section adjacent to the portion already quilted. Always work from the center out to the edges. The quilting is done in the lap, generally in an easy chair. For a small quilt (65 × 65 inches), the lap frame works well; but for the larger bed covers, the traditional frame is recommended.

The oval frame, $16\frac{1}{2} \times 27$ inches, is basically the same as the round frame, but has a floor stand attached to it. The quilter sits at the frame on a regular chair and quilts from the center to the outer borders, moving the hoops to unquilted areas as with the lap frame.

The quality of these frames depends on how taut you can get the work in the frame. If the frame loosens up when being worked on, then it is of little value.

How to Quilt

The purpose of quilting is to unite a loose batting material between two layers of fabric. Quilt stitching contains the batting material in a small pocket of stitches. Each time the quilted item is washed, the batting material will remain in the same place. How small the pockets must be depends on the quality of the batting material and its' resistance to lumping together in that pocket of quilt stitches. That is where polyester fiber reigns supreme. It has the greatest ability to puff up and fill the pocket in which it is contained.

The actual stitch used is a running stitch. There are three aids to good quilting. The first is the use of a strong thread with a hard finished surface. It is called "quilting thread." The second aid is a small needle with a wide eye called a *between*. The smaller the better, as it will force the quilter to make small stitches. The wide eye will allow for easy threading. The third aid is the tautness of the quilting frame. The frame holds the work in one place allowing the two hands to be free. In a multilayered item such as a quilt, it holds the three layers stationary. Try to quilt toward yourself when you start. In time you will learn to quilt away from yourself with even stitches.

The first thing to understand about the stitching is that both hands are used. Each one of us has an educated hand and an uneducated hand. The educated hand has greater dexterity than the uneducated hand, which needs more eye coordination to help it in its tasks. Most of us are right-handed; this is our educated hand.

In the most popular method, the running stitch, the uneducated hand is placed below the work and the index or middle finger is pushed up against the back of the work where the stitches are to be made. This provides a pressing together of the

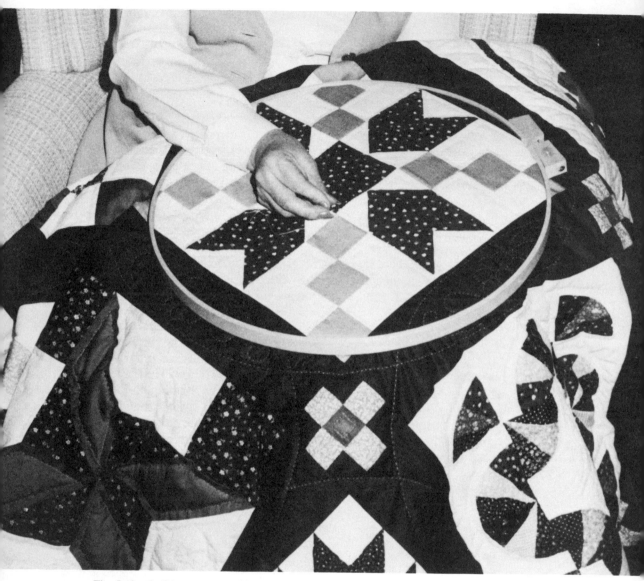

Fig. 5-13 *Quilting on a round lap frame, good for smaller quilts.*

210

three layers and makes the surface easier to stitch. On the surface the educated hand can pick up one to three small stitches at a time on the needle (Fig. 5-14). The thread need not be pulled through each time a few stitches are made, but can wait until there are many stitches. The thread is pulled ever so lightly to make a depression. This is how the texture is created.

The alternate method of stitching is called the *up and down* method. Here the educated hand, the one that can work better without the eye to guide it, is placed under the frame. The uneducated hand is placed above the frame with the needle and thread. The upper hand places the needle at a 90°-angle to the cloth (Fig. 5-15). The needle is passed straight down through the layers. It is received by the hand below and with that educated hand it is passed back up through the layers to be received on the top. It is said that masters of this method can make the smallest stitches of all; however, due to its reliance on greater dexterity, it is not the most popular method. It is used many times in conjunction with the more popular running stitch method. It can be used very effectively where the fabric layers become very thick. The running stitches cannot be kept the same size where the layers are very thick so the up and down method is employed.

If a quilter can get five to seven stitches to the inch, that is standard. More stitches per inch will increase the quilt's intrinsic value. It is important to note that the evenness of the stitches is most important. Even stitching creates greater symmetry that ultimately results in a more unified effect on the surface.

Fig. 5-14 *Quilting a running stitch on the marked lines. The uneducated hand works below and educated hand makes two to three stitches at a time.*

Starting and Ending the Stitches

For a long time the tried and true way to start any line of stitchery was with a knot. The very old information we have tells the quilter to start with a knot and pull it through the backing. That may have been a fine practice when the backing materials were very thin and loosely woven, but today they are closely woven and the knots do not easily slip through to be caught in the batting. So that while starting with a small knot on the back of the quilt is acceptable, another method has become more popular with good quilters everywhere. It utilizes one long thread that would be double the amount that normally is used before get-

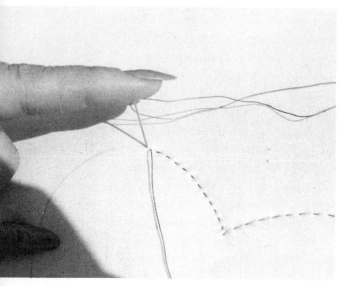

Fig. 5-15 *Quilting with the up and down method. At left, the uneducated hand passes the needle down. At right, the educated hand returns the needle to the hand waiting above.*

ting badly frayed (about 36 inches). The thread is folded in half and a pin is placed in the middle of an area to be worked. The folded loop of the thread is caught around the pin head and circled back and forth between the pin point and head in a figure-8 fashion, thus securing the thread in a stationary position on the face of the quilt (Fig. 5-16a). The needle is threaded on one half of the thread. The stitches are worked in one direction. When that thread is used up, the pin is withdrawn and the remainder of the thread is used in the opposite direction or in a paralleling line. Both threads are finished with a hidden backstitch and rewoven. When the thread has reached the

end of its use, place a half-sized stitch in the quilt and then cover it with a full stitch. The tail of the thread is rewoven back through the last few stitches that have been made. Make one long stitch under the face, through the batting coming out again on the top of the quilt, the tail is cut. It will take a long time for this tail to pull out (Fig. 5-16). This puts all the work on the top of the quilt and a knot is unnecessary. Many people who work on lap frames will finish the tails of the thread on the backing side. The thread is sent to the back, when it can no longer be worked, the frame is turned over and the reweaving is done on the wrong side.

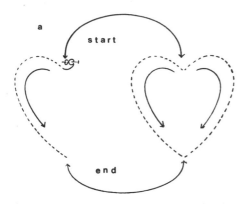

Fig. 5-16 *(a) To start quilting, use a double length of thread; catch center around pin in figure 8-fashion; quilt to one side then the other. (b) Reweave back a few stitches and pass needle under the face but not through backing; coming up on face, clip at X mark.*

Where to Quilt

The textural element of quilting enhances the color and design of the patterns used in the blocks. Remember all the seams in this craft are $\frac{1}{4}$ inch and that is for good reason. Most of the easy quilting is carried out $\frac{1}{4}$ inch off the seam line so that the stitches are made through three layers of fabric. Otherwise, with the seam allowances and the face, batting and backing, there would be five layers of material to stitch through. This extra thickness would force the running stitches to be larger.

Patchwork Quilting

The most popular method is to outline most of the individual pieces of patchwork. If the pattern has many common-colored pieces in one block, then only portions of the block need be quilted. Many times the background is quilted, causing a depression of that portion and leaving the remaining portions of the pattern to stand up in relief (Fig. 2-26). For the large open elements of a pattern, quilting of a more picturesque nature can be used. It may be an intricate medallion (Fig. 2-51) or picture type such as a butterfly (Fig. 2-64). Some of the pieces may have several concentric lines of quilting applied within one portion of a block (Fig. 2-29). To quilt patchwork, it is easy to follow $\frac{1}{4}$ inch away from the straight lines of the seams with no additional markings. If a decorative pattern is to be added, then a template will have to be made. (See Templates, Chapter 3.) Generally when quilting patchwork, it is important to keep the graphic line feeling to the type of quilting patterns used. The ease of quilting patchwork by following its seamlines attracts many people who are looking for easy quilting.

Quilting Sawtooth Edge Patchwork

It would appear that the quilting is started and finished separately for each triangle. This is not so. It would be too time consuming and the stitching would not be very strong. Instead, a double length of thread is used to quilt a line of five to ten individual triangles. Double the length of thread at the midpoint and loop it over a pin at the top or right-hand side of the sawtooth row. Make a figure-8 several times over the pin. Thread the needle on one side and begin to stitch along the bottom of the first triangle (Fig. 5-17a). When reaching the other side of the first triangle, do not start upward but rather slip the needle under the seam through the batting and come up on the other side of the seam at a place where the quilting will start again along the bottom of the second triangle. Keep the quilting running across the bottom until reaching a set number of triangles. Backstitch and reweave tail (Fig. 5-17a). Slip the remaining thread off the pin at the beginning point and start to quilt the zigzag portion of the sawtooth. When the thread runs out, finish with a backstitch and reweave the tail (Fig. 5-17b). If the distance under the seamline is too great for the needle to pass easily, then slip the needle into the seam and take hidden stitches in the seam line. Proceed to quilt again when you get to the next piece in the patchwork. After a while you will become very adept at se-

lecting the length of thread needed. Slipping from one area through the batting is an old quilting trick. It will become apparent where this technique will fit into other areas of quilt stitching (Fig. 5-18).

Pieced Applique Quilting

Here the shapes to be quilted are softer but the main portions of the blocks are patchwork. Keep the patchwork portions very graphic. The patchwork is applied to a background and may be outlined $\frac{1}{4}$ inch off the seam line. Then the background is free for more imaginative quilting. Simple hearts or small florals can be put into the corners of the Friendship Ring or small fan patterns. Another attractive device is the use of two or three concentric lines that echo the perimeter of the applied patchwork (Fig. 5-19 to Fig. 5-21).

All of these patterns can have a form of quilting called quilting in the valley. It means that instead of working $\frac{1}{4}$ inch off the seam line, the quilting is placed on the seamline. Since the seams have been pressed to one side, the quilter will be going through only three layers. It is more difficult to push the needle and it's hard to get the stitches small and even, but the effect is stunning for certain design blocks. All wedge design patterns would have very fine definition if the patchwork part were handled this way and open areas could be handled with more picturesque design. The pattern that benefits most from this kind of quilting is the Log Cabin which is all patchwork. When it is quilted in the valley, the logs seem to puff up and roll outward as real logs would. This may be quilted

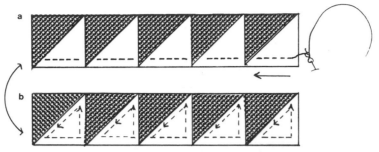

Fig. 5-17 *Quilting sawtooth squares. (a) First, stitch along bottom of triangles with half of the doubled length of thread. (b) With the other half of thread, quilt the sawtooth sections.*

just off the line around each log but the valley quilting gives a more interesting effect. The drawback to this kind of quilting is that, even though the quilt will have a very textured feeling, the stitches are not seen. Some people feel that the quilt stitches should be seen. Try it in your sampler quilt and see what you think.

Applique Quilting

Because this is a picture-making technique, it stands to reason that the quilting will also be very picturesque in nature. First and foremost, all appliques are outlined $\frac{1}{4}$ inch around the edge on the background. Because applique is structurally the weakest type design, it is often outlined within each of the appliques as well. Use the quilt stitches to create petal-like outlines on the larger flowers or create the illusion of veins on the leaves. Many times quilting on the appliques is used for definition.

Very often the appliques are repeated in a quilt one after the other without bordering bands between. This creates a very large open background area to be filled with textural quilting. There are several popular designs of a simple nature that will fill the background. The cross bar is just diagonal lines intersecting each other (Fig. 3-24). The chevron pipeline utilizes straight lines that meet in a chevron pattern (Fig. 5-22). The use of concentric lines is also popular (Fig. 4-10). These just keep moving out beyond each applique until the lines meet each other and form smaller designs. There are still more intricate motifs that involve complicated leaf and vine patterns and extended floral medallions (Fig. 5-35).

The applique patterns that have been chosen and graded to fit the 16-inch block for the sampler quilt will fill up the block with a minimum of quilting. In a sampler quilt, outlining is all that is necessary, but many quilters like to run a row of quilt stitches $\frac{1}{4}$ inch off the edges of the bordering bands on the background material of the applique block.

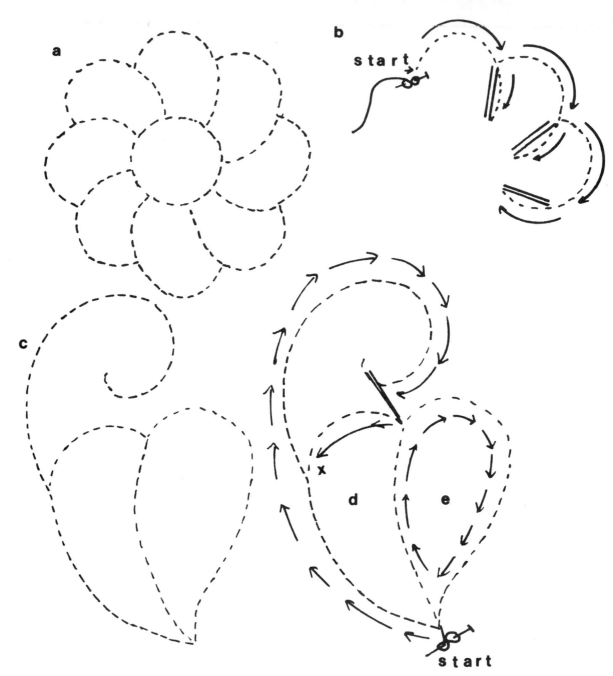

Fig. 5-18 *Quilting intricate forms. (a) Pattern of flower to be quilted. (b) Start double length of thread on pin at point marked* start. *Quilt to the right, outlining the first petal. Return needle through the batting (marked with double lines) to start the second petal. Continue until all right hand petals are completed. Release pin and quilt the left hand petals and the center circle. (c) A complicated leaf pattern. (d) Start at the bottom point of the leaf, with double length of thread caught on pin. Move up left side of the leaf and over top of the vine. Come back through the batting (marked with double lines) to reach center top of leaf, quilt to the left and finish thread at X. (e) Release pin with second half of thread and start at bottom point. Stitch in an oval direction, completing center vein and proceed back down to bottom point where you started this second portion of the leaf, finish thread. (See Earth Tones quilt in color section.)*

Fig. 5-19 *Assorted small quilting patterns to be used as fill-in behind applique. They can be reduced or enlarged. Run them one after the other in board bands. Combine with long curves to elongate. (a) rose; (b) lazy daisy; (c) combined diamonds; (d) eight-point star (half given).*

Fig. 5-20 *Fill-in quilting patterns (e) butterfly; (f) hearts in any size are good fillers; (g) tulip on curved stem fits well around curved patterns and softens geometric shapes (see Clay's Choice); (h) novelty flower; (k) a pansy type flower, another leaf can be added to the left or use flower alone.*

Fig. 5-21 *Fill-in quilting patterns (l) grouped hearts; (m) small floral bouquet (very good to enlarge for a wide solid outer border); (n) bird has nice crescent shapes to work with flowers or fill-in behind appliques; (o) the curved leaf, with or without additional side veins; (p) novelty flower shape to fill-in on a corner.*

Border Band Quilting

Many quilts and, in particular, sampler quilts have bands that intersect to create frames. This area should be quilted. The two easiest designs to accomplish this are diamonds and ovals (Fig. 5-23). Here a double length of thread is wound on a pin as described in Fig. 5-16 and the design is worked along one side and then the other thread is released from the pin and it is worked on the reverse portions.

Patterns of a little more intricate nature are shown in Fig. 5-23 to Fig. 5-25. The quilt called Earth Tones uses a small nine-patch in the corner intersections (Fig. 5-25). The four outer corners use the same background material as the bands. This offers an opportunity to allow the quilting of the bands to form intersecting circles around each block. The double arc formed by the design allows for an additional quilt design to be used in the band center. The bands may also have elongated designs of leaves and florals to fill the space (Fig. 5-26 and Fig. 5-27).

The Outer Border Design

The top of the sampler quilt is often so busy in its design that the portions that hang over the side of the bed should be a solid color or broad stripes. If an assortment of stripes is used around the quilt, keep the quilting in the print portions rather simple (Fig. 5-23) and use more intricate designs for the solid colors (Fig. 5-26 and 5-27). If the drop is a wide solid color, then make good use of this area for beautiful quilt designs (Fig. 5-31 to Fig. 5-40).

Finding Quilt Designs

Designs for quilting are plentiful. Libraries abound in picture books of floral designs, folk art and tole painting designs. Paper folding yields some very interesting designs. Fold the paper four or five times and cut various designs. Make sure the paper will fit in the open space needing quilting. One of the most accessible sources for florals can be found on dishes. The people that have to create the designs are masters at both central figures and border designs. Jewelry offers another source for soft flowing lines; study pins and pendants for upright designs, chains and bracelets for border designs.

If you see a pattern in a book that you want to use, but it is too large, many copying machines at the libraries can reduce the patterns. An alternate method is to draw the pattern selected onto graph paper and then use either larger or smaller graph paper to reduce or enlarge it. Number all the vertical and horizontal lines on each of the graph papers to keep the lines in the same relationships. Copy the drawing box for box.

Making Solid Templates for Quilting Designs

Most of the time a design is selected from a base drawing that will fit the space requiring quilting. Many patterns for quilting are given on paper such as in a book or from supply companies (see source list). These can be traced on to strong, lightweight art board such as bristol board or oak tag. Cut each element out to make a

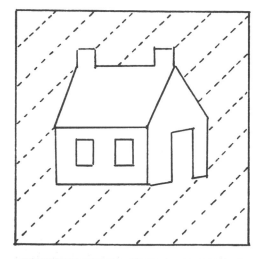

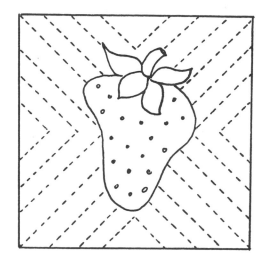

Fig. 5-22 *Chevron quilting fills in background. If lines are used all in one direction on a diagonal, it's called pipeline quilting. Photo shows pipeline quilting with floral design center.*

separate template of each part (see Fig. 5-28). Here the flower is cut out on the outside and the inside. Note that the center of the flower has a line across as that indicates the middle of the band. Two of the flower petals also have small notches. This will indicate where the heart-shaped leaves will be placed. On one side of the flower, the leaf will be placed right side up and on the other side the leaf will be reversed. This notching of a pattern is a popular tech-

nique. For a running border using a single shape, the notching makes it easy to draw the pattern (Fig. 5-29). The solid template is notched on top and bottom. The first figure is marked on the quilt with the notch marks included. The next one is placed so that the notch marks on the top of the template fit into the notch marks on the lower portion of the drawn shape. Each one is added in this manner.

When working on the bordering bands

Fig. 5-24 *The Album quilt uses a flower and double leaves at intersection (see color section).*

Fig. 5-25 *Earth Tones quilt uses a flower and two leaves in the band, surrounded by an arc shape outline that joins one band to the adjoining bands (Fig. 5-18 pattern).*

or the outer border portions of a quilt, draw the size of the band on paper and then sketch in the designs to see how they will look when placed against the quilt. When designing a template for the long narrow outer borders, take the measurement of the width and length that will require quilting. Find a common number that divides into both and make a pattern that can be repeated an even number of times.

Stencil Templates

These are quite popular today because they are being made of clear plastic. There are many designs and they can be had from many manufactured sources (see source list). They are used for intricate patterns

Fig. 5-23 *Simple border band quilt designs. Top to bottom: diamonds, ovals, combined semicircles, lightning stripes, interlocking circles, running leaf, twisted rope.*

of vines and leaves and interconnecting circles. These more complicated designs can be made very successfully at home. They utilize a solid piece of cardboard or plastic upon which a full design is drawn or a portion of a design is drawn. Using an art knife, such as an X-acto brand, cut small slits on the drawn lines, or entire areas can be cut out such as a leaf or a flower. The template is then placed over the area to be quilted and a pencil used to trace the cut out spaces (Fig. 5-30).

Study the suggested quilting designs in Fig. 5-31 to Fig. 5-41 for ideas for wide and narrow bands and drops, the sections that cover the sides of the beds. If a design is particularly liked but is too narrow, it may have an additional design like a running leaf added above and/or below. It may be further enhanced with additional material. These are my original designs but that does not mean they can't be improved

Fig. 5-27 *Intricate design for border bands. Floral and vine for a more open effect. Flower in center with vine on either side in reverse position for 4" × 16" band.*

Fig. 5-26 *Intricate designs for border bands. Floral and leaf with small tight lines. Use two in 16" × 4" band, placed in reversed positions.*

Fig. 5-28 *Solid template showing notched markings for placement. Leaf is reversed for other side (only two templates needed).*

or altered. Using contrast color thread, the drop may add more definition to the design. Study the designs and make templates that you will be comfortable using. Mark the center; most templates are just folded over and repeated one after the other. Remember that while quilting adds a textural element, it also pockets the batting in small areas.

Also study the color photos for additional ideas. See Fig. 5-22 for ideas on straight lines. Figure 5-23 offers designs that may be enlarged and used on drops too. These are the popular, most often used designs.

Binding the Finished Quilt

When a quilt is taken out of the frame after all the quilting is finished, the raw edges will have to be bound. The simplest method is to cut all the edges even with the face and add a bias binding around the edge. The binding may be purchased or homemade, about $\frac{1}{2}$ inch to a full inch. Place the binding with its right side against the right side of the quilt and stitch around the entire quilt by hand or machine. Overlap the ends of the bias on the diagonal where they meet. Turn the bias to the wrong side of the quilt. Turn in $\frac{1}{4}$ inch on the remaining raw edge, pin in place, then finish with an overcast or hidden slipstitch.

An alternate method that is popular today is to use the backing as a binding. This requires a little forethought and planning. If the backing is to be used on the front, it will have to be compatible with the design and color of the face of the quilt. When laying out the three layers for basting, make sure that about 2 inches of the backing extends beyond the face. After quilting, trim the backing so an even amount appears around the perimeter of the face. Turn the raw edge of the backing $\frac{1}{4}$ inch to $\frac{1}{2}$ inch to its wrong side. Baste this down.

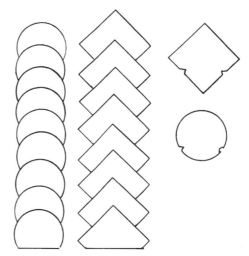

Fig. 5-29 *Solid template with notched edges fit into each other to form a chain effect along an outer border.*

225

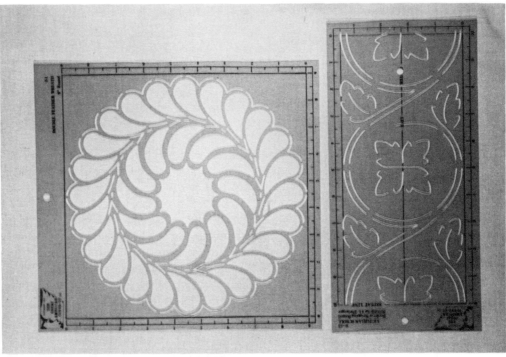

Fig. 5-30 *Dye cut stencils are made of tinted transparent plastic and ruled for easy measure. (a) The square on left of the double feathered wreath pattern which comes in many sizes and border pattern on right called victorian scroll are both from Come Quilt With Me (see source list). (b) Open window template for the tulip quilt pattern cut out and two solid patterns used for tracing.*

Trim the batting away to half the depth of the extended backing. Turn the backing over the batting and $\frac{1}{4}$ to $\frac{1}{2}$ inch over the raw edge of the face. Pin in place, mitering the corners and stitch down with a hidden slipstitch. This extension of the batting helps to protect the raw edges of the face. If wear does occur, then it will fray the edge of the extended backing and the batting. This can be trimmed away and bias bound. This technique may finish with as small as $\frac{1}{4}$ inch showing or as wide as $1\frac{1}{4}$ inches on the front. Anything larger than this would require quilting to hold the batting in place. For further information on binding and finishing, refer to *The Quilting Primer*, a general purpose text which I wrote for Chilton Book Company, 1979.

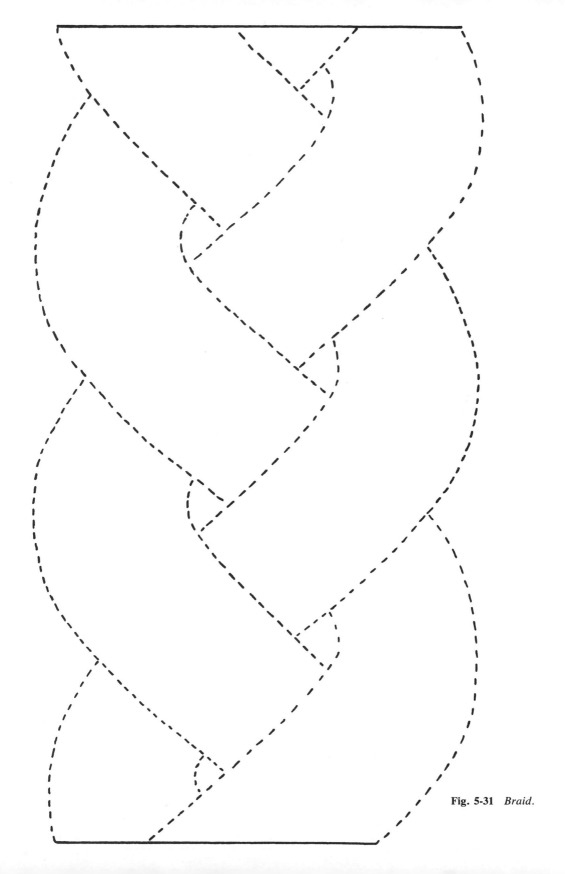

Fig. 5-31 *Braid.*

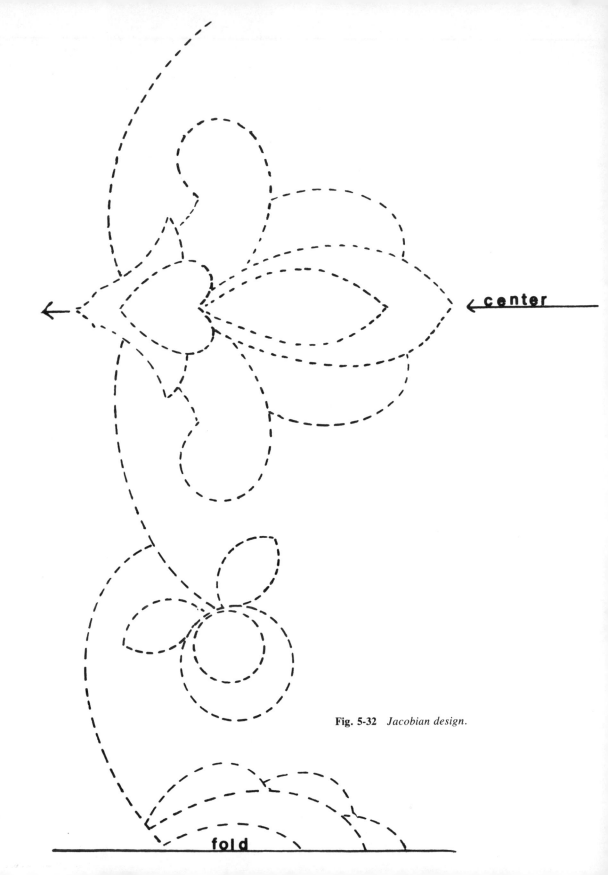

center

Fig. 5-32 *Jacobian design.*

fold

Fig. 5-33 *Large floral basket with floral fill-in at base. Butterflies going in one direction may be added at top (use Fig. 5-20e).*

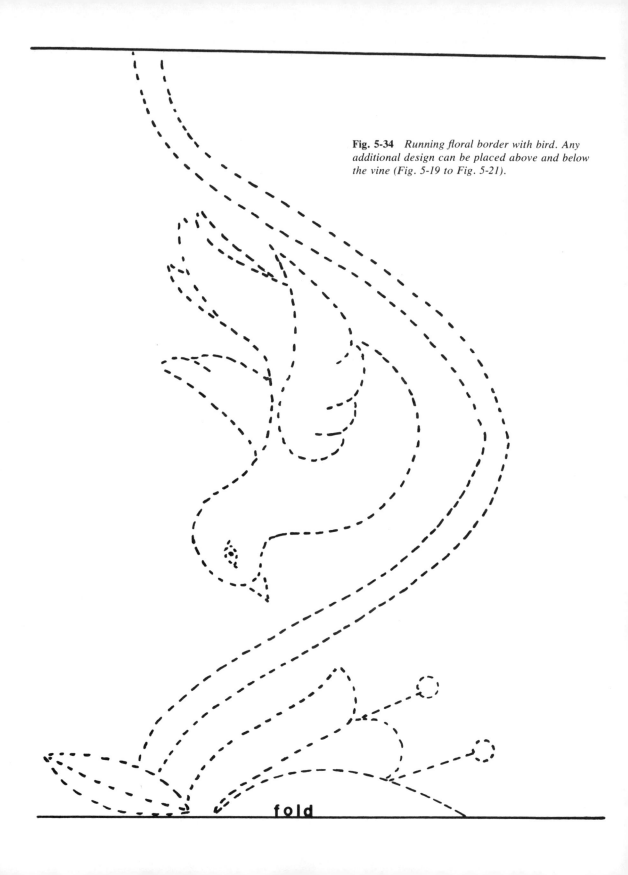

Fig. 5-34 *Running floral border with bird. Any additional design can be placed above and below the vine (Fig. 5-19 to Fig. 5-21).*

fold

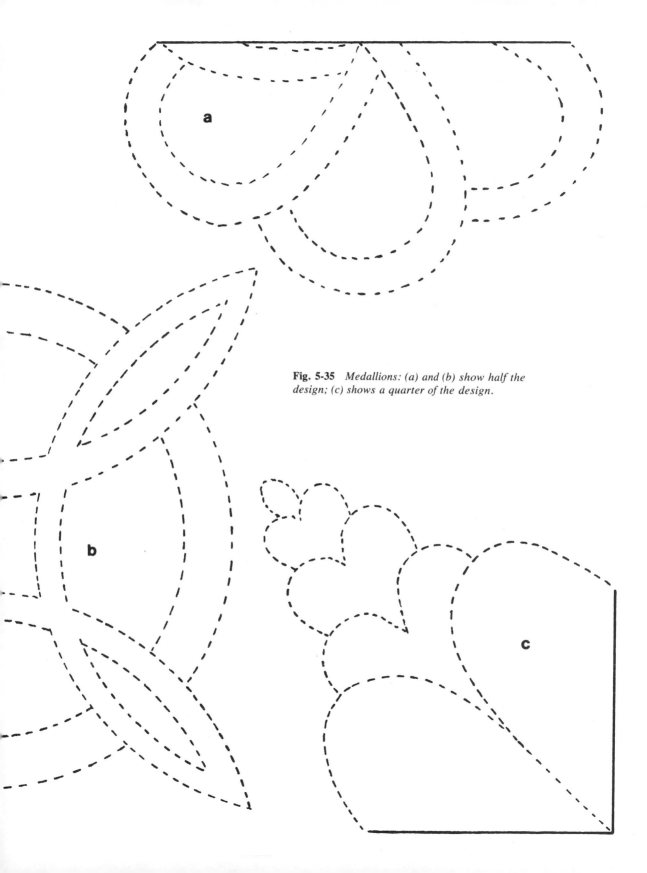

Fig. 5-35 *Medallions: (a) and (b) show half the design; (c) shows a quarter of the design.*

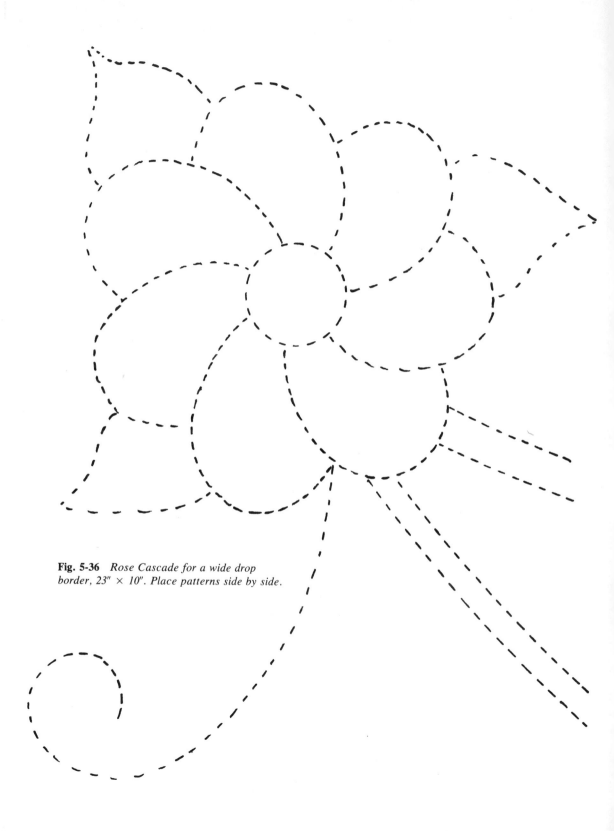

Fig. 5-36 *Rose Cascade for a wide drop border, 23″ × 10″. Place patterns side by side.*

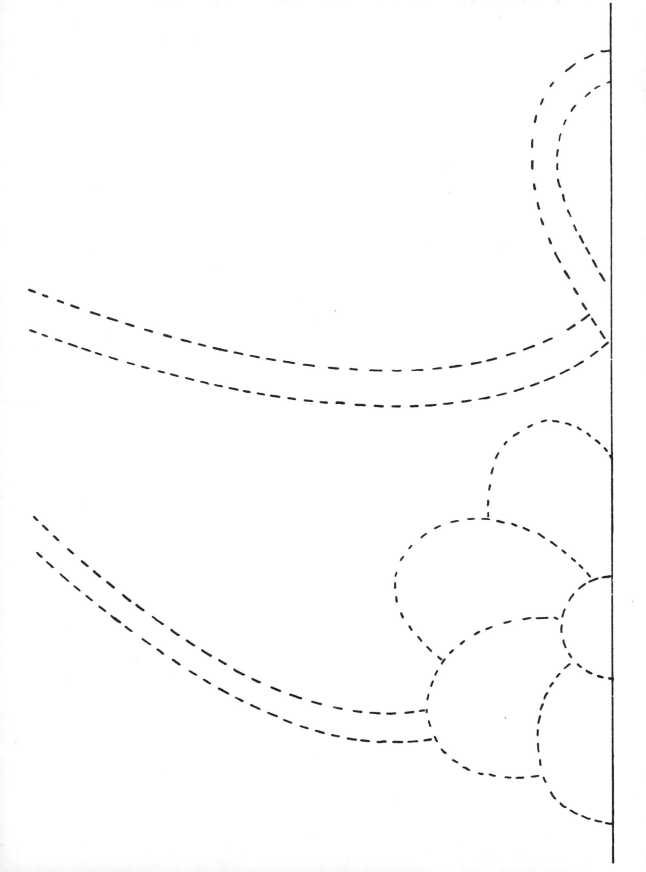

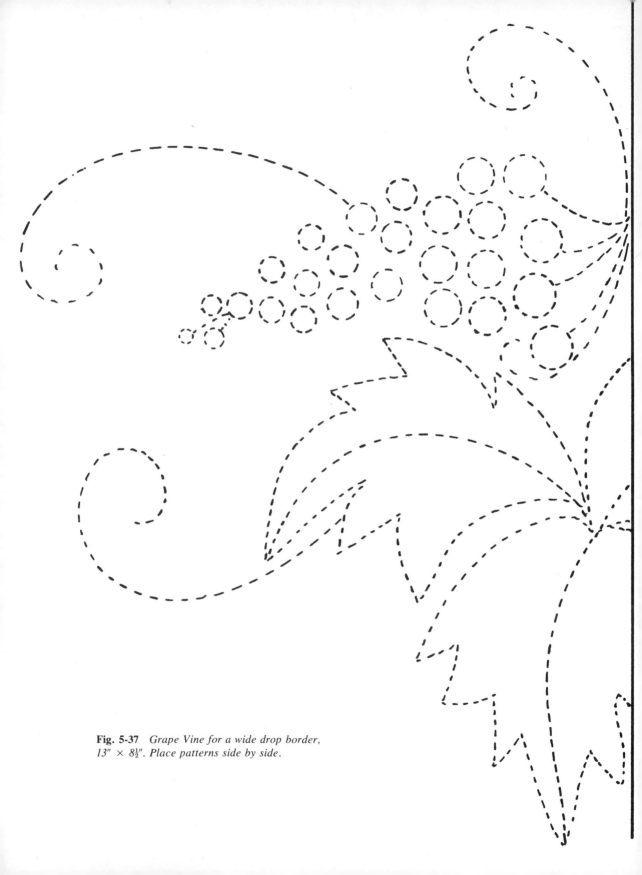

Fig. 5-37 *Grape Vine for a wide drop border,*
13″ × 8½″. Place patterns side by side.

Fig. 5-38 *Bell Flower, 24″ × 8½″. Place patterns side by side.*

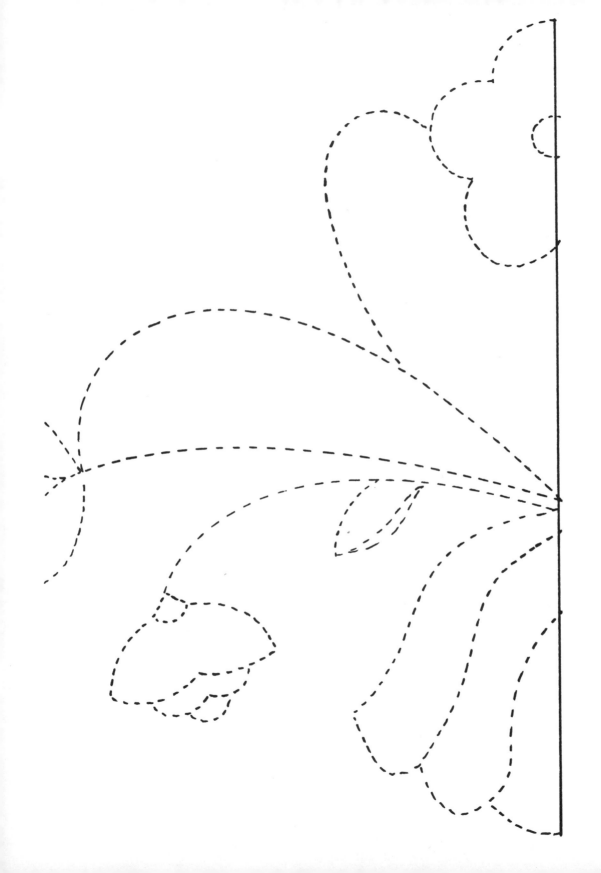

Fig. 5-39 *Bird in the Tulip Tree, 11" × 8½".
Place patterns side by side.*

Fig. 5-40 *Spring Heart and Flower.*

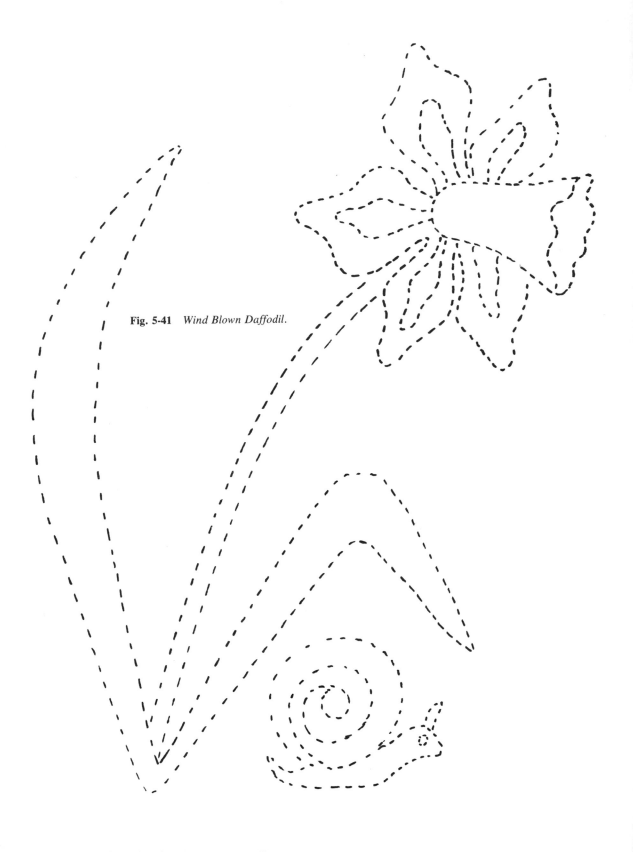

Fig. 5-41 *Wind Blown Daffodil.*

SOURCE LIST

Quilters Newsletter Magazine
Wheat Ridge, CO 80033

Monthly magazine for quilters

Quilts and Other Comforts
Box 394, Wheat Ridge, CO 80033

Full supply source, write for brochure

Stearns and Foster Company
Lockland, Cincinnati, OH 45215

*Supplier of Mountain Mist Batting, write for
brochure*

Come Quilt With Me
Box 1063, Cadman Plaza Station
Brooklyn, NY 11202

*Full line of mail-order supply, write for
brochure*

Quilt Country U.S.A.
13 Union Street, Rockaway, NJ 07866

Full line of supplies

Bear's Paw Quilt Shop
Rd 1, Box 817, Lafayette, NJ 07848

Large selection of quilt supplies

Nassau's of Ridgewood
235 East Ridgewood Ave., Ridgewood, NJ
07450

*Very large selection of quilt fabrics and
supplies*

Contemporary Quilt
2863 N. Clark Street, Chicago, IL 60657

Contemporary Quilt
Lombard Pines Plaza,
Main St. & Roosevelt Rd., Lombard, IL
60148

Full line of supplies

Ginger Snap Station
Box 81086
Atlanta, GA 30366

Highland Needlecrafts
Rt. 9 and Snake Hill Road, NY 10524

Mail-order catalog called Cross Patch

Marilyn Califfs Contemporary Quilts
5305 Denwood Avenue
Memphis, TN 38119

*Full line of supplies, write for catalog with
    photos of 150 quilts*

Annie's
703 Albany Avenue, Kingston, NY 12401

Full line of supplies

Woodstock Patchworks
Rock City Road, Woodstock, NY 12498

Full line of supplies

INDEX

Page numbers in **boldface** refer to illustrations

Album sampler quilt, 185, 193, **223**
Applique, 131–199
  basting, **105,** 107
  Bird in the Bush design, 175, **175,
    176–177**
  Bridal Wreath design, 159, **160, 162**
  Butterfly design, 148, **148, 149,** 150
  Cat design, 150, **150–156,** 157
  central floral designs, 178–181
  common center designs, 140–144
  crossed diagonal designs, 133–142
  Crossed Tulip design, 133–134, **134, 135,**
    137
  curve lines in, 133
  definition, 3, 103
  Dutch Tulip design, 134, **134, 136,** 137
  fabrics for, 104
  finishing, 109

Applique, *cont'd.*
  Heart All Round design, 142, **142, 143,**
    144
  hidden slipstitch for, 107–109, **108**
  history of, 131–132
  Laurel Leaf Wreath design, 162–163, **164**
  making patterns for, 132–133
  marking fabric for, 17
  motifs for, 148–157
  needles for, 18
  North Carolina Lily design, 182, 185,
    183–184
  Oak Leaf and Reel design, 146, **146,** 148
  opaque fabric for, 106–107, **107**
  pictorial designs, 185, **186–192,** 193–194
  pieced, *see* Pieced applique
  Pineapple design, 140, **140, 141,** 142
  Pomegranates design, **174,** 175, **175**

Applique, *cont'd.*
placement of, 107
President's Wreath design, **161**, 162, **162, 163**
quilting, 215, **221**
Reel and Buds design, 144, **144, 145,** 146
reel designs, 144–148
Rose Wreath design, 157–159, **158, 159**
slashing and mitering, 106, **106**
slipstitch for, 109
templates and fabric marking for, 104
thread for, 18
Triple Tulip design, 171, **171, 172–173**
Turkey Tracks design, 137, **137–139,** 140
upright patterns, 164–165, **166–170**
wedge designs for, *see* Wedge designs
Whig Rose design, 178, **178, 179–180**
wreath designs, 157–164
Assembly of quilts, *see under specific designs*
Aunt Sukey's Choice design, 26
assembly of, 68, **69**
materials and cutting, 67
pattern for, **70–71**
quilting suggestions for, 68
Autograph design, 79–81, **79, 80**
pattern for, **82, 83**

Baby quilts, 5
Background fabric, 8–9
Backing, 3
assembly of, 201–202
as a binding, 225–226
selection of, 200–201
Bands, *see* Border bands
Barn Raising setting, 97, **98**
Basting
appliques, **105,** 107
of face, batting, and backing, 201–202, **203, 204**
Batiste, 8
Batting, 3
assembly of, 201–202

Batting, *cont'd.*
cotton versus polyester, 201
sizes of, 201
Bear's Paw design
assembly of, 58–59, **59**
colors for, 57
materials and cutting, 57–58
pattern for, **60–61**
quilting suggestions for, 59–60
sawtooth edge for, **58,** 58–59
Bell Flower border, **236–237**
Between needle, 18, 211
Bias grain, 17, **18**
Binding, 225–226
Bird in the Bush design, 175, **175**
pattern for, **176–177**
Bird in the Tulip Tree border, **238–239**
Birds, 30
Border bands, 9–12
colors for, 5
quilting, 220, **221–224**
size of quilt and, 5–7
yardage for, 9
Braid border, **229**
Bridal Wreath design, 159, **160**
pattern for, **162**
Broadcloth
colors of, 7
in cotton and polyester blends, 7
for secondary color, 4
Buildings, 193
Butterfly design, 148, **148,** 150
pattern for, **149**
Butting the backing together, 201

Cactus Rose, 95
Calico Corners quilt, 98
Calicoes, 7
Cat design, 150, **150,** 157
pattern for, **151–156**
Central floral designs, 178–181
Chinese Fan, **85**
curved seams in, 81, 83, **83, 84,** 85
pattern for, **84**

Clay's Choice design, 25, **25**, 31
  assembly of, 33, **33**, 35
  materials and cutting, 33, **34**
  pattern for, **34**
  quilting suggestions for, 35
Color(s), 3
  of background, 8
  for border bands, 5
  choosing, 4–5
  for corners, 10, 11
  setting, 7
Colorfastness, 7
Common center designs, 140–144
Corners
  on border bands, 10
  three-pieced, 65–67, **66**
Cotton batting, 201
Cotton fabrics, 7
Cotton-and-polyester blend fabrics, 7
Country Roads design, 47, 49–51, **49, 50**
  pattern for, **52**
Crossed diagonal designs, 133–142
Crossed Tulip design, 133–134, **134**, 137
  pattern for, **135**
Curved seam patchwork, 81, 83, **83, 84,** 85
Cutting fabrics
  for border bands, 10, **10,** 11
  grain line and, 17–18, **18**
  See also Scissors; *and under specific*
    designs

Dahlia design, 94–95, **94, 95**
  center pattern pieces for, **96**
  pattern for background pieces, **91**
Deer in the Woods design, 49
Design, 3
Diagonal designs
  crossed, 133–142
  effective use of, 181–182
Diamond setting, Log Cabin quilt in, 98, **99**
Double bed size, 5–6
Double solid templates, 15, **17**
Dressmaker thread, 18
Dressmarkers, 16

Drunkard's Path
  curved seams in, 81, 83, **83, 84,** 85
  pattern for, **84**
Duck and Ducklings design, 23, **24,** 40
  assembly of, 42–43, **43**
  materials and cutting, 42
  pattern for, **44–45**
  quilting suggestions for, 43
Duck's Foot in the Mud design, 57
Dutchman's Puzzle design, 30–31
  pattern for, **32**
Dutch Tulip design, 134, **134,** 137
  pattern for, **136**

Earth Tones quilt, 220, **223**
Eight-Point Star, **87, 89**
  assembly of, **88,** 89, 92
  marking, 87
  materials and cutting, 89
  pattern for, **90, 91**
  See also Dahlia design; Le Moyne design
Everyone Has Eyelashes quilt, 198

Fabrics, 7–9
  for applique, 104
  for background, 8–9
  for backing, 200–201
  cutting, *see* Cutting fabrics
  marking, 16–17, 104
  opaque, for applique, 106, **107**
Face, 3, 200
Faces and Fashion quilt, 187, **199**
Facial features, 193
Fan designs, *see* Small fans; Victorian fans
Felt-tip marker, 17
Floral basket border, **229**
Floral Border with bird, **230**
Four-patch block design, **22,** 23, 30–35
Frame(s), 202–205, **205**
  round and oval, 209, **210**
  strapping the quilt on, 207–208, **208**
Friendship Ring, 109, **109,** 112
  patterns for, **111**
Friendship Sampler, 182

Garden of Eden design, 23, **24**
Geese, 30
General Israel Putnam, **198**
Ginghams, 8
Grading of patterns, 13
Grain line, 17–18, **18**
  applique and, 104
  stripes and, 47, 49
  tumbling block patch and, 117–118
Grandmother's Flower Garden quilt, **121, 122**
  assembly of, 121, **123,** 123–124
  materials and cutting, 121
  pattern for, **124**
  quilting suggestions for, 124
Grape Vine border, **234–235**

Hand sewing, advantages of, 28
Hearts All Round design, 142, **142,** 144
  pattern form, **143**
Hidden slipstitch, 107–109, **108**
Honey Bee design, 124–125, **124, 125**

Jack and Jill design, 164–165, **166–171**
  assembly of, 164–165, 171
  materials and cutting, 164
  patterns for, **166–171**
Jacobian design for border, **228**

Laurel Leaf Wreath design, 162–163, **162**
  pattern for, **163**
Le Moyne Star design, 92, **92, 93**
  pattern for, **90, 91**
Log Cabin design, 95, 97–102
  assembly of, 100–102, **100**
  Barn Raising setting for, 97
  diamond setting for, 98, **99**
  quilting suggestions for, 102
  string technique for, **97,** 99–102, **99–101**
Logs, 95
Ludington Mill, **196**

Machine sewing, 28–29, **29**
Man and His Horse, **186**

Man and His Horse, *cont'd.*
  pattern for, **189–192**
Marking fabric, 16–17, 207
  for applique, 104
Medallions for borders, **231**
Mitering, for applique, 106, **106**
Mixed media, *see* Pieced applique
Mohawk Trail design, 86–87, **86**
Monkey Wrench design, 23, **24,** 35–36, **35, 36**
  patterns for, **37**
Moon center piece, 40, 42
Muslin, 4, 7–8
  for backing, 202

Needles, 18
Nine-patch block design, 23, **24,** 25
  even size, 35–40
  uneven size, 40–47
North Carolina Lily design, 95, 182, 185
  pattern for, **183–184**

Oak Leaf and Reel design, 146, **146, 147,** 148
  pattern for, **147**
Opaque fabric, for applique, 106–107, **107**
Orange Basket design, 128, **128, 129,** 130
Outer borders, 6, 12–13, **12, 14**
  designs for, 220, **222, 227–241**

Parallelograms, *see* Tumbling blocks
Pascack Valley Historical Society quilt, 195
Patches, definition of, 23
Patchwork, 20–102
  assembly techniques for, 25–28, **26–28**
  Aunt Sukey's Choice, 67–68, **67, 69–71**
  autograph, 79–81, **79, 80, 82, 83**
  basic design formula for, 21, 23
  Chinese Fan, 81, 83, **83, 84,** 85, **85**
  Clay's Choice, 31, 33, **33, 34,** 35
  Country Roads, 47, 49–51, **49, 50**
  curved seams, 81, 83, **83, 84,** 85
  cutting fabric for, 17–18

Patchwork, *cont'd.*
  Dahlia design, 94–95, **94, 95**
  definition of, 3, 103
  Drunkard's Path, 81, 83, **83, 84,** 85–86, **86**
  Duck and Ducklings, 40, 42–43, **42–45**
  Dutchman's Puzzle, 30–31, **30–32**
  Eight-Point Stars, 87, **87–91,** 89, 92
  four-patch block design for, **22,** 23, 30–35
  hand sewing vs. machine sewing, 28–29, **29**
  history of, 20–21
  Le Moyne Star, **90–93,** 92
  Log Cabin, 95, 97–102, **97–101**
  marking fabric for, 16–17
  mixed stripes for, 47, 49, 50, **50,** 51
  Mohawk Trail, 86–87, **86**
  Monkey Wrench, 35–36, **35, 36**
  nine-patch block design for, 23, **24,** 25, 35–47
  Pine Tree, 56–57, **57,** 60, 62–63, **62–64,** 65
  pressing seams for, 29–30
  quilting, 213–214
  sawtooth edge for, 53–54, 56–57, **56, 57**
  Stepping Stones, 46–47, **46, 47**
  three-pieced corners for, 65–67, **66**
  Union Square, 73, 75–77, **76–78,** 79
  Variable Star and Star-Within-a-Star, 36, 38–40, **38, 40, 41**
  Water Wheel, 51, 53–54, **53–55**
  Weathervane, 68, 71–72, **72, 73**
  Whirling Star, **90, 91,** 93–94, **93, 94**
  working from the center out with, 73
Patterns
  choice of, for this book, 2
  grading of, 13
  technical skill building with, 2
  See also Templates
People, 185
Pictorial designs, 185, 186–192
  assembly of, 194
  buildings, 193
  deciding what to represent in, 185
  facial features, 193

Pictorial designs, *cont'd.*
  Pascack Valley Historical Society quilt, 194
  people, 185
  placement of, 193–194
  Putnam County quilt, **195,** 198
  size of drawing for, 185
Picture-frame template, *see* Window-frame templates
Pieced applique, 103–130
  basting the applique to the background in, 107
  definition of, 3
  Grandmother's Flower Garden, 121, **121–124,** 123–124
  hidden slipstitch for, 107–109, **108**
  Honey Bee design, 124–125, **124–127**
  Orange Basket design, 128, **128, 129,** 130
  quilting, 214–215, **216–219**
  slipstitches for, 109
  templates and fabric markings for, 104
  tumbling blocks design, 117–119, **117–120**
  wedge designs for, *see* Wedge designs
  working order for, 104, **105,** 106
  See also Applique
Pieces, definition of, 23
Pineapple design, 140, **140,** 142
  pattern for, **141**
Pine Tree design, **57**
  assembly of, 63, **63,** 65
  colors for, 60, 62
  materials and cutting, 62
  pattern for, **64**
  quilting suggestions for, 65
  sawtooth edge for, 56–57, **57**
Pinning, 25–26, **26**
  for machine sewing, 28–29
Pins, 18
Polyester batting, 203
Pomegranates design, 175, **175**
  pattern for, **174**
Pre-folded square method, 107
President's Wreath design, 162, **162**
  pattern for, **161**

Pressing seams, for patchwork, 29–30
Putnam County quilt, **195,** 198

Quilt
    assembling the face, batting, and backing
        of, 200–202, **203, 204**
    definition of, 3
    finding designs for, 220
    size of, 5–7, **5**
    steps in making, 200
Quilter, The, **186**
    pattern for, **187–188**
Quilt frame, *see* Frame
Quilting
    applique, 215, **221**
    border band, 220, **221–224**
    definition of, 21
    patchwork, 213–214
    pieced applique, 214–215, **216–219**
    sawtooth edge patchwork, 214, **215**
    in the valley, 214–215
Quilting bee, 79
Quilting thread, *see* Thread

Rails, 202–205, **205, 207,** 208
Raised seams, 26–28, **27**
Reel and Buds design, 144, **144,** 146
    pattern for, **145**
Reel designs, 144–148
Rising Sun center piece, 40, 42
Rose Cascade border, **232–233**
Rose Wreath design, 157–159, **159**
    pattern for, 158
Ruler, 15
Running stitch, 209, 211, **211**

Sampler quilt(s)
    experimenting with, 2
    as learning tool, 3–4
    as teaching tool, 1–2
Sawtooth edge, 53–54, 56–57, **56, 57**
    for Bear's Paw, **58,** 58–59
    for Pine Tree design, 56–57, **57**
    quilting, 214, **215**

Scissors, 18
Scraps, 4
    for Water Wheel design, 51
Seam(s)
    curved, 81, 83, **83, 84,** 85
    pinning, 25–26, **26**
    pressing, for patchwork, 29–30
    raised, 26–28, **27**
Seam allowance, 9, 25, 213
Sewing, *see* Stitching
Shoo Fly design, 23, **24**
Silk and silk-like blends, 8
Single motif designs, 148–157
Single templates, 15–16, **16**
Size of a quilt, 5–7, **5**
Slashing, for applique, 106, **106**
Small fans, 112–114, **112–114**
    patterns for, **111**
Snider, De Ette, 187, **199**
Spring Heart and Flower border, **240**
Stage Coach, **195**
Star, eight-point, *see* Eight-Point Star
Star-Within-a-Star, **38,** 39
    pattern for, **41**
Stencil templates, 223, 225, **226**
Stepping Stones design, 23, **24,** 46–47, **46,**
    47
    pattern for, **48**
Stitch(ing), 209
    from the center out, 28, **28,** 73
    of face, batting, and backing, 201–202,
        203, 204
    hand vs. machine, 28–29, **29**
    hidden slipstitch, 107–109, **108**
    number of stitches per inch, 211
    from raw edge to raw edge, 26, **26**
    on the seam line only, 26, **26**
    starting and ending, 211–212, **213**
    up and down method of, 211, **212**
Strapping the quilt, 207–208, **208**
Stretcher bars, 202–203, **205,** 205–207
String technique, for Log Cabin quilts, **97,**
    99–102, **99–101**
Striped fabric, 47

Stripes, 5
    mixed, 47, 49, 50, **50**, 51
    for Water Wheel design, 49, 51, **54**
Sunburst pattern, for basting three layers
       together, 201–202, **202**

Tearing of fabric, 11
Templates
    for applique, 104, 133
    double solid, 15, **17**
    single, 15–16, **16**
    solid, 220–221, 223, **225**
    window-frame, 13, 15, **15**, 16
Thimble, 18
Thread, 3, 19, 209
Three-pieced corners, 65–67, **66**
Time-saving methods
    for mixed stripes, 47, 49, 50, **50**, 51
    for sawtooth edge, 53–54, 56–57, **56**, **57**
Tree of Life design, *see* Pine Tree design
Triple Tulip design, 171, **171**
    pattern for, **172–173**
Tumbling blocks design, 117–119, **117–119**
    pattern for, **120**
Turkey Tracks design, 137, **137**, **138**, 140
    pattern for, **139**
Twin size quilt, size of, 5

Union Square design, 75, **76**
    assembly of, 76–77, **77**
    materials and cutting, 76
    pattern for, **78**
    quilting suggestions for, 77, 79
    working from the center out with, 73, **76**
Upright patterns, 164–165, **166–170**

Variable Star design, 36, 38, **38**
    assembly of, 39, **40**

Variable Star design, *cont'd.*
    materials and cutting, 39
    pattern for, **41**
    quilting suggestions for, 39–40
Victorian Fan, 114–115, **114**, **115**, 117
    embroidered bow for, **116**, 117
    pattern for, **116**

Wall hanging, **6**
    size of, 5
Water Wheel design, 52, 53–57
    assembly of, 53, **54**
    materials and cutting, 53
    pattern for, **55**
    stripes for, 49, 51, **54**
Weathervane design, 68, 71–72, **72**, **73**
    pattern for, **74–75**
Wedge designs, 109–117
    Friendship Ring, 109, **109**, **111**
    small fans, **111–114**, 112–114
    Victorian Fan, 114, **114–116**
Whig Rose design, 178, **178**, **179–180**
    pattern for, **179–180**
Whirling Star design, 93–94, **93**, **94**
    pattern for, **90**, **91**
Wind Blown Daffodil border, **241**
Window-frame templates, 13, 15, **15**, **16**
Wool, 8
Wreath designs, 157–162

Yardage
    for border bands, 9
    for outer borders, 12
    for quilts, 5–6
    for solid color bands, 11

Zigzagging, 29, **29**

The Complete Book of Machine Quilting
Tony & Robbie Fanning

Combine machine versatility with a beautiful and authentic American folk art: quilting. No other book offers so much valuable information on easy, fast methods that enable even the busiest person to create lovely, durable, practical items for the home. Includes over two dozen fresh, vibrant projects to make in a day, a weekend, or a week. Tells you what can go wrong and how to avoid it, and how to quilt on any machine without buying fancy attachments. Features traditional and contemporary designs. 356 pages, 300 illustrations, color insert.

Book Code: 6802/hardcover $15.95
Book Code: 6803/paperback $10.95

Quilt as You Go
Sandra Millett

This is a technique book, teaching the first successful (patented) method for assembling quilted modules. Traditional and contemporary quilt patterns can be successfully assembled using Sandra Millett's strip-assembly technique. The secret is in the portable lap frame that can be built in ten minutes and used for years to quilt strips rather than individual blocks. With this book, it is possible to learn how to cut, piece, assemble a strip, and quilt, all in the same day. 256 pages, over 200 illustrations, color insert.

Book Code: 7101/hardcover $15.95
Book Code: 7102/paperback $10.95

The Quilting Primer 2nd Edition
Dorothy Frager

Expanded and revised, this heavily illustrated edition contains the most up-to-date information on quilting. The wide range of techniques covered offers something for the quilter at every level of expertise. Special features include 58 quilts shown, with detailed instructions for 30; 8 new pictorial quilt patterns, with descriptions of over 200 blocks; 5 new sampler quilts and descriptions of 100 blocks; 67 accessory items; and 70 full-size, ready-to-work patterns. 256 pages, 16 color photos, 190 black and white illustrations.

Book Code: 6826/hardcover $14.95
Book Code: 6827/paperback $10.95

The Book of Sampler Quilts
Dorothy Frager

Quilters who have relied on Dorothy Frager's *The Quilting Primer* will find this the most comprehensive book published on sampler quilting. Both a technique and a pattern book, it teaches 24 skill-building techniques, from the basics of patchwork to advanced pictorial applique. The introduction discusses colors, fabrics, yardage, patternmaking, and materials. Following chapters discuss Patchwork, Pieced Applique, and Applique. Over 50 individual block designs are included. 224 pages, 200 illustrations, color insert.

Book Code: 7267/hardcover $16.95
Book Code: 7268/paperback $11.95

Chilton's Needlework books are available at your local bookstore or craft shop or by mailing a check/money order for the price of the book plus **$1.50** for postage and handling to:

CHILTON BOOK COMPANY
Dept. DM Radnor, PA 19089

NOTE: *When ordering be sure to include name & address, book code & title*